2014 Case Supplement

Constitutional Law: Cases in Context,
Second Edition

Constitutional Rights: Cases in Context

Constitutional Structure: Cases in Context

EDITORIAL ADVISORS

2014 Case Supplement

Constitutional Law: Cases in Context, Second Edition

Constitutional Rights: Cases in Context

Constitutional Structure: Cases in Context

Randy E. Barnett
Carmack Waterhouse Professor of Legal Theory
Georgetown University Law Center

Wolters Kluwer
Law & Business

Published by Wolters Kluwer Law & Business in New York.

Wolters Kluwer Law & Business serves customers worldwide with CCH, Aspen Publishers, and Kluwer Law International products. (www.wolterskluwerlb.com)

To contact Customer Service, e-mail customer.service@wolterskluwer.com, call 1-800-234-1660, fax 1-800-901-9075, or mail correspondence to:

Wolters Kluwer Law & Business
Attn: Order Department
PO Box 990
Frederick, MD 21705

Printed in the United States of America.

1 2 3 4 5 6 7 8 9 0

ISBN 978-1-4548-4167-8

About Wolters Kluwer Law & Business

Wolters Kluwer Law & Business is a leading global provider of intelligent information and digital solutions for legal and business professionals in key specialty areas, and respected educational resources for professors and law students. Wolters Kluwer Law & Business connects legal and business professionals as well as those in the education market with timely, specialized authoritative content and information-enabled solutions to support success through productivity, accuracy and mobility.

Serving customers worldwide, Wolters Kluwer Law & Business products include those under the Aspen Publishers, CCH, Kluwer Law International, Loislaw, ftwilliam.com and MediRegs family of products.

CCH products have been a trusted resource since 1913, and are highly regarded resources for legal, securities, antitrust and trade regulation, government contracting, banking, pension, payroll, employment and labor, and healthcare reimbursement and compliance professionals.

Aspen Publishers products provide essential information to attorneys, business professionals and law students. Written by preeminent authorities, the product line offers analytical and practical information in a range of specialty practice areas from securities law and intellectual property to mergers and acquisitions and pension/benefits. Aspen's trusted legal education resources provide professors and students with high-quality, up-to-date and effective resources for successful instruction and study in all areas of the law.

Kluwer Law International products provide the global business community with reliable international legal information in English. Legal practitioners, corporate counsel and business executives around the world rely on Kluwer Law journals, looseleafs, books, and electronic products for comprehensive information in many areas of international legal practice.

Loislaw is a comprehensive online legal research product providing legal content to law firm practitioners of various specializations. Loislaw provides attorneys with the ability to quickly and efficiently find the necessary legal information they need, when and where they need it, by facilitating access to primary law as well as state-specific law, records, forms and treatises.

ftwilliam.com offers employee benefits professionals the highest quality plan documents (retirement, welfare and non-qualified) and government forms (5500/PBGC, 1099 and IRS) software at highly competitive prices.

MediRegs products provide integrated health care compliance content and software solutions for professionals in healthcare, higher education and life sciences, including professionals in accounting, law and consulting.

Wolters Kluwer Law & Business, a division of Wolters Kluwer, is headquartered in New York. Wolters Kluwer is a market-leading global information services company focused on professionals.

Contents

2014 Case Supplement

Constitutional Law: Cases in Context,
Second Edition

Constitutional Rights: Cases in Context

Constitutional Structure: Cases in Context

Chapter 1

The Founding: Further Readings on the Origins of the Constitution

ASSIGNMENT S-1

1. John Locke: On the State of Nature and the Origin and Purpose of Civil Society and Government

The Founders were very much influenced by such natural rights thinkers as John Locke, Hugo Grotious, Samuel von Pufendorf, and Emmerich de Vattel. Following are the fuller passages from which the excerpts appearing in the casebook were taken.

Study Guide:

- What do you suppose is the persistent appeal of "state of nature" theorizing?
- How does Locke's vision of the "state of nature" differ from that of Hobbes (as it appears in the casebook)?
- Can you imagine why these words of Locke would be considered so great a threat to the established authority in general and of the Crown in particular?
- What is Locke's argument for government?
- What does he say is lacking in the state of nature?
- What is his argument for majority rule?
- Can a majority form a government over a dissenting minority?
- Finally, notice how Locke identifies the separation of legislative, executive, and judicial powers.

JOHN LOCKE, SECOND TREATISE OF GOVERNMENT: AN ESSAY CONCERNING THE TRUE ORIGINAL, EXTENT AND END OF CIVIL GOVERNMENT, 1690

CHAPTER 2
Of the State of Nature

§4. To understand political power right, and derive it from its original, we must consider, what state all men are naturally in, and that is, a state of perfect freedom to order their actions, and dispose of their possessions and persons, as they think fit, within the bounds of the law of nature, without asking leave, or depending upon the will of any other man.

A state also of equality, wherein all the power and jurisdiction is reciprocal, no one having more than another; there being nothing more evident, than that creatures of the same species and rank, promiscuously born to all the same advantages of nature, and the use of the same faculties, should also be equal one amongst another without subordination or subjection, unless the lord and master of them all should, by any manifest declaration of his will, set one above another, and confer on him, by an evident and clear appointment, an undoubted right to dominion and sovereignty. . . .

§6. But though this be a state of liberty, yet it is not a state of licence: though man in that state have an uncontroulable liberty to dispose of his person or possessions, yet he has not liberty to destroy himself, or so much as any creature in his possession, but where some nobler use than its bare preservation calls for it. The state of nature has a law of nature to govern it, which obliges every one: and reason, which is that law, teaches all mankind, who will but consult it, that being all equal and independent, no one ought to harm another in his life, health, liberty, or possessions: for men being all the workmanship of one omnipotent, and infinitely wise maker; all the servants of one sovereign master, sent into the world by his order, and about his business; they are his property, whose workmanship they are, made to last during his, not one another's pleasure: and being furnished with like faculties, sharing all in one community of nature, there cannot be supposed any such subordination among us, that may authorize us to destroy one another, as if we were made for one another's uses, as the inferior ranks of creatures are for ours. Every one, as he is bound to preserve himself, and not to quit his station wilfully, so by the like reason, when his own preservation comes not in competition, ought he, as much as he can, to preserve the rest of mankind, and may not, unless it be to do justice on an offender, take away, or impair the life, or what tends to the preservation of the life, the liberty, health, limb, or goods of another.

§7. And that all men may be restrained from invading others' rights, and from doing hurt to one another, and the law of nature be observed, which willeth the peace and preservation of all mankind, the execution of the law of nature is, in that state, put into every man's hands, whereby every one has a right to punish the transgressors of that law to such a degree, as may hinder its violation: for the law of nature would, as all other laws that concern men in this world be in vain, if there were no body that in the state of nature had a power to execute that law, and thereby preserve the innocent and restrain offenders. And if any one in the state of nature may punish another for any evil he has done, every one may do so: for in that state of perfect equality, where naturally there is no superiority or jurisdiction of one over another, what any may do in prosecution of that law, every one must needs have a right to do.

§8. And thus, in the state of nature, one man comes by a power over another; but yet no absolute or arbitrary power, to use a criminal, when he has got him in his hands, according to the passionate heats, or boundless extravagancy of his own will; but only to retribute to him, so far as calm reason and conscience dictate, what is proportionate to his transgression, which is so much as may serve for reparation and restraint: for these two are the only reasons, why one man may lawfully do harm to another, which is that we call punishment. In transgressing the law of nature, the offender declares himself to live by another rule than that of reason and common equity, which is that measure God has set to the actions of men, for their mutual security; and so he becomes dangerous to mankind, the tye, which is to secure them from injury and violence, being slighted and broken by him. Which being a trespass against the whole species, and the peace and safety of it, provided for by the law of nature, every man upon this score, by the right he hath to preserve mankind in general, may restrain, or where it is necessary, destroy things noxious to them, and so may bring such evil on any one, who hath transgressed that law, as may make him repent the doing of it, and thereby deter him, and by his example others, from doing the like mischief. And in the case, and upon this ground, EVERY MAN HATH A RIGHT TO PUNISH THE OFFENDER, AND BE EXECUTIONER OF THE LAW OF NATURE. . . .

§11. From these two distinct rights, the one of punishing the crime for restraint, and preventing the like offence, which right of punishing is in every body; the other of taking reparation, which belongs only to the injured party, comes it to pass that the magistrate, who by being magistrate hath the common right of punishing put into his hands, can often, where the public good demands not the execution of the law, remit the punishment of criminal offences by his own authority, but yet cannot remit the satisfaction due to any private man for the damage he has received. That, he who has suffered the damage has a right to demand in his own name. . . .

§13. To this strange doctrine, viz. That in the state of nature every one has the executive power of the law of nature, I doubt not but it will be objected, that it is unreasonable for men to be judges in their own cases, that self-love will make men partial to themselves and their friends: and on the other side, that ill nature, passion and revenge will carry them too far in punishing others; and hence nothing but confusion and disorder will follow, and that therefore God hath certainly appointed government to restrain the partiality and violence of men. I easily grant, that civil government is the proper remedy for the inconveniencies of the state of nature, which must certainly be great, where men may be judges in their own case, since it is easy to be imagined, that he who was so unjust as to do his brother an injury, will scarce be so just as to condemn himself for it: but I shall desire those who make this objection, to remember, that absolute monarchs are but men; and if government is to be the remedy of those evils, which necessarily follow from men's being judges in their own cases, and the state of nature is therefore not to be endured, I desire to know what kind of government that is, and how much better it is than the state of nature, where one man, commanding a multitude, has the liberty to be judge in his own case, and may do to all his subjects whatever he pleases, without the least liberty to any one to question or controul those who execute his pleasure and in whatsoever he doth, whether led by reason, mistake or passion, must be submitted to. Much better it is in the state of nature, wherein men are not bound to submit to the unjust will of another. And if he that judges, judges amiss in his own, or any other case, he is answerable for it to the rest of mankind.

§14. It is often asked as a mighty objection, where are, or ever were there any men in such a state of nature? To which it may suffice as an answer at present, that since all princes and rulers of independent governments all through the world, are in a state of nature, it is plain the world never was, nor ever will be, without numbers of men in that state. I have named all governors of independent communities, whether they are, or are not, in league with others: for it is not every compact that puts an end to the state of nature between men, but only this one of agreeing together mutually to enter into one community, and make one body politic; other promises, and compacts, men may make one with another, and yet still be in the state of nature. The promises and bargains for truck, &c. between the two men in the desert island, mentioned by Garcilasso de la Vega, in his history of Peru; or between a Swiss and an Indian, in the woods of America, are binding to them, though they are perfectly in a state of nature, in reference to one another: for truth and keeping of faith belongs to men, as men, and not as members of society. . . .

CHAPTER 8
Of the Beginning of Political Societies

§95. Men being, as has been said, by nature, all free, equal, and independent, no one can be put out of this estate, and subjected to the political power of another, without his own consent. The only way whereby any one divests himself of his natural liberty, and puts on the bonds of civil society, is by agreeing with other men to join and unite into a community for their comfortable, safe, and peaceable living one amongst another, in a secure enjoyment of their properties, and a greater security against any, that are not of it. This any number of men may do, because it injures not the freedom of the rest; they are left as they were in the liberty of the state of nature. When any number of men have so consented to make one community or government, they are thereby presently incorporated, and make one body politic, wherein the majority have a right to act and conclude the rest.

§96. For when any number of men have, by the consent of every individual, made a community, they have thereby made that community one body, with a power to act as one body, which is only by the will and determination of the majority: for that which acts any community, being only the consent of the individuals of it, and it being necessary to that which is one body to move one way; it is necessary the body should move that way whither the greater force carries it, which is the consent of the majority: . . . and so every one is bound by that consent to be concluded by the majority. . . .

§97. And thus every man, by consenting with others to make one body politic under one government, puts himself under an obligation, to every one of that society, to submit to the determination of the majority, and to be concluded by it; or else this original compact, whereby he with others incorporates into one society, would signify nothing, and be no compact, if he be left free, and under no other ties than he was in before in the state of nature. . . .

§98. For if the consent of the majority shall not, in reason, be received as the act of the whole, and conclude every individual; nothing but the consent of every individual can make any thing to be the act of the whole: but such a consent is next to impossible ever to be had, if we consider the infirmities of health, and avocations of business, which in a number, though much less than that of a commonwealth, will necessarily keep many away from the public assembly. To which if we add the variety of opinions, and contrariety of interests, . . . [s]uch a constitution as this would make the mighty Leviathan of a shorter duration, than the feeblest creatures, and not let it outlast the day it was born. . . .

§99. Whosoever therefore out of a state of nature unite into a community, must be understood to give up all the power, necessary to the ends for which they unite into society, to the majority of the community, unless they expressly agreed in any number greater than the majority. And this is done by barely agreeing to unite into one political society, which is all the compact that is, or needs be, between the individuals, that enter into, or make up a commonwealth. And thus that, which begins and actually constitutes any political society, is nothing but the consent of any number of freemen capable of a majority to unite and incorporate into such a society. And this is that, and that only, which did, or could give beginning to any lawful government in the world. . . .

CHAPTER 9
Of the Ends of Political Society and Government

§123. If man in the state of nature be so free, as has been said; if he be absolute lord of his own person and possessions, equal to the greatest, and subject to no body, why will he part with his freedom? Why will he give up this empire, and subject himself to the dominion and controul of any other power? To which it is obvious to answer, that though in the state of nature he hath such a right, yet the enjoyment of it is very uncertain, and constantly exposed to the invasion of others: for all being kings as much as he, every man his equal, and the greater part no strict observers of equity and justice, the enjoyment of the property he has in this state is very unsafe, very unsecure. This makes him willing to quit a condition, which, however free, is full of fears and continual dangers: and it is not without reason, that he seeks out, and is willing to join in society with others, who are already united, or have a mind to unite, for the mutual preservation of their lives, liberties and estates, which I call by the general name, property.

§124. The great and chief end, therefore, of men's uniting into commonwealths, and putting themselves under government, is the preservation of their property. To which in the state of nature there are many things wanting.

First, There wants an established, settled, known law, received and allowed by common consent to be the standard of right and wrong, and the common measure to decide all controversies between them: for though the law of nature be plain and intelligible to all rational creatures; yet men being biassed by their interest, as well as ignorant for want of study of it, are not apt to allow of it as a law binding to them in the application of it to their particular cases.

§125. Secondly, In the state of nature there wants a known and indifferent judge, with authority to determine all differences according to the established law: for every one in that state being both judge and executioner of the law of nature, men being partial to themselves, passion and revenge is very apt to carry them too far, and with too much heat, in their own cases; as well as negligence, and unconcernedness, to make them too remiss in other men's.

§126. Thirdly, In the state of nature there often wants power to back and support the sentence when right, and to give it due execution, They who by any injustice offended, will seldom fail, where they are able, by force to make good their injustice; such resistance many times makes the punishment dangerous, and frequently destructive, to those who attempt it.

§127. Thus mankind, notwithstanding all the privileges of the state of nature, being but in an ill condition, while they remain in it, are quickly driven into society. Hence it comes to pass, that we seldom find any number of men live any time together in this state. The inconveniencies that they are therein exposed to, by the irregular and uncertain exercise of the power every man has of punishing the transgressions of others, make them take sanctuary under the established laws of government, and therein seek the preservation of their property. It is this makes them so willingly give up every one his single power of punishing, to be exercised by such alone, as shall be appointed to it amongst them; and by such rules as the community, or those authorized by them to that purpose, shall agree on. And in this we have the original right and rise of both the legislative and executive power, as well as of the governments and societies themselves.

§128. For in the state of nature, to omit the liberty he has of innocent delights, a man has two powers.

The first is to do whatsoever he thinks fit for the preservation of himself, and others within the permission of the law of nature: by which law, common to them all, he and all the rest of mankind are one community, make up one society, distinct from all other creatures. And were it not for the corruption and vitiousness of degenerate men, there would be no need of any other; no necessity that men should separate from this great and natural community, and by positive agreements combine into smaller and divided associations.

The other power a man has in the state of nature, is the power to punish the crimes committed against that law. Both these he gives up, when he joins in a private, if I may so call it, or particular politic society, and incorporates into any common wealth, separate from the rest of mankind.

§129. The first power, viz. of doing whatsoever he thought for the preservation of himself, and the rest of mankind, he gives up to be regulated by laws made by the society, so far forth as the preservation of himself, and the rest of that society shall require; which laws of the society in many things confine the liberty he had by the law of nature.

§130. Secondly, The power of punishing he wholly gives up, and engages his natural force, (which he might before employ in the execution of the law of nature, by his own single authority, as he thought fit) to assist the executive power of the society, as the law thereof shall require: for being now in a new state, wherein he is to enjoy many conveniencies, from the labour, assistance, and society of others in the same community, as well as protection from its whole strength; he is to part also with as much of his natural liberty, in providing for himself, as the good, prosperity, and safety of the society shall require; which is not only necessary, but just, since the other members of the society do the like.

§131. But though men, when they enter into society, give up the equality, liberty, and executive power they had in the state of nature, into the hands of the society, to be so far disposed of by the legislative, as the good of the society shall require; yet it being only with an intention in every one the better to preserve himself, his liberty and property; (for no rational creature can be supposed to change his condition with an intention to be worse) the power of the society, or legislative constituted by them, can never be supposed to extend farther, than the common good; but is obliged to secure every one's property, by providing against those three defects above mentioned, that made the state of nature so unsafe and uneasy. And so whoever has the legislative or supreme power of any commonwealth, is bound to govern by established standing laws, promulgated and known to the people, and not by extemporary decrees; by indifferent and upright judges, who are to decide controversies by those laws; and to employ the force of the community at home, only in the execution of such laws, or abroad to prevent or redress foreign injuries, and secure the community from inroads and invasion. And all this to be directed to no other end, but the peace, safety, and public good of the people.

ASSIGNMENT S-2

2. James Madison: On the Alleged Failure of the Articles of Confederation

Prior to the adoption of the Constitution, the United States was governed by the Articles of Confederation (which appear in the beginning of the casebook). During the post-Revolutionary period, many Americans became unhappy with the general state of the economy and with the behavior of state governments. In an essay prepared in advance of the Philadelphia convention, Madison summarized what he and others perceived as the deficiencies or "vices" in the form of government defined by the Articles. That the Articles were deficient in these ways was one of the principal assumptions underlying the formulation and eventual adoption of the Constitution. The list he provided is a useful summary of these defenses.

Madison also addresses an important problem with then-prevalent political theory: how to explain the adoption of bad policies and widespread violations of rights by state governments that are "republican" in form and therefore accountable to "the People." At the time, state governments were largely run by a single popularly elected assembly, to which the executive and judiciary were subservient. Such governments were widely thought to be the proper alternative to rule by an aristocracy as the means of protecting the retained rights of the people. Yet, those who favored a new constitutional structure believed these republican governments to be pervasively violating the people's rights, which was simply not supposed to happen.

In this essay (summarized by bullet points in the casebook), Madison attempts to answer this question with an early version of the argument he later presents in *The Federalist, No. 10*: his theory of "faction" that explains how majoritarian rule can come to violate unjustly the rights of the people.

Study Guide:

- When reading Madison's complaints about the Articles, you must keep in mind that a great many people either did not share these complaints, or thought that they could be cured by making changes to the Articles, rather than by replacing them altogether. For this reason, when the Constitution was proposed, it was also bitterly opposed.
- There is much of interest in this essay that presages the new Constitution, as well as future constitutional controversies. One is Madison's strong concern for commerce. Another is his belief that a constitution should be ratified by the people. Why was that deemed by him to be so important?
- What is Madison's proposed solution to the problem of faction?

JAMES MADISON, VICES OF THE POLITICAL SYSTEM OF THE UNITED STATES, APRIL 1787: 1. *Failure of the States to comply with the Constitutional requisitions.* This evil has been so fully experienced both during the war and since the peace, results so naturally from the number and independent authority of the States and has been so uniformly exemplified in every similar Confederacy, that it may be considered as not less radically and permanently inherent in, than it is fatal to the object of, the present System.

2. *Encroachments by the States on the federal authority.* Examples of this are numerous and repetitions may be foreseen in almost every case where any favorite object of a State shall present a temptation. Among these examples are the wars and Treaties of Georgia with the Indians—The unlicensed compacts between Virginia and Maryland, and between Pena. & N. Jersey—the troops raised and to be kept up by Massts.

3. *Violations of the law of nations and of treaties.* From the number of Legislatures, the sphere of life from which most of their members are taken, and the circumstances under which their legislative business is carried on,

irregularities of this kind must frequently happen. Accordingly not a year has passed without instances of them in some one or other of the States. The Treaty of peace—the treaty with France—the treaty with Holland have each been violated. The causes of these irregularities must necessarily produce frequent violations of the law of nations in other respects.

As yet foreign powers have not been rigorous in animadverting on us. This moderation however cannot be mistaken for a permanent partiality to our faults, or a permanent security agst. those disputes with other nations, which being among the greatest of public calamities, it ought to be least in the power of any part of the Community to bring on the whole.

4. *Trespasses of the States on the rights of each other.* These are alarming symptoms, and may be daily apprehended as we are admonished by daily experience. See the law of Virginia restricting foreign vessels to certain ports—of Maryland in favor of vessels belonging to her own citizens—of N. York in favor of the same.

Paper money, instalments of debts, occlusion of Courts, making property a legal tender, may likewise be deemed aggressions on the rights of other States. As the Citizens of every State aggregately taken stand more or less in the relation of Creditors or debtors, to the Citizens of every other States, Acts of the debtor State in favor of debtors, affect the Creditor State, in the same manner, as they do its own citizens who are relatively creditors towards other citizens. This remark may be extended to foreign nations. If the exclusive regulation of the value and alloy of coin was properly delegated to the federal authority, the policy of it equally requires a controul on the States in the cases above mentioned. It must have been meant 1. to preserve uniformity in the circulating medium throughout the nation. 2. to prevent those frauds on the citizens of other States, and the subjects of foreign powers, which might disturb the tranquility at home, or involve the Union in foreign contests.

The practice of many States in restricting the commercial intercourse with other States, and putting their productions and manufactures on the same footing with those of foreign nations, though not contrary to the federal articles, is certainly adverse to the spirit of the Union, and tends to beget retaliating regulations, not less expensive & vexatious in themselves, than they are destructive of the general harmony.

5. *Want of concert in matters where common interest requires it.* This defect is strongly illustrated in the state of our commercial affairs. How much has the national dignity, interest, and revenue suffered from this cause? Instances of inferior moment are the want of uniformity in the laws concerning naturalization & literary property; of provision for national seminaries, for grants of incorporation for national purposes, for canals and other works of general utility, wch. may at present be defeated by the perverseness of particular States whose concurrence is necessary.

6. *Want of guaranty to the States of their Constitutions & laws against internal violence.* The confederation is silent on this point and therefore by the second article the hands of the federal authority are tied. According to Republican Theory, Right and power being both vested in the majority, are held to be

synonimous. According to fact and experience a minority may in an appeal to force, be an overmatch for the majority. 1. If the minority happen to include all such as possess the skill and habits of military life, & such as possess the great pecuniary resources, one third only may conquer the remaining two thirds. 2. One third of those who participate in the choice of the rulers, may be rendered a majority by the accession of those whose poverty excludes them from a right of suffrage, and who for obvious reasons will be more likely to join the standard of sedition than that of the established Government. 3. Where slavery exists the republican Theory becomes still more fallacious.

7. *Want of sanction to the laws, and of coercion in the Government of the Confederacy.* A sanction is essential to the idea of law, as coercion is to that of Government. The federal system being destitute of both, wants the great vital principles of a Political Cons[ti]tution. Under the form of such a Constitution, it is in fact nothing more than a treaty of amity of commerce and of alliance, between so many independent and Sovereign States. From what cause could so fatal an omission have happened in the articles of Confederation? from a mistaken confidence that the justice, the good faith, the honor, the sound policy, of the several legislative assemblies would render superfluous any appeal to the ordinary motives by which the laws secure the obedience of individuals: a confidence which does honor to the enthusiastic virtue of the compilers, as much as the inexperience of the crisis apologizes for their errors. The time which has since elapsed has had the double effect, of increasing the light, and tempering the warmth, with which the arduous work may be revised. It is no longer doubted that a unanimous and punctual obedience of 13 independent bodies, to the acts of the federal Government, ought not be calculated on. Even during the war, when external danger supplied in some degree the defect of legal & coercive sanctions, how imperfectly did the States fulfil their obligations to the Union? In time of peace, we see already what is to be expected. How indeed could it be otherwise? In the first place, Every general act of the Union must necessarily bear unequally hard on some particular member or members of it. Secondly the partiality of the members to their own interests and rights, a partiality which will be fostered by the Courtiers of popularity, will naturally exaggerate the inequality where it exists, and even suspect it where it has no existence. Thirdly a distrust of the voluntary compliance of each other may prevent the compliance of any, although it should be the latent disposition of all. Here are causes & pretexts which will never fail to render federal measures abortive. If the laws of the States, were merely recommendatory to their citizens, or if they were to be rejudged by County authorities, what security, what probability would exist, that they would be carried into execution? Is the security or probability greater in favor of the acts of Congs. which depending for their execution on the will of the state legislatures, wch. are tho' nominally authoritative, in fact recommendatory only.

8. *Want of ratification by the people of the articles of Confederation.* In some of the States the Confederation is recognized by, and forms a part of the constitution. In others however it has received no other sanction than that of the Legislative authority. From this defect two evils result: 1. Whenever a law of a State happens to be repugnant to an act of Congress, particularly when the latter

is of posterior date to the former, it will be at least questionable whether the latter must not prevail; and as the question must be decided by the Tribunals of the State, they will be most likely to lean on the side of the State. 2. As far as the Union of the States is to be regarded as a league of sovereign powers, and not as a political Constitution by virtue of which they are become one sovereign power, so far it seems to follow from the doctrine of compacts, that a breach of any of the articles of the confederation by any of the parties to it, absolves the other parties from their respective obligations, and gives them a right if they chuse to exert it, of dissolving the Union altogether.

9. *Multiplicity of laws in the several States*. . . . Among the evils . . . of our situation may well be ranked the multiplicity of laws from which no State is exempt. As far as laws are necessary, to mark with precision the duties of those who are to obey them, and to take from those who are to administer them a discretion, which might be abused, their number is the price of liberty. As far as the laws exceed this limit, they are a nusance: a nusance of the most pestilent kind. Try the Codes of the several States by this test, and what a luxuriancy of legislation do they present. The short period of independency has filled as many pages as the century which preceded it. Every year, almost every session, adds a new volume. This may be the effect in part, but it can only be in part, of the situation in which the revolution has placed us. A review of the several codes will shew that every necessary and useful part of the least voluminous of them might be compressed into one tenth of the compass, and at the same time be rendered tenfold as perspicuous.

10. *Mutability of the laws of the States*. . . . We daily see laws repealed or superseded, before any trial can have been made of their merits: and even before a knowledge of them can have reached the remoter districts within which they were to operate. In the regulations of trade this instability becomes a snare not only to our citizens but to foreigners also.

11. *Injustice of the laws of States*. If the multiplicity and mutability of laws prove a want of wisdom, their injustice betrays a defect still more alarming: more alarming not merely because it is a greater evil in itself, but because it brings more into question the fundamental principle of republican Government, that the majority who rule in such Governments, are the safest Guardians both of public Good and of private rights. To what causes is this evil to be ascribed?

These causes lie 1. in the Representative bodies. 2. in the people themselves.

1. Representative appointments are sought from 3 motives. 1. ambition 2. personal interest. 3. public good. Unhappily the two first are proved by experience to be most prevalent. Hence the candidates who feel them, particularly, the second, are most industrious, and most successful in pursuing their object: and forming often a majority in the legislative Councils, with interested views, contrary to the interest, and views, of their Constituents, join in a perfidious sacrifice of the latter to the former. A succeeding election it might be supposed, would displace the offenders, and repair the mischief. But how easily are base and selfish measures, masked by pretexts of public good and apparent expediency? How frequently will a repetition of the same arts and industry which succeeded in the first instance, again prevail on the unwary to misplace their confidence?

How frequently too will the honest but unenlightened representative be the dupe of a favorite leader, veiling his selfish views under the professions of public good, and varnishing his sophistical arguments with the glowing colours of popular eloquence?

2. A still more fatal if not more frequent cause lies among the people themselves. All civilized societies are divided into different interests and factions, as they happen to be creditors or debtors—Rich or poor—husbandmen, merchants or manufacturers—members of different religious sects—followers of different political leaders—inhabitants of different districts—owners of different kinds of property &c. &c. In republican Government the majority however composed, ultimately give the law. Whenever therefore an apparent interest or common passion unites a majority what is to restrain them from unjust violations of the rights and interests of the minority, or of individuals? Three motives only:

> 1. a prudent regard to their own good as involved in the general and permanent good of the Community. This consideration although of decisive weight in itself, is found by experience to be too often unheeded. It is too often forgotten, by nations as well as by individuals that honesty is the best policy.
>
> 2dly. respect for character. However strong this motive may be in individuals, it is considered as very insufficient to restrain them from injustice. In a multitude its efficacy is diminished in proportion to the number which is to share the praise or the blame. Besides, as it has reference to public opinion, which within a particular Society, is the opinion of the majority, the standard is fixed by those whose conduct is to be measured by it. The public opinion without the Society, will be little respected by the people at large of any Country. Individuals of extended views, and of national pride, may bring the public proceedings to this standard, but the example will never be followed by the multitude. Is it to be imagined that an ordinary citizen or even an assemblyman of R. Island in estimating the policy of paper money, ever considered or cared in what light the measure would be viewed in France or Holland; or even in Massts or Connect.? It was a sufficient temptation to both that it was for their interest: it was a sufficient sanction to the latter that it was popular in the State; to the former that it was so in the neighbourhood.
>
> 3dly. will Religion the only remaining motive be a sufficient restraint? It is not pretended to be such on men individually considered. Will its effect be greater on them considered in an aggregate view? quite the reverse. The conduct of every popular assembly acting on oath, the strongest of religious Ties, proves that individuals join without remorse in acts, against which their consciences would revolt if proposed to them under the like sanction, separately in their closets. When indeed Religion is kindled into enthusiasm, its force like that of other passions, is increased by the sympathy of a multitude. But enthusiasm is only a temporary state of religion, and while it lasts will hardly be seen with pleasure at the helm of Government. Besides as religion in its coolest state, is not infallible, it may become a motive to oppression as well as a restraint from injustice.

Place three individuals in a situation wherein the interest of each depends on the voice of the others, and give to two of them an interest opposed to the rights of the third? Will the latter be secure? The prudence of every man would shun the danger. The rules & forms of justice suppose & guard against it. Will two thousand in a like situation be less likely to encroach on the rights of one thousand? The contrary is witnessed by the notorious factions & oppressions which take place in corporate towns limited as the opportunities are, and in little republics when uncontrouled by apprehensions of external danger. If an enlargement of the sphere is found to lessen the insecurity of private rights, it is not because the impulse of a common interest or passion is less predominant in this case with the majority; but because a common interest or passion is less apt to be felt and the requisite combinations less easy to be formed by a great than by a small number. The Society becomes broken into a greater variety of interests, of pursuits, of passions, which check each other, whilst those who may feel a common sentiment have less opportunity of communication and concert. It may be inferred that the inconveniences of popular States contrary to the prevailing Theory, are in proportion not to the extent, but to the narrowness of their limits.

The great desideratum in Government is such a modification of the Sovereignty as will render it sufficiently neutral between the different interests and factions, to controul one part of the Society from invading the rights of another, and at the same time sufficiently controuled itself, from setting up an interest adverse to that of the whole Society. In absolute Monarchies, the prince is sufficiently, neutral towards his subjects, but frequently sacrifices their happiness to his ambition or his avarice. In small Republics, the sovereign will is sufficiently controuled from such a Sacrifice of the entire Society, but is not sufficiently neutral towards the parts composing it. As a limited Monarchy tempers the evils of an absolute one; so an extensive Republic meliorates the administration of a small Republic.

An auxiliary desideratum for the melioration of the Republican form is such a process of elections as will most certainly extract from the mass of the Society the purest and noblest characters which it contains; such as will at once feel most strongly the proper motives to pursue the end of their appointment, and be most capable to devise the proper means of attaining it.

Chapter 2

Enumerated Powers

ASSIGNMENT S-3

The Roberts Court

The Commerce and Necessary and Proper Clauses

Study Guide:

- The next case is noteworthy, not for its majority opinion that is based on statutory interpretation, but for the concurring opinion by Justice Thomas in which he discusses the scope of the Indian Commerce Clause.
- Some scholars have contended that, because the first statute regulating "intercourse" with Indian tribes reflected a broader meaning of "commerce" than Justice Thomas attributed to the Interstate Commerce Clause, his interpretation of "commerce" is refuted.
- What follows is a brief point-counterpoint by Jack Balkin and Robert Natelson discussing the 1790 statute.

ADOPTIVE COUPLE v. BABY GIRL

No. 12-399

Argued Apr. 16, 2013 | Decided June 25, 2013

Justice Alito delivered the opinion of the Court.

This case is about a little girl (Baby Girl) who is classified as an Indian because she is 1.2% (3/256) Cherokee. Because Baby Girl is classified in this way, the South Carolina Supreme Court held that certain provisions of the federal Indian Child Welfare Act of 1978 required her to be taken, at the age of 27 months, from the only parents she had ever known and handed over to her biological father, who had attempted to relinquish his parental rights and who had no prior contact with the child. The provisions of the federal statute at issue here do not demand this result. Contrary to the State Supreme Court's ruling, we hold that 25 U.S.C. §1912(f)—which bars involuntary termination of a parent's rights in the absence of a heightened showing that serious harm to the Indian child is likely to result from the parent's "continued custody" of the child—does not apply when, as here, the relevant parent never had custody of the child. We further hold that §1912(d)—which conditions involuntary termination of parental rights with respect to an Indian child on a showing that remedial efforts have been made to prevent the "breakup of the Indian family"—is inapplicable when, as here, the parent abandoned the Indian child before birth and never had custody of the child. Finally, we clarify that §1915(a), which provides placement preferences for the adoption of Indian children, does not bar a non-Indian family like Adoptive Couple from adopting an Indian child when no other eligible candidates have sought to adopt the child. We accordingly reverse the South Carolina Supreme Court's judgment and remand for further proceedings. . . .

The Indian Child Welfare Act was enacted to help preserve the cultural identity and heritage of Indian tribes, but under the State Supreme Court's reading, the Act would put certain vulnerable children at a great disadvantage solely because an ancestor—even a remote one—was an Indian. As the State Supreme Court read §§1912(d) and (f), a biological Indian father could abandon his child *in utero* and refuse any support for the birth mother—perhaps contributing to the mother's decision to put the child up for adoption—and then could play his ICWA trump card at the eleventh hour to override the mother's decision and the child's best interests. If this were possible, many prospective adoptive parents would surely pause before adopting any child who might possibly qualify as an Indian under the ICWA. Such an interpretation would raise equal protection concerns, but the plain text of §§1912(f) and (d) makes clear that neither provision applies in the present context. Nor do §1915(a)'s rebuttable adoption preferences apply when no alternative party has formally sought to adopt the child. We therefore reverse the judgment of the South Carolina Supreme Court and remand the case for further proceedings not inconsistent with this opinion.

It is so ordered.

JUSTICE THOMAS, concurring.

I join the Court's opinion in full but write separately to explain why constitutional avoidance compels this outcome. Each party in this case has put forward a plausible interpretation of the relevant sections of the Indian Child Welfare Act (ICWA). However, the interpretations offered by respondent Birth Father and the United States raise significant constitutional problems as applied to this case. Because the Court's decision avoids those problems, I concur in its interpretation.

I

This case arises out of a contested state-court adoption proceeding. Adoption proceedings are adjudicated in state family courts across the country every day, and "domestic relations" is "an area that has long been regarded as a virtually exclusive province of the States." *Sosna v. Iowa* (1975). Indeed, "[t]he whole subject of the domestic relations of husband and wife, parent and child, belongs to the laws of the States and not to the laws of the United States." *In re Burrus* (1890). Nevertheless, when Adoptive Couple filed a petition in South Carolina

Family Court to finalize their adoption of Baby Girl, Birth Father, who had relinquished his parental rights via a text message to Birth Mother, claimed a federal right under the ICWA to block the adoption and to obtain custody.

The ICWA establishes "federal standards that govern state-court child custody proceedings involving Indian children." The ICWA defines "Indian child" as "any unmarried person who is under age eighteen and is either (a) a member of an Indian tribe or (b) is eligible for membership in an Indian tribe and is the biological child of a member of an Indian tribe." As relevant, the ICWA defines "child custody proceeding," §1903(1), to include "adoptive placement," which means "the permanent placement of an Indian child for adoption, including any action resulting in a final decree of adoption," §1903(1)(iv), and "termination of parental rights," which means "any action resulting in the termination of the parent-child relationship," §1903(1)(ii).

The ICWA restricts a state court's ability to terminate the parental rights of an Indian parent in two relevant ways. Section 1912(f) prohibits a state court from involuntarily terminating parental rights "in the absence of a determination, supported by evidence beyond a reasonable doubt, including testimony of qualified expert witnesses, that the continued custody of the child by the parent or Indian custodian is likely to result in serious emotional or physical damage to the child." Section 1912(d) prohibits a state court from terminating parental rights until the court is satisfied "that active efforts have been made to provide remedial services and rehabilitative programs designed to prevent the breakup of the Indian family and that these efforts have proved unsuccessful." A third provision creates specific placement preferences for the adoption of Indian children, which favor placement with Indians over other adoptive families. §1915(a). Operating together, these requirements often lead to different outcomes than would result under state law. That is precisely what happened here. See *ante* ("It is undisputed that, had Baby Girl not been 3/256 Cherokee, Biological Father would have had no right to object to her adoption under South Carolina law").

The ICWA recognizes States' inherent "jurisdiction over Indian child custody proceedings," §1901(5), but asserts that federal regulation is necessary because States "have often failed to recognize the essential tribal relations of Indian people and the cultural and social standards prevailing in Indian communities and families." However, Congress may regulate areas of traditional state concern only if the Constitution grants it such power. Admt. 10 ("The powers not delegated to the United States by the Constitution, nor prohibited by it to the States, are reserved to the States respectively, or to the people"). The threshold question, then, is whether the Constitution grants Congress power to override state custody law whenever an Indian is involved.

II

The ICWA asserts that the Indian Commerce Clause, Art. I, §8, cl. 3, and "other constitutional authority" provides Congress with "plenary power over Indian affairs." §1901(1). The reference to "other constitutional authority" is not illuminating, and I am aware of no other enumerated power that could even arguably support Congress' intrusion into this area of traditional state authority. See Fletcher, The Supreme Court and Federal Indian Policy, 85 Neb. L. Rev. 121, 137 (2006) ("As a matter of federal constitutional law, the Indian Commerce Clause grants Congress the only explicit constitutional authority to deal with Indian tribes"); Natelson, The Original Understanding of the Indian Commerce Clause, 85 Denver U. L. Rev. 201, 210 (2007) (hereinafter Natelson) (evaluating, and rejecting, other potential sources of authority supporting congressional power over Indians). The assertion of plenary authority must, therefore, stand or fall on Congress' power under the Indian Commerce Clause. Although this Court has said that the "central function of the Indian Commerce Clause is to provide Congress with plenary power to legislate in the field of Indian affairs," *Cotton Petroleum Corp. v. New Mexico* (1989), neither the text nor the original understanding of the Clause supports Congress' claim to such "plenary" power.

A

The Indian Commerce Clause gives Congress authority "[t]o regulate *Commerce* . . . with the Indian tribes." Art. I, §8, cl. 3 (emphasis added). "At the time the original Constitution was ratified, 'commerce' consisted of selling, buying, and bartering, as well as transporting for these purposes." *United States v. Lopez* (1995) (Thomas, J., concurring). See also 1 S. Johnson, A Dictionary of the English Language 361 (4th rev. ed. 1773) (reprint 1978) (defining commerce as "Intercourse; exchange of one thing for another; interchange of any thing; trade; traffick"). "[W]hen Federalists and Anti-Federalists discussed the Commerce Clause during the ratification period, they often used trade (in its selling/bartering sense) and commerce interchangeably." *Lopez* (Thomas, J., concurring). The term "commerce" did not include economic activity such as "manufacturing and agriculture," let alone noneconomic activity such as adoption of children.

Furthermore, the term "commerce with Indian tribes" was invariably used during the time of the founding to mean "'trade with Indians.'" See, *e.g.*, Natelson (citing 18th-century sources); Report of Committee on Indian Affairs (Feb. 20, 1787), in 32 Journals of the Continental Congress 1774-1789 (R. Hill ed. 1936) (hereinafter J. Cont'l Cong.) (using the phrase "commerce with the Indians" to mean trade with the Indians). And regulation of Indian commerce generally referred to legal structures governing "the conduct of the merchants engaged in the Indian trade, the nature of the goods they sold, the prices charged, and similar matters." Natelson.

The Indian Commerce Clause contains an additional textual limitation relevant to this case: Congress is given the power to regulate Commerce "with the Indian *tribes*." The Clause does not give Congress the power to regulate commerce with all Indian *persons* any more than the Foreign Commerce Clause gives Congress the power to regulate commerce with all foreign nationals traveling within the United States. A straightforward reading of the text, thus, confirms that Congress may only regulate commercial interactions — "commerce"—taking place with established Indian communities — "tribes." That power is far from "plenary."

B

Congress' assertion of "plenary power" over Indian affairs is also inconsistent with the history of the Indian Commerce Clause. At the time of the founding, the Clause was understood to reserve to the States general police powers with respect to Indians who were citizens of the several States. The Clause instead conferred on Congress the much narrower power to regulate trade with Indian tribes—that is, Indians who had not been incorporated into the body-politic of any State.

1

Before the Revolution, most Colonies adopted their own regulations governing Indian trade. See Natelson (citing colonial laws). Such regulations were necessary because colonial traders all too often abused their Indian trading partners, through fraud, exorbitant prices, extortion, and physical invasion of Indian territory, among other things. See 1 F. Prucha, The Great Father (1984) (hereinafter Prucha). These abuses sometimes provoked violent Indian retaliation. To mitigate these conflicts, most Colonies extensively regulated traders engaged in commerce with Indian tribes. See *e.g.*, Ordinance to Regulate Indian Affairs, Statutes of South Carolina (Aug. 31, 1751), in 16 Early American Indian Documents: Treaties and Laws, 1607-1789 (A. Vaughan and D. Rosen eds. 1998).[1] Over time, commercial regulation at the colonial level proved largely ineffective, in part because "[t]here was no uniformity among the colonies, no two sets of like regulations." Prucha.

Recognizing the need for uniform regulation of trade with the Indians, Benjamin Franklin proposed his own "articles of confederation" to the Continental Congress on July 21, 1775, which reflected his view that central control over Indian affairs should predominate over local control. 2 J. Cont'l Cong. (W. Ford ed. 1905). Franklin's proposal was not enacted, but in November 1775, Congress empowered a committee to draft regulations for the Indian trade. On July 12, 1776, the committee submitted a draft of the Articles of Confederation to Congress, which incorporated many of Franklin's proposals. The draft prohibited States from waging offensive war against the Indians without congressional authorization and granted Congress the exclusive power to acquire land from the Indians outside state boundaries, once those boundaries had been established. This version

---

1. South Carolina, for example, required traders to be licensed, to be of good moral character, and to post a bond. Ordinance to Regulate Indian Affairs. A potential applicant's name was posted publicly before issuing the license, so anyone with objections had an opportunity to raise them. Restrictions were placed on employing agents and names of potential agents had to be disclosed. Traders who violated these rules were subject to substantial penalties.

also gave Congress "the sole and exclusive Right and Power of . . . Regulating the Trade, and managing all Affairs with the Indians."

On August 20, 1776, the Committee of the Whole presented to Congress a revised draft, which provided Congress with "the sole and exclusive right and power of . . . regulating the trade, and managing all affairs with the Indians." Some delegates feared that the Articles gave Congress excessive power to interfere with States' jurisdiction over affairs with Indians residing within state boundaries. After further deliberation, the final result was a clause that included a broad grant of congressional authority with two significant exceptions: "The United States in Congress assembled shall also have the sole and exclusive right and power of . . . regulating the trade and managing all affairs with the Indians, not members of any of the States, provided that the legislative right of any State within its own limits be not infringed or violated." Articles of Confederation, Art. IX, cl. 4. As a result, Congress retained exclusive jurisdiction over Indian affairs outside the borders of the States; the States retained exclusive jurisdiction over relations with Member-Indians;[2] and Congress and the States "exercise[d] concurrent jurisdiction over transactions with tribal Indians within state boundaries, but congressional decisions would have to be in compliance with local law." Natelson 230. The drafting of the Articles of Confederation reveals the delegates' concern with protecting the power of the States to regulate Indian persons who were politically incorporated into the States. This concern for state power reemerged during the drafting of the Constitution.

2

The drafting history of the Constitutional Convention also supports a limited construction of the Indian Commerce Clause. On July 24, 1787, the convention elected a drafting committee—the Committee of Detail—and charged it to "report a Constitution conformable to the Resolutions passed by the Convention." 2 Records of the Federal Convention of 1787 (M. Farrand rev. 1966) (J. Madison). During the Committee's deliberations, John Rutledge, the chairman, suggested incorporating an Indian affairs power into the Constitution. The first draft reported back to the convention, however, provided Congress with authority "[t]o regulate commerce with foreign nations, and among the several States," *id.* (Madison) (Aug. 6, 1787), but did not include any specific Indian affairs clause. On August 18, James Madison proposed that the Federal Government be granted several additional powers, including the power "[t]o regulate *affairs* with the Indians as well within as without the limits of the U. States." *Id.* (J. Madison) (emphasis added). On August 22, Rutledge delivered the Committee of Detail's second report, which modified Madison's proposed

2. Although Indians were generally considered "members" of a State if they paid taxes or were citizens, see Natelson, the precise definition of the term was "not yet settled" at the time of the founding and was "a question of frequent perplexity and contention in the federal councils," The Federalist No. 42 (J. Madison).

clause. The Committee proposed to add to Congress' power "[t]o regulate commerce with foreign nations, and among the several States" the words, "and with Indians, within the Limits of any State, not subject to the laws thereof." The Committee's version, which echoed the Articles of Confederation, was far narrower than Madison's proposal. On August 31, the revised draft was submitted to a Committee of Eleven for further action. That Committee recommended adding to the Commerce Clause the phrase, "and with the Indian tribes," which the Convention ultimately adopted.

It is, thus, clear that the Framers of the Constitution were alert to the difference between the power to regulate trade with the Indians and the power to regulate all Indian affairs. By limiting Congress' power to the former, the Framers declined to grant Congress the same broad powers over Indian affairs conferred by the Articles of Confederation. See Prakash, Against Tribal Fungibility, 89 Cornell L. Rev. 1069, 1090 (2004).

During the ratification debates, opposition to the Indian Commerce Clause was nearly nonexistent. See Natelson (noting that Robert Yates, a New York Anti-Federalist was "almost the only writer who objected to any part [of] of the Commerce Clause—a clear indication that its scope was understood to be fairly narrow"). Given the Anti-Federalists' vehement opposition to the Constitution's other grants of power to the Federal Government, this silence is revealing. The ratifiers almost certainly understood the Clause to confer a relatively modest power on Congress—namely, the power to regulate trade with Indian tribes living beyond state borders. And this feature of the Constitution was welcomed by Federalists and Anti-Federalists alike due to the considerable interest in expanding trade with such Indian tribes. See, *e.g.,* The Federalist No. 42 (J. Madison) (praising the Constitution for removing the obstacles that had existed under the Articles of Confederation to federal control over "*trade* with Indians" (emphasis added)); 3 J. Elliot, The Debates in the Several State Conventions on the Adoption of the Federal Constitution 580 (2d ed. 1863) (Adam Stephens, at the Virginia ratifying convention, June 23, 1788, describing the Indian tribes residing near the Mississippi and "the variety of articles which might be obtained to advantage by trading with these people"); The Federalist No. 24 (A. Hamilton) (arguing that frontier garrisons would "be keys to the trade with the Indian nations"); Brutus (Letter) X, N.Y. J., Jan. 24, 1788 (conceding that there must be a standing army for some purposes, including "trade with Indians"). There is little evidence that the ratifiers of the Constitution understood the Indian Commerce Clause to confer anything resembling plenary power over Indian affairs. See Natelson 247-250.

III

In light of the original understanding of the Indian Commerce Clause, the constitutional problems that would be created by application of the ICWA here are evident. First, the statute deals with "child custody proceedings," §1903(1), not "commerce." It was enacted in response to concerns that "an alarmingly high percentage of Indian families [were] broken up by the removal, often unwarranted, of their children from them by nontribal public and private agencies." §1901(4). The perceived problem was that many Indian children were "placed in non-Indian foster and adoptive homes and institutions." This problem, however, had nothing to do with commerce.

Second, the portions of the ICWA at issue here do not regulate Indian tribes as tribes. [They] apply to all child custody proceedings involving an Indian child, regardless of whether an Indian tribe is involved. This case thus does not directly implicate Congress' power to "legislate in respect to Indian *tribes*." *United States v. Lara* (2004) (emphasis added). Baby Girl was never domiciled on an Indian Reservation, and the Cherokee Nation had no jurisdiction over her. Although Birth Father is a registered member of The Cherokee Nation, he did not live on a reservation either. He was, thus, subject to the laws of the State in which he resided (Oklahoma) and of the State where his daughter resided during the custody proceedings (South Carolina). Nothing in the Indian Commerce Clause permits Congress to enact special laws applicable to Birth Father merely because of his status as an Indian.

Because adoption proceedings like this one involve neither "commerce" nor "Indian tribes," there is simply no constitutional basis for Congress' assertion of authority over such proceedings. Also, the notion that Congress can direct state courts to apply different rules of evidence and procedure merely because a person of Indian descent is involved raises absurd possibilities. Such plenary power would allow Congress to dictate specific rules of criminal procedure for state-court prosecutions against Indian defendants. Likewise, it would allow Congress to substitute federal law for state law when contract disputes involve Indians. But the Constitution does not grant Congress power to override state law whenever that law happens to be applied to Indians. Accordingly, application of the ICWA to these child custody proceedings would be unconstitutional.

* * *

Because the Court's plausible interpretation of the relevant sections of the ICWA avoids these constitutional problems, I concur.

JACK M. BALKIN, COMMERCE, 109 MICH. L. REV. 1 (2010): Some contemporary originalists like Justice Clarence Thomas have argued that the original meaning of "commerce" is very narrow, essentially limited to the trade or exchange of goods and commodities. Thus, it would not include manufacturing, mining, or agriculture, much less any noneconomic activities. This reading is anachronistic: by focusing on the disposition of commodities it reflects a modern conception of commerce viewed as a subset of economic activity; it completely misses the eighteenth-century dimensions of commerce as a form of social intercourse. . . .

If we view the Commerce Clause through the lens of the central reasons for forming the Constitution and the central questions that faced the new nation — foreign affairs and dealings with Indian tribes — reading "commerce" to mean "intercourse" or "interactions" makes the most sense. The Clause enabled "Congress to regulate all interactions (and altercations) with foreign nations and Indian tribes," which "if improperly handled by a single state acting on its own, might lead to needless wars or compromise the interests of sister states."

One of the first things the new government did, for example, was to regulate its interactions with the Indian tribes, through a series of Trade and Intercourse Acts beginning in 1790. The title of these acts was apt: they not only required licenses for trade with Indians, but also punished "any crime upon, or trespass against, the person or property of any peaceable and friendly Indian or Indians." These crimes did not necessarily involve trade or even economic activity; they could involve assault, murder, or rape. Note as well that even if the point of regulating these crimes was because of their likely effects on trade with the Indian tribes, the activities regulated were themselves not economic. And note finally that the 1790 and 1793 Trade and Intercourse Acts could not be justified as legislation designed to enforce treaties; they applied to crimes against Indians whether or not they had signed treaties with the United States. Congress clearly believed that it could reach both economic and noneconomic activity under the Indian Commerce Clause; at the very least it believed that it could regulate noneconomic activity in order to protect trade and diplomatic relations that would further trade. This is hardly surprising. It was assumed in international law at the time of the founding that international intercourse included both commercial and noncommercial aspects that were inevitably intertwined.

Neither the trade theory nor the economic theory can explain why the early Trade and Intercourse Acts would be constitutional unless we assume that Congress has the auxiliary power to regulate noneconomic (or nontrade) activity that affects foreign or Indian commerce. That is, we must assume that Congress can reach activities that do not involve trade or are not economic in order to protect its powers to regulate trade or other economic activity, perhaps under the Necessary and Proper Clause. If so, then the two theories essentially merge into the interaction theory. Note, however, that the Clause says that Congress can regulate "commerce" with foreign nations and with the Indian tribes, not "activity that affects commerce" with foreign nations and with the Indian tribes. The interaction theory is therefore more consistent with the text.

ROBERT G. NATELSON, THE ORIGINAL UNDERSTANDING OF THE INDIAN COMMERCE CLAUSE, 85 DENV. U. L. REV. 201 (2007): In contending for an expansive view of the commerce power, some have argued that a portion of the Indian Intercourse Act of 1790 shows an intended meaning for Indian "commerce" that goes beyond mere trade. . . . [T]he fundamental problem with arguing that the Indian Intercourse Act sheds light on the Commerce Clause is this: the Indian Intercourse Act was not adopted pursuant to the Commerce Clause. It was adopted pursuant to the Treaty Power.

In 1785 and 1786 Congress entered into the three "Hopewell" treaties with the Cherokees, Chickasaws, and Choctaws. By the terms of all these treaties, the United States had promised to regulate trade between the United States and the Natives "[f]or the benefit and comfort of the Indians, and for the prevention of injuries or oppressions on the part of the citizens or Indians." The tribes, President Washington, and Secretary of War Henry Knox all were unhappy over white abuses that continued in defiance of the treaties, and became convinced that enforcement legislation was needed.

On August 22, 1789, the President entered the chamber of the Senate and consulted its members on Indian affairs. After reciting the tribes' dissatisfaction, he noted that the Cherokees lived primarily in North Carolina, which had not yet joined the union, and added:

> The commissioners for negotiating with the Southern Indians may be instructed to transmit a message to the Cherokees, stating to them, as far as may be proper, the difficulties arising from the local claims of North Carolina, and to assure them that the United States are not unmindful of the treaty at Hopewell. . . .
>
> The Commissioners may be instructed to transmit messages to the said tribes, containing our assurances of the continuance of the friendship of the United States, and that measures will soon be taken for extending a trade to them agreeably to the treaties of Hopewell.

The President then proceeded to impress upon his listeners the importance of an early agreement with the Creeks. He returned two days later for further consultation. Congress responded the following summer by enacting the Indian Intercourse Act.

Hence, the first three sections of the Act were designed to fulfill the promise of the United States to regulate trade for the benefit of the Indians. Section 4 was, by its terms, designed to effectuate Indian treaties. Section 5—the substantive criminal provision—loosely tracked the language in another provision of the Hopewell pacts, which required that United States citizens who committed crimes in Indian country be tried and punished as if they had committed those crimes against fellow citizens. Provisions in treaties that defined and provided for punishment of crimes were well precedented.

The trade and criminal portions of the Indian Intercourse Act applied to all Native Americans, not merely the Hopewell tribes. But that was because none of the treaties limited their primary benefits to members of the signatory tribes. The trade provisions in the treaties referred generally to "the Indians," and the criminal sections referred to "any Indian." Further, the broad statutory language was appropriate because the government apparently planned to apply the Hopewell language as a template for future agreements: very similar terms were contained in a fourth treaty, signed only a few days later with the Creeks, and in a fifth, concluded the following year with the Cherokees.

A law enacted to execute the Treaty Power cannot be said to represent an interpretation of the Commerce Clause. . . .

Chapter 3

The Separation of Powers

ASSIGNMENT S-4

The Appointments Power

STUDY GUIDE:

- As in *Morrison v. Olson*, the majority claims to be applying a functional rather than a textualist or originalist analysis, although unlike *Morrison*, the result of the case is consistent with that urged by Justice Scalia in his concurring opinion.
- Does this case represent the repudiation of originalism? Can you see the interpretive conclusion of Justice Breyer that enables him to employ a functional analysis? Do you think at least some of the Justices might have voted to uphold the President's recess appointments here had they not been confronting the textualist and originalist analysis accepted by the Court of Appeals and the four concurring Justices?
- Given that they have not previously employed an originalist analysis in their opinions, it is perhaps noteworthy that Chief Justice Roberts and Justice Alito join Justice Scalia's concurrence.

NATIONAL LABOR RELATIONS BOARD v. NOEL CANNING

No. 12-1281

Argued Jan. 13, 2014 | Decided June 26, 2014

JUSTICE BREYER delivered the opinion of the Court.

Ordinarily the President must obtain "the Advice and Consent of the Senate" before appointing an "Office[r] of the United States." U.S. Const., Art. II, §2, cl. 2. But the Recess Appointments Clause creates an exception. It gives the President alone the power "to fill up all Vacancies that may happen during the Recess of the Senate, by granting Commissions which shall expire at the End of their next Session." Art. II, §2, cl. 3. We here consider three questions about the application of this Clause.

The first concerns the scope of the words "recess of the Senate." Does that phrase refer only to an inter-session recess (*i.e.*, a break between formal sessions of Congress), or does it also include an intra-session recess, such as a summer recess in the midst of a session? We conclude that the Clause applies to both kinds of recess.

The second question concerns the scope of the words "vacancies that may happen." Does that phrase refer only to vacancies that first come into existence during a recess, or does it also include vacancies that arise prior to a recess but continue to exist during the recess? We conclude that the Clause applies to both kinds of vacancy.

The third question concerns calculation of the length of a "recess." The President made the appointments here at issue on January 4, 2012. At that time the Senate was in recess pursuant to a December 17, 2011, resolution providing for a series of brief recesses punctuated by "*pro forma* session[s]," with "no business . . . transacted," every Tuesday and Friday through January 20, 2012. In calculating the length of a recess are we to ignore the *pro forma* sessions, thereby treating the series of brief recesses as a single, month-long recess? We conclude that we cannot ignore these *pro forma* sessions.

Our answer to the third question means that, when the appointments before us took place, the Senate was in the midst of a 3-day recess. Three days is too short a time to bring a recess within the scope of the Clause. Thus we conclude that the President lacked the power to make the recess appointments here at issue.

I

The case before us arises out of a labor dispute. The National Labor Relations Board (NLRB) found that a Pepsi-Cola distributor, Noel Canning, had unlawfully refused to reduce to writing and execute a collective-bargaining agreement with a labor union. The Board ordered the distributor to execute the agreement and to make employees whole for any losses.

The Pepsi-Cola distributor subsequently asked the Court of Appeals for the District of Columbia Circuit to set the Board's order aside. It claimed that three of the five Board members had been invalidly appointed, leaving the Board without the three lawfully appointed members necessary for it to act.

The three members in question were Sharon Block, Richard Griffin, and Terence Flynn. In 2011 the President had nominated each of them to the Board. As of January 2012, Flynn's nomination had been pending in the Senate awaiting confirmation for approximately a year. The nominations of each of the other two had been pending for a few weeks. On January 4, 2012, the President, invoking the Recess Appointments Clause, appointed all three to the Board.

The distributor argued that the Recess Appointments Clause did not authorize those appointments. It pointed out that on December 17, 2011, the Senate, by unanimous consent, had adopted a resolution providing that it would take a series of brief recesses beginning the following day. Pursuant to that resolution, the Senate held *pro forma* sessions every Tuesday and Friday until it returned for ordinary business on January 23, 2012. The President's January 4 appointments were made between the January 3 and January 6 *pro forma* sessions. In the distributor's view, each *pro forma* session terminated the immediately preceding recess. Accordingly, the appointments were made during a 3-day adjournment, which is not long enough to trigger the Recess Appointments Clause.

The Court of Appeals agreed that the appointments fell outside the scope of the Clause. But the court set forth different reasons. It held that the Clause's words "the recess of the Senate" do not include recesses that occur *within* a formal session of Congress, *i.e.*, intra-session recesses. Rather those words apply only to recesses *between* those formal sessions, *i.e.*, inter-session recesses. Since the second session of the 112th Congress began on January 3, 2012, the day before the President's appointments, those appointments occurred during an intra-session recess, and the appointments consequently fell outside the scope of the Clause.

The Court of Appeals added that, in any event, the phrase "vacancies that may happen during the recess" applies only to vacancies that come into existence during a recess. The vacancies that Members Block, Griffin, and Flynn were appointed to fill had arisen before the beginning of the recess during which they were appointed. For this reason too the President's appointments were invalid. And, because the Board lacked a quorum of validly appointed members when it issued its order, the order was invalid.

We granted the Solicitor General's petition for certiorari. We asked the parties to address not only the Court of Appeals' interpretation of the Clause but also the distributor's initial argument, namely, "[w]hether the President's recess-appointment power may be exercised when the Senate is convening every three days in *pro forma* sessions."

We shall answer all three questions presented.

II

Before turning to the specific questions presented, we shall mention two background considerations that we find relevant to all three. First, *the Recess Appointments Clause sets forth a subsidiary, not a primary, method for appointing officers of the United States.* The immediately preceding Clause—Article II, Section 2, Clause 2—provides the primary method of appointment. It says that the President "shall nominate, *and by and with the Advice and Consent of the Senate,* shall appoint Ambassadors, other public Ministers and Consuls, Judges of the supreme Court, and all other Officers of the United States" (emphasis added).

The Federalist Papers make clear that the Founders intended this method of appointment, requiring Senate approval, to be the norm (at least for principal officers). Alexander Hamilton wrote that the Constitution vests the power of *nomination* in the President alone because "one man of discernment is better fitted to analise and estimate the peculiar qualities adapted to particular offices, than a body of men of equal, or perhaps even of superior discernment." The Federalist No. 76, p. 510 (J. Cooke ed. 1961). At the same time, the need to secure Senate approval provides "an excellent check upon a spirit of favoritism in the President, and would tend greatly to preventing the appointment of unfit characters from State prejudice, from family connection, from personal attachment, or from a view to popularity." *Id.* Hamilton further explained that the

> ordinary power of appointment is confided to the President and Senate *jointly,* and can therefore only be exercised during the session of the Senate; but as it would have been improper to oblige this body to be continually in session for the appointment of officers; and as vacancies might happen *in their recess,* which it might be necessary for the public service to fill without delay, the succeeding clause is evidently intended to authorise the President *singly* to make temporary appointments. *Id.,* No. 67.

Thus the Recess Appointments Clause reflects the tension between, on the one hand, the President's continuous need for "the assistance of subordinates," *Myers v. United States* (1926), and, on the other, the Senate's practice, particularly during the Republic's early years, of meeting for a single brief session each year. We seek to interpret the Clause as granting the President the power to make appointments during a recess but not offering the President the authority routinely to avoid the need for Senate confirmation.

Second, *in interpreting the Clause, we put significant weight upon historical practice.* For one thing, the interpretive questions before us concern the allocation of power between two elected branches of Government. Long ago Chief Justice Marshall wrote that

> a doubtful question, one on which human reason may pause, and the human judgment be suspended, in the decision of which the great principles of liberty are not concerned, but the respective powers of those who are equally the representatives of the people, are to be adjusted; if not put at rest by the practice of the government, ought to receive a considerable impression from that practice. *McCulloch v. Maryland* (1819).

And we later confirmed that "[l]ong settled and established practice is a consideration of great weight in a proper interpretation of constitutional provisions" regulating the relationship between Congress and the President. *The Pocket Veto Case* (1929).

We recognize, of course, that the separation of powers can serve to safeguard individual liberty, and that it is the "duty of the judicial department"—in a separation-of-powers case as in any other—"to say what the law is," *Marbury v. Madison* (1803). But it is equally true that the longstanding "practice of the government," *McCulloch,* can inform our determination of "what the law is," *Marbury.*

That principle is neither new nor controversial. As James Madison wrote, it "was foreseen at the birth of the Constitution, that difficulties and differences of opinion might occasionally arise in expounding terms & phrases necessarily used in such a charter . . . and that it might require a regular course of practice to liquidate & settle the meaning of some of them." Letter to Spencer Roane (Sept. 2, 1819). And our cases have continually confirmed Madison's view.

These precedents show that this Court has treated practice as an important interpretive factor even when the nature or longevity of that practice is subject to dispute, and even when that practice began after the founding era.

There is a great deal of history to consider here. Presidents have made recess appointments since the beginning of the Republic. Their frequency suggests that the Senate and President have recognized that recess appointments can be both necessary and appropriate in certain circumstances. We have not previously interpreted the Clause, and, when doing so for the first time in more than 200 years, we must hesitate to upset the compromises and working arrangements that the elected branches of Government themselves have reached.

III

The first question concerns the scope of the phrase "*the recess* of the Senate." Art. II, §2, cl. 3 (emphasis added). The Constitution provides for congressional elections every two years. And the 2-year life of each elected Congress typically consists of two formal 1-year sessions, each separated from the next by an "inter-session recess." The Senate or the House of Representatives announces an inter-session recess by approving a resolution stating that it will "adjourn *sine die,*" *i.e.,* without specifying a date to return (in which case Congress will reconvene when the next formal session is scheduled to begin).

The Senate and the House also take breaks in the midst of a session. The Senate or the House announces any such "intra-session recess" by adopting a resolution stating that it will "adjourn" to a fixed date, a few days or weeks or even months later. All agree that the phrase "the recess of the Senate" covers inter-session recesses. The question is whether it includes intra-session recesses as well.

In our view, the phrase "the recess" includes an intra-session recess of substantial length. Its words taken literally can refer to both types of recess. Founding-era dictionaries define the word "recess," much as we do today, simply as "a period of cessation from usual work." 13 The Oxford English Dictionary 322-323 (2d ed. 1989) (hereinafter OED) (citing 18th- and 19th-century sources for that definition of "recess"); 2 N. Webster, An American Dictionary of the English Language (1828) ("[r]emission or suspension of business or procedure"); 2 S. Johnson, A Dictionary of the English Language 1602-1603 (4th ed. 1773) (hereinafter Johnson) (same). The Founders themselves used the word to refer to intra-session, as well as to inter-session, breaks. See, *e.g.,* 3 Records of the Federal Convention of 1787 (M. Farrand rev. 1966) (hereinafter Farrand) (letter from George Washington to John Jay using "the recess" to refer to an intra-session break of the Constitutional Convention); *id.* (speech of Luther Martin with a similar usage); 1 T. Jefferson, A Manual of Parliamentary Practice §LI (2d ed. 1812) (describing a "recess by adjournment" which did *not* end a session).

We recognize that the word "the" in "*the* recess" might suggest that the phrase refers to the single break separating formal sessions of Congress. That is because the word "the" frequently (but not always) indicates "a particular thing." 2 Johnson 2003. But the word can also refer "to a term used generically or universally." 17 OED 879. The Constitution, for example, directs the Senate to choose a President *pro tempore* "in *the* Absence of the Vice-President." Art. I, §3, cl. 5 (emphasis added). And the Federalist Papers refer to the chief magistrate of an ancient Achaean league who "administered the government in *the* recess of the Senate." The Federalist No. 18 (J. Madison) (emphasis added). Reading "the" generically in this way, there is no linguistic problem applying the Clause's phrase to both kinds of recess. And, in fact, the phrase "the recess" was used to refer to intra-session recesses at the time of the founding. See, *e.g.,* 3 Farrand 76 (letter from Washington to Jay); New Jersey Legislative-Council Journal, 5th Sess., 1st Sitting 70, 2d Sitting 9 (1781) (twice referring to a 4-month, intra-session break as "the Recess").

The constitutional text is thus ambiguous. And we believe the Clause's purpose demands the broader interpretation. The Clause gives the President authority to make appointments during "the recess of the Senate" so that the President can ensure the continued functioning of the Federal Government when the Senate is away. The Senate is equally away during both an inter-session and an intra-session recess, and its capacity to participate in the appointments process has nothing to do with the words it uses to signal its departure.

History also offers strong support for the broad interpretation. We concede that pre-Civil War history is not helpful. But it shows only that Congress generally took long breaks between sessions, while taking no significant intra-session breaks at all (five times it took a break of a week or so at Christmas). Obviously, if there are no significant intra-session recesses, there will be no intra-session recess appointments. In 1867 and 1868, Congress for the first time took substantial, nonholiday intra-session breaks, and President Andrew Johnson made dozens of recess appointments. The Federal Court of Claims upheld one of those specific appointments, writing "[w]e have *no doubt* that a vacancy occurring while the Senate was thus temporarily adjourned" during the "first session of the Fortieth Congress" was "legally filled by appointment of the President alone." *Gould v. United States* (1884) (emphasis added). Attorney General Evarts also issued three opinions concerning the constitutionality of President Johnson's appointments, and it apparently did not occur to him that the distinction between intra-session and inter-session recesses was significant. Similarly, though the 40th Congress impeached President Johnson on charges relating to his appointment power, he was not accused of violating the Constitution by making intra-session recess appointments. Hartnett, Recess Appointments of Article III Judges: Three Constitutional Questions, 26 Cardozo L. Rev. 377, 409 (2005).

In all, between the founding and the Great Depression, Congress took substantial intra-session breaks (other than holiday breaks) in four years: 1867, 1868, 1921, and 1929. And in each of those years the President made intra-session recess appointments.

Since 1929, and particularly since the end of World War II, Congress has shortened its inter-session breaks as it has taken longer and more frequent intra-session breaks; Presidents have correspondingly made more intra-session recess appointments. Indeed, if we include military appointments, Presidents have made thousands of intra-session recess appointments. . . .

Not surprisingly, the publicly available opinions of Presidential legal advisers that we have found are nearly unanimous in determining that the Clause authorizes these appointments. . . .

We must note one contrary opinion authored by President Theodore Roosevelt's Attorney General Philander Knox. Knox advised the President that the Clause did not cover a 19-day intra-session Christmas recess. But in doing so he relied heavily upon the use of the word "the," a linguistic point that we do not find determinative. And Knox all but confessed that his interpretation ran contrary to the basic purpose of the Clause. For it would permit the Senate to adjourn for "several months," to a fixed date, and thereby "seriously curtail the President's power of making recess appointments." Moreover, only three days before Knox gave his opinion, the Solicitor of the Treasury came to the opposite conclusion. We therefore do not think Knox's isolated opinion can disturb the consensus advice within the Executive Branch taking the opposite position.

What about the Senate? Since Presidents began making intra-session recess appointments, individual Senators have taken differing views about the proper definition of "the recess." But neither the Senate considered as a body nor its committees, despite opportunities to express opposition to the practice of intra-session recess appointments, has done so. Rather, to the extent that the Senate or a Senate committee has expressed a view, that view has favored a functional definition of "recess," and a functional definition encompasses intra-session recesses.

Most notably, in 1905 the Senate Committee on the Judiciary objected strongly to President Theodore Roosevelt's use of the Clause to make more than 160 recess appointments during a "fictitious" inter-session recess. At noon on December 7, 1903, the Senate President *pro tempore* had "declare[d]" a formal, "extraordinary session" of the Senate "adjourned without day," and the next formal Senate session began immediately afterwards. President Roosevelt made over 160 recess appointments during the instantaneous inter-session interval. The Judiciary Committee, when stating its strong objection, defined "recess" in functional terms as

> the period of time when the Senate is not sitting in regular or extraordinary session as a branch of the Congress . . . ; when its members owe no duty of attendance; when its Chamber is empty; when, because of its absence, it can not receive communications from the President or participate as a body in making appointments.

That functional definition encompasses intra-session, as well as inter-session, recesses. Justice Scalia is right that the 1905 Report did not specifically address the distinction between inter-session and intra-session recesses. But the animating principle of the Report—that "recess" should be practically construed to mean a time when the Senate is unavailable to participate in the appointments process—is inconsistent with the formalistic approach that Justice Scalia endorses.

Similarly, in 1940 the Senate helped to enact a law regulating the payment of recess appointees, and the Comptroller General of the United States has interpreted that law functionally. An earlier 1863 statute had denied pay to individuals appointed to fill up vacancies first arising prior to the beginning of a recess. The Senate Judiciary Committee then believed that those vacancies fell outside the scope of the Clause. In 1940, however, the Senate amended the law to permit many of those recess appointees to be paid. . . .

The upshot is that restricting the Clause to inter-session recesses would frustrate its purpose. It would make the President's recess-appointment power dependent on a formalistic distinction of Senate procedure. Moreover, the President has consistently and frequently interpreted the word "recess" to apply to intra-session recesses, and has acted on that interpretation. The Senate as a body has done nothing to deny the validity of this practice for at least three-quarters of a century. And three-quarters of a century of settled practice is long enough to entitle a practice to "great weight in a proper interpretation" of the constitutional provision. . . .

[S]ome argue that the Founders would likely have intended the Clause to apply only to inter-session recesses, for they hardly knew any other. See, *e.g.*, Brief for Originalist Scholars as *Amici Curiae*. Indeed, from the founding until the Civil War inter-session recesses were the only kind of significant recesses that Congress took. The problem with this argument, however, is that it does not fully describe the relevant founding intent. The question is not: Did the Founders at the time think about intra-session recesses? Perhaps they did not. The question is: Did the Founders intend to restrict the scope of the Clause to the form of congressional recess then prevalent, or did they intend a broader scope permitting the Clause to apply, where appropriate, to somewhat changed circumstances? The Founders knew they were writing a document designed to apply to ever-changing circumstances over centuries. After all, a Constitution is "intended to endure for ages to come," and must adapt itself to a future that can only be "seen dimly," if at all. *McCulloch,* 4 Wheat., at 415, 4 L. Ed. 579. We therefore think the Framers likely did intend the Clause to apply to a new circumstance that so clearly falls within its essential purposes, where doing so is consistent with the Clause's language. . . .

The greater interpretive problem is determining how long a recess must be in order to fall within the Clause. Is a break of a week, or a day, or an hour too short to count as a "recess"? The Clause itself does not say. And Justice Scalia claims that this silence itself shows that the Framers intended the Clause to apply only to an inter-session recess. *Post.*

We disagree. For one thing, the most likely reason the Framers did not place a textual floor underneath the word "recess" is that they did not foresee the *need* for one. They might have expected that the Senate would meet for a single session lasting at most half a year. The Federalist No. 84 (A. Hamilton). And they might not have anticipated that intra-session recesses would become lengthier and more significant than inter-session ones. The Framers' lack of clairvoyance on that point is not dispositive. Unlike Justice Scalia, we think it most consistent with our constitutional structure to presume that the Framers would have allowed intra-session recess appointments where there was a long history of such practice. . . .

The Recess Appointments Clause seeks to permit the Executive Branch to function smoothly when Congress is unavailable. And though Congress has taken short breaks for almost 200 years, and there have been many thousands of recess appointments in that time, we have not found a single example of a recess appointment made during an intra-session recess that was shorter than 10 days. Nor has the Solicitor General. Indeed, the Office of Legal Counsel once informally advised against making a recess appointment during a 6-day intra-session recess. The lack of examples suggests that the recess-appointment power is not needed in that context.

There are a few historical examples of recess appointments made during inter-session recesses shorter than 10 days. . . . There may be others of which we are unaware. But when considered against 200 years of settled practice, we regard these few scattered examples as anomalies. We therefore conclude, in light of historical practice, that a recess of more than 3 days but less than 10 days is presumptively too short to fall within the Clause. We add the word "presumptively" to leave open the possibility that some very unusual circumstance—a national catastrophe, for instance, that renders the Senate unavailable but calls for an urgent response—could demand the exercise of the recess-appointment power during a shorter break. (It should go without saying—except that Justice Scalia compels us to say it—that political opposition in the Senate would not qualify as an unusual circumstance.)

In sum, we conclude that the phrase "the recess" applies to both intra-session and inter-session recesses. If a Senate recess is so short that it does not require the consent of the House, it is too short to trigger the Recess Appointments Clause. And a recess lasting less than 10 days is presumptively too short as well.

IV

The second question concerns the scope of the phrase "vacancies *that may happen* during the recess of the Senate." Art. II, §2, cl. 3 (emphasis added). All agree that the phrase applies to vacancies that initially occur during a recess. But does it also apply to vacancies that initially occur before a recess and continue to exist during the recess? In our view the phrase applies to both kinds of vacancy.

We believe that the Clause's language, read literally, permits, though it does not naturally favor, our broader interpretation. We concede that the most natural meaning of "happens" as applied to a "vacancy" (at least to a modern ear) is that the vacancy "happens" when it initially occurs. See 1 Johnson 913 (defining "happen" in relevant part as meaning "[t]o fall out; to chance; to come to pass"). But that is not the only possible way to use the word.

Thomas Jefferson wrote that the Clause is "certainly susceptible of [two] constructions." Letter to Wilson Cary Nicholas (Jan. 26, 1802). It "may mean 'vacancies that may happen to be' or 'may happen to fall'" during a recess. Jefferson used the phrase in the first sense when he wrote to a job seeker that a particular position was unavailable, but that he (Jefferson) was "happy that *another vacancy happens* wherein I can . . . avail the public of your integrity & talents," for "the office of Treasurer of the US. *is vacant* by the resignation of mr Meredith." Letter to Thomas Tudor Tucker (Oct. 31, 1801) (emphasis added).

Similarly, when Attorney General William Wirt advised President Monroe to follow the broader interpretation, he wrote that the "expression seems not perfectly clear. It may mean 'happen to take place:' that is, '*to originate*,'" or it "may mean, also, without violence to the sense, 'happen to exist.'" 1 Op. Atty. Gen. (1823). The broader interpretation, he added, is "most accordant with" the Constitution's "reason and spirit."

We can still understand this earlier use of "happen" if we think of it used together with another word that, like "vacancy," can refer to a continuing state, say, a financial crisis. A statute that gives the President authority to act in respect to "any financial crisis that may happen during his term" can easily be interpreted to include crises that arise before, and continue during, that term. Perhaps that is why the Oxford English Dictionary defines "happen" in part as "chance *to be*," rather than "chance to occur." OED (emphasis added); see also OED (defining "vacancy" as the "condition of an office or post being . . . vacant").

In any event, the linguistic question here is not whether the phrase can be, but whether it must be, read more narrowly. The question is whether the Clause is ambiguous. And the broader reading, we believe, is at least a permissible reading of a "'doubtful'" phrase. We consequently go on to consider the Clause's purpose and historical practice.

The Clause's purpose strongly supports the broader interpretation. That purpose is to permit the President to obtain the assistance of subordinate officers when the Senate, due to its recess, cannot confirm them. . . . At the same time, we recognize one important purpose-related consideration that argues in the opposite direction. A broad interpretation might permit a President to avoid Senate confirmations as a matter of course. If the Clause gives the President the power to "fill up all vacancies" that occur before, and continue to exist during, the Senate's recess, a President might not submit any nominations to the Senate. He might simply wait for a recess and then provide all potential nominees with recess appointments. He might thereby routinely avoid the constitutional need to obtain the Senate's "advice and consent." . . .

[S]uch temptations should not often arise. It is often less desirable for a President to make a recess appointment. A recess appointee only serves a limited term. That, combined with the lack of Senate approval, may diminish the recess appointee's ability, as a practical matter, to get a controversial job done. And even where the President and Senate are at odds over politically sensitive appointments, compromise is normally possible. . . . In an unusual instance, where a matter is important enough to the Senate, that body can remain in session, preventing recess appointments by refusing to take a recess. In any event, the Executive Branch has adhered to the broader interpretation for two centuries, and Senate confirmation has always remained the norm for officers that require it.

While we concede that both interpretations carry with them some risk of undesirable consequences, we believe the narrower interpretation risks undermining constitutionally conferred powers more seriously and more often. It would prevent the President from making any recess appointment that arose before a recess, no matter who the official, no matter how dire the need, no matter how uncontroversial the appointment, and no matter how late in the session the office fell vacant. Overall, . . . we believe the broader interpretation more consistent with the Constitution's "reason and spirit."

Historical practice over the past 200 years strongly favors the broader interpretation. The tradition of applying the Clause to pre-recess vacancies dates at least to President James Madison. There is no undisputed record of Presidents George Washington, John Adams, or Thomas Jefferson making such an appointment, though the Solicitor General believes he has found records showing that Presidents Washington and Jefferson did so. We know that Edmund Randolph, Washington's Attorney General, favored a narrow reading of the Clause. Randolph believed that the "Spirit of the Constitution favors the participation of the Senate in all appointments," though he did not address — let alone answer — the powerful purposive and structural arguments subsequently made by Attorney General Wirt.

President Adams seemed to endorse the broader view of the Clause in writing, though we are not aware of any appointments he made in keeping with that view. See Letter to J. McHenry (Apr. 16, 1799). His Attorney General, Charles Lee, later informed Jefferson that, in the Adams administration, "whenever an office became vacant so short a time before Congress rose, as not to give an opportunity of enquiring for a proper character, they let it lie always till recess." We know that President Jefferson thought that the broad interpretation was linguistically supportable, though his actual practice is not clear. But the evidence suggests that James Madison — as familiar as anyone with the workings of the Constitutional Convention — appointed Theodore Gaillard to replace a district judge who had left office before a recess began. It also appears that in 1815 Madison signed a bill that created two new offices prior to a recess which he then filled later during the recess. He also made recess appointments to "territorial" United States attorney and marshal positions, both of which had been created when the Senate was in session more than two years before. Justice Scalia refers to "written evidence of Madison's own beliefs," but in fact we have no direct evidence of what President Madison believed. We only know that he declined to make one appointment to a pre-recess vacancy after his Secretary of War advised him that he lacked the power. On the other hand, he *did* apparently make at least five other appointments to pre-recess vacancies, as Justice Scalia does not dispute.

The next President, James Monroe, received and presumably acted upon Attorney General Wirt's advice, namely that "all vacancies which, from any casualty, happen to exist at a time when the Senate cannot be consulted as to filling them, may be temporarily filled by the President." Nearly every subsequent Attorney General to consider the question throughout the Nation's history has thought the same. Indeed, as early as 1862, Attorney General Bates advised President Lincoln that his power to fill pre-recess vacancies was "settled . . . as far . . . as a constitutional question can be settled," and a century later Acting Attorney General Walsh gave President Eisenhower the same advice "without any doubt." . . .

Common sense also suggests that many recess appointees filled vacancies that arose before the recess began. We have compared the list of *intra*-session recess appointments in the Solicitor General's brief with the chart of congressional recesses. Where a specific date of appointment can be ascertained, more than half of those intra-session appointments were made within two weeks of the beginning of a recess. That short window strongly suggests that many of the vacancies initially arose prior to the recess. . . . Further, with research assistance from the Supreme Court Library, we have examined a random sample of the recess appointments made by our two most recent Presidents, and have found that almost all of those appointments filled pre-recess vacancies: Of a sample of 21 recess appointments, 18 filled pre-recess vacancies and only 1 filled a vacancy that arose during the recess in which he was appointed. The precise date on which 2 of the vacancies arose could not be determined. Taken together, we think it is a fair inference that a large proportion of the recess appointments in the history of the Nation have filled pre-existing vacancies. . . .

The upshot is that the President has consistently and frequently interpreted the Recess Appointments Clause to apply to vacancies that initially occur before, but continue to exist during, a recess of the Senate. The Senate as a body has not countered this practice for nearly three-quarters of a century, perhaps longer. The tradition is long enough to entitle the practice "to great regard in determining the true construction" of the constitutional provision. *The Pocket Veto Case*. And we are reluctant to upset this traditional practice where doing so would seriously shrink the authority that Presidents have believed existed and have exercised for so long.

In light of some linguistic ambiguity, the basic purpose of the Clause, and the historical practice we have described, we conclude that the phrase "all vacancies" includes vacancies that come into existence while the Senate is in session.

V

The third question concerns the calculation of the length of the Senate's "recess." On December 17, 2011, the Senate by unanimous consent adopted a resolution to convene "*pro forma* session[s]" only, with "no business . . . transacted," on every Tuesday and Friday from December 20, 2011, through January 20, 2012. At the end of each *pro forma* session, the Senate would "adjourn until" the following *pro forma* session. During that period, the Senate convened and adjourned as agreed. It held *pro forma* sessions on December 20, 23, 27, and 30, and on January 3, 6, 10, 13, 17, and 20; and at the end of each *pro forma* session, it adjourned until the time and date of the next.

The President made the recess appointments before us on January 4, 2012, in between the January 3 and the January 6 *pro forma* sessions. We must determine the significance of these sessions—that is, whether, for purposes of the Clause, we should treat them as periods when the Senate was in session or as periods when it was in recess. If the former, the period between January 3 and January 6 was a 3-day recess, which is too short to trigger the President's recess-appointment power. If the latter, however, then the 3-day period was part of a much longer recess during which the President did have the power to make recess appointments.

The Solicitor General argues that we must treat the *pro forma* sessions as periods of recess. He says that these "sessions" were sessions in name only because the Senate was in recess as a *functional* matter. The Senate, he contends, remained in a single, unbroken recess from January 3, when the second session of the 112th Congress began by operation of the Twentieth Amendment, until January 23, when the Senate reconvened to do regular business.

In our view, however, the *pro forma* sessions count as sessions, not as periods of recess. We hold that, for purposes of the Recess Appointments Clause, the Senate is in session when it says it is, provided that, under its own rules, it retains the capacity to transact Senate business. The Senate met that standard here.

The standard we apply is consistent with the Constitution's broad delegation of authority to the Senate to determine how and when to conduct its business. The Constitution explicitly empowers the Senate to "determine the Rules of its Proceedings." Art. I, §5, cl. 2. And we have held that "all matters of method are open to the determination" of the Senate, as long as there is "a reasonable relation between the mode or method of proceeding established by the rule and the result which is sought to be attained" and the rule does not "ignore constitutional restraints or violate fundamental rights." *United States v. Ballin* (1892).

In addition, the Constitution provides the Senate with extensive control over its schedule. There are only limited exceptions. The Constitution thus gives the Senate wide latitude to determine whether and when to have a session, as well as how to conduct the session. This suggests that the Senate's determination about what constitutes a session should merit great respect. . . .

For these reasons, we conclude that we must give great weight to the Senate's own determination of when it is and when it is not in session. But our deference to the Senate cannot be absolute. When the Senate is without the *capacity* to act, under its own rules, it is not in session even if it so declares. In that circumstance, the Senate is not simply unlikely or unwilling to act upon nominations of the President. It is *unable* to do so. The purpose of the Clause is to ensure the continued functioning of the Federal Government while the Senate is unavailable. This purpose would count for little were we to treat the Senate as though it were in session even when it lacks the ability to provide its "advice and consent." Art. II, §2, cl. 2. Accordingly, we conclude that when the Senate declares that it is in session and possesses the capacity, under its own rules, to conduct business, it is in session for purposes of the Clause.

Applying this standard, we find that the *pro forma* sessions were sessions for purposes of the Clause. First, the Senate said it was in session. The Journal of the Senate and the Congressional Record indicate that the Senate convened for a series of twice-weekly "sessions" from December 20 through January 20. . . .

Second, the Senate's rules make clear that during its *pro forma* sessions, despite its resolution that it would conduct no business, the Senate retained the power to conduct business. During any *pro forma* session, the Senate could have conducted business simply by passing a unanimous consent agreement. The Senate in fact conducts much of its business through unanimous consent. Senate rules presume that a quorum is present unless a present Senator questions it. And when the Senate has a quorum, an agreement is unanimously passed if, upon its proposal, no present Senator objects. It is consequently unsurprising that the Senate *has* enacted legislation during *pro forma* sessions even when it has said that no business will be transacted. Indeed, the Senate passed a bill by unanimous consent during the second *pro forma* session after its December 17 adjournment. And that bill quickly became law.

By way of contrast, we do not see how the Senate could conduct business during a recess. It could terminate the recess and then, when in session, pass a bill. But in that case, of course, the Senate would no longer be in recess. It would be in session. And that is the crucial point. Senate rules make clear that, once in session, the Senate can act even if it has earlier said that it would not. . . .

[T]he Recess Appointments Clause is not designed to overcome serious institutional friction. It simply provides a subsidiary method for appointing officials when the Senate is away during a recess. Here, as in other contexts, friction between the branches is an inevitable consequence of our constitutional structure. That structure foresees resolution not only through judicial interpretation and compromise among the branches but also by the ballot box.

VI

The Recess Appointments Clause responds to a structural difference between the Executive and Legislative Branches: The Executive Branch is perpetually in operation, while the Legislature only acts in intervals separated by recesses. The purpose of the Clause is to allow the Executive to continue operating while the Senate is unavailable. We believe that the Clause's text, standing alone, is ambiguous. It does not resolve whether the President may make appointments during intra-session recesses, or whether he may fill pre-recess vacancies. But the broader reading better serves the Clause's structural function. Moreover, that broader reading is reinforced by centuries of history, which we are hesitant to disturb. We thus hold that the Constitution empowers the President to fill any existing vacancy during any recess—intra-session or inter-session—of sufficient length.

Justice Scalia would render illegitimate thousands of recess appointments reaching all the way back to the founding era. More than that: Calling the Clause an "anachronism," he would basically read it out of the Constitution. He performs this act of judicial excision in the name of liberty. We fail to see how excising the Recess Appointments Clause preserves freedom. In fact, Alexander Hamilton observed in the very first Federalist Paper that "the vigour of government is essential to the security of liberty." The Federalist No. 1. And the Framers included the Recess Appointments Clause to preserve the "vigour of government" at times when an important organ of Government, the United States Senate, is in recess. Justice Scalia's interpretation of the Clause would defeat the power of the Clause to achieve that objective.

The foregoing discussion should refute Justice Scalia's claim that we have "embrace[d]" an "adverse-possession theory of executive power." Instead, as in all cases, we interpret the Constitution in light of its text, purposes, and "our whole experience" as a Nation. *Missouri v. Holland* (1920). And we look to the actual practice of Government to inform our interpretation.

Given our answer to the last question before us, we conclude that the Recess Appointments Clause does not give the President the constitutional authority to make the appointments here at issue. Because the Court of Appeals reached the same ultimate conclusion (though for reasons we reject), its judgment is affirmed.

It is so ordered.

JUSTICE SCALIA, with whom THE CHIEF JUSTICE, JUSTICE THOMAS, and JUSTICE ALITO join, concurring in the judgment. . . .

Today's Court agrees that the appointments were invalid, but for the far narrower reason that they were made during a 3-day break in the Senate's session. On its way to that result, the majority sweeps away the key textual limitations on the recess-appointment power. It holds, first, that the President can make appointments without the Senate's participation even during short breaks in the middle of the Senate's session, and second, that those appointments can fill offices that became vacant long before the break in which they were filled. The majority justifies those atextual results on an adverse-possession theory of executive authority: Presidents have long claimed the powers in question, and the Senate has not disputed those claims with sufficient vigor, so the Court should not "upset the compromises and working arrangements that the elected branches of Government themselves have reached."

The Court's decision transforms the recess-appointment power from a tool carefully designed to fill a narrow and specific need into a weapon to be wielded by future Presidents against future Senates. To reach that result, the majority casts aside the plain, original meaning of the constitutional text in deference to late-arising historical practices that are ambiguous at best. The majority's insistence on deferring to the Executive's untenably broad interpretation of the power is in clear conflict with our precedent and forebodes a diminution of this Court's role in controversies involving the separation of powers and the structure of government. I concur in the judgment only.

I. OUR RESPONSIBILITY

Today's majority disregards two overarching principles that ought to guide our consideration of the questions presented here.

First, the Constitution's core, government-structuring provisions are no less critical to preserving liberty than are the later adopted provisions of the Bill of Rights. Indeed, "[s]o convinced were the Framers that liberty of the person inheres in structure that at first they did not consider a Bill of Rights necessary." *Clinton v. City of New York* (1998) (Kennedy, J., concurring). Those structural provisions reflect the founding generation's deep conviction that "checks and balances were the foundation of a structure of government that would protect liberty." *Bowsher v. Synar* (1986). It is for that reason that "the claims of individuals—not of Government departments—have been the principal source of judicial decisions concerning separation of powers and checks and balances." *Bond v. United States* (2011). Second and relatedly, when questions involving the Constitution's government-structuring provisions are presented in a justiciable case, it is the solemn responsibility of the Judicial Branch " 'to say what the law is.' " *Zivotofsky v. Clinton* (2012) (quoting *Marbury v. Madison* (1803)). This Court does not defer to the other branches' resolution of such controversies; as Justice Kennedy has previously written, our role is in no way "lessened" because it might be said that "the two political branches are adjusting their own powers between themselves." *Clinton* (concurring opinion). Since the separation of powers exists for the protection of individual liberty, its vitality "does not depend" on "whether 'the encroached-upon branch approves the encroachment.' " [*Free Enterprise Fund v. Public Company Accounting Oversight Bd.* (2010).] . . .

Ignoring our more recent precedent in this area, which is extensive, the majority relies on *The Pocket Veto Case* (1929), for the proposition that when interpreting a constitutional provision "regulating the relationship between Congress and the President," we must defer to the settled practice of the political branches if the provision is "in any respect of doubtful meaning." The language the majority quotes from that case was pure dictum. The *Pocket Veto* Court had to decide whether a bill passed by the House and Senate and presented to the President less than 10 days before the adjournment of the first session of a particular Congress, but neither signed nor vetoed by the President, became a law. Most of the opinion analyzed that issue like any other legal question and concluded that treating the bill as a law would have been inconsistent with the text and structure of the Constitution. Only near the end of the opinion did the Court add that its conclusion was "confirmed" by longstanding Presidential practice in which Congress appeared to have acquiesced. We did not suggest that the case would have come out differently had the longstanding practice been otherwise.

II. Intra-Session Breaks

The first question presented is whether "the Recess of the Senate," during which the President's recess-appointment power is active, is (a) the period between two of the Senate's formal sessions, or (b) any break in the Senate's proceedings. I would hold that "the Recess" is the gap between sessions and that the appointments at issue here are invalid because they undisputedly were made *during* the Senate's session. The Court's contrary conclusion—that "the Recess" includes "breaks in the midst of a session,"—is inconsistent with the Constitution's text and structure, and it requires judicial fabrication of vague, unadministrable limits on the recess-appointment power (thus defined) that overstep the judicial role. And although the majority relies heavily on "historical practice," no practice worthy of our deference supports the majority's conclusion on this issue.

A. PLAIN MEANING

A sensible interpretation of the Recess Appointments Clause should start by recognizing that the Clause uses the term "Recess" in contradistinction to the term "Session." As Alexander Hamilton wrote: "The time within which the power is to operate 'during the recess of the Senate' and the duration of the appointments 'to the end of the next session' of that body, conspire to elucidate the sense of the provision." The Federalist No. 67.

In the founding era, the terms "recess" and "session" had well-understood meanings in the marking-out of legislative time. The life of each elected Congress typically consisted (as it still does) of two or more formal sessions separated by adjournments "*sine die*," that is, without a specified return date. The period *between* two sessions was known as "the recess." As one scholar has thoroughly demonstrated, "in government practice the phrase 'the Recess' *always* referred to the gap between sessions." Natelson, The Origins and Meaning of "Vacancies that May Happen During the Recess" in the Constitution's Recess Appointments Clause, 37 Harv. J.L. & Pub. Pol'y 199, 213 (2014) (hereinafter Natelson). By contrast, other provisions of the Constitution use the verb "adjourn" rather than "recess" to refer to the commencement of breaks *during* a formal legislative session. See, *e.g.*, Art. I, §5, cl. 1; *id.*, §5, cl. 4.

To be sure, in colloquial usage both words, "recess" and "session," could take on alternative, less precise meanings. A session could include any short period when a legislature's members were "assembled for business," and a recess could refer to any brief "suspension" of legislative "business." 2 N. Webster, American Dictionary of the English Language (1828). So the Continental Congress could complain of the noise from passing carriages disrupting its "daily Session," 29 Journals of the Continental Congress 1774-1789 (1785), and the House could "take a recess" from 4 o'clock to 6 o'clock, Journal of the House of Representatives, 17th Cong., 2d Sess. (1823). But as even the majority acknowledges, the Constitution's use of "the word 'the' in '*the* [R]ecess' " tends to suggest "that the phrase refers to the single break separating formal sessions."

More importantly, neither the Solicitor General nor the majority argues that the Clause uses "session" in its loose, colloquial sense. And if "the next Session" denotes a *formal* session, then "the Recess" must mean the break *between* formal sessions. As every commentator on the Clause until the 20th century seems to have understood, the "Recess" and the "Session" to which the Clause refers are mutually exclusive, alternating states.

Besides being linguistically unsound, the majority's reading yields the strange result that an appointment made during a short break near the beginning of one official session will not terminate until the end of the *following* official session, enabling the appointment to last for up to two years. . . .

One way to avoid the linguistic incongruity of the majority's reading would be to read both "the Recess" and "the next Session" colloquially, so that the recess-appointment power would be activated during any temporary suspension of Senate proceedings, but appointments made pursuant to that power would last only until the beginning of the next suspension (which would end the next colloquial session). See, *e.g.*, Rappaport, The Original Meaning of the Recess Appointments Clause, 52 UCLA L. Rev. 1487, 1569 (2005) (hereinafter Rappaport, Original Meaning). That approach would be more linguistically defensible than the majority's. But it would not cure the most fundamental problem with giving "Recess" its colloquial, rather than its formal, meaning: Doing so leaves the recess-appointment power without a textually grounded principle limiting the time of its exercise.

The dictionary definitions of "recess" on which the majority relies provide no such principle. On the contrary, they make clear that in colloquial usage, a recess could include *any* suspension of legislative business, no matter how short. Webster even provides a stark illustration: "[T]he house of representatives had a *recess* of half an hour." The notion that the Constitution empowers the President to make unilateral appointments every time the Senate takes a half-hour lunch break is so absurd as to be self-refuting. But that, in the majority's view, is what the text authorizes.

The boundlessness of the colloquial reading of "the Recess" thus refutes the majority's assertion that the Clause's "purpose" of "ensur[ing] the continued functioning of the Federal Government" demands that it apply to intra-session breaks as well as inter-session recesses. The majority disregards another self-evident purpose of the Clause: to preserve the Senate's role in the appointment process—which the founding generation regarded as a critical protection against " 'despotism,' " [*Freytag v. Commissioner* (1991)] —by clearly delineating the times when the President can appoint officers without the Senate's consent. Today's decision seriously undercuts *that* purpose. In doing so, it demonstrates the folly of interpreting constitutional provisions designed to establish "a structure of government that would protect liberty," *Bowsher*, on the narrow-minded assumption that their only purpose is to make the government run as efficiently as possible. "Convenience and efficiency," we have repeatedly recognized, "are not the primary objectives" of our constitutional framework. *Free Enterprise Fund*.

Relatedly, the majority contends that the Clause's supposed purpose of keeping the wheels of government turning demands that we interpret the Clause to maintain its relevance in light of the "new circumstance" of the Senate's taking an increasing number of intra-session breaks that exceed three days. Even if I accepted the canard that courts can alter the Constitution's meaning to accommodate changed circumstances, I would be hard pressed to see the relevance of that notion here. The rise of intra-session adjournments has occurred in tandem with the development of modern forms of communication and transportation that mean the Senate "is always available" to consider nominations, even when its Members are temporarily dispersed for an intra-session break. Tr. of Oral Arg. (Ginsburg, J.). The Recess Appointments Clause therefore is, or rather, should be, an anachronism—"essentially an historic relic, something whose original purpose has disappeared." *Id.* (Kagan, J.). The need it was designed to fill no longer exists, and its only remaining use is the ignoble one of enabling the President to circumvent the Senate's role in the appointment process. That does not justify "read[ing] it out of the Constitution" and, contra the majority, I would not do so; but neither would I distort the Clause's original meaning, as the majority does, to ensure a prominent role for the recess-appointment power in an era when its influence is far more pernicious than beneficial.

To avoid the absurd results that follow from its colloquial reading of "the Recess," the majority is forced to declare that some intra-session breaks—though undisputedly within the phrase's colloquial meaning—are simply "too short to trigger the Recess Appointments Clause." But it identifies no textual basis whatsoever for limiting the length of "the Recess," nor does it point to any clear standard for determining how short is too short. It is inconceivable that the Framers would have left the circumstances in which the President could exercise such a significant and potentially dangerous power so utterly indeterminate. Other structural provisions of the Constitution that turn on duration are quite specific: Neither House can adjourn "for more than three days" without the other's consent. Art. I, §5, cl. 4. The President must return a passed bill to Congress "within ten Days (Sundays excepted)," lest it become a law. *Id.,* §7, cl. 2. Yet on the majority's view, when the first Senate considered taking a 1-month break, a 3-day weekend, or a half-hour siesta, it had no way of knowing whether the President would be constitutionally authorized to appoint officers in its absence. And any officers appointed in those circumstances would have served under a cloud, unable to determine with any degree of confidence whether their appointments were valid.[1]

Fumbling for some textually grounded standard, the majority seizes on the Adjournments Clause, which bars either House from adjourning for more than three days without the other's consent. *Id.,* §5, cl. 4. According to the majority, that clause establishes that a 3-day break is *always* "too short" to trigger the Recess Appointments Clause. It goes without saying that nothing in the constitutional text supports that disposition. If (as the majority concludes) "the Recess" means a recess in the colloquial sense, then it necessarily includes breaks shorter than three days. And the fact that the Constitution includes a 3-day limit in one clause but omits it from the other weighs strongly against finding such a limit to be implicit in the clause in which it does not appear. In all events, the dramatically different contexts in which the two clauses operate make importing the 3-day limit from the Adjournments Clause into the Recess Appointments Clause "both arbitrary and mistaken." Rappaport, Original Meaning.

1. The majority insists that "the most likely reason the Framers did not place a textual floor underneath the word 'recess' is that they did not foresee the *need* for one" because they did not anticipate that intra-session breaks "would become lengthier and more significant than inter-session ones." The majority's logic escapes me. The Framers' supposed failure to anticipate "length[y]" intra-session breaks might explain why (as I maintain) they did not bother to authorize recess appointments during intra-session breaks at all; but it cannot explain why (as the majority holds) they would have enacted a text that authorizes appointments during *all* intra-session breaks—even the short ones the majority says they *did* anticipate—without placing a temporal limitation on that power.

And what about breaks longer than three days? The majority says that a break of four to nine days is "presumptively too short" but that the presumption may be rebutted in an "unusual circumstance," such as a "national catastrophe . . . that renders the Senate unavailable but calls for an urgent response." The majority must hope that the *in terrorem* effect of its "presumptively too short" pronouncement will deter future Presidents from making any recess appointments during 4-to-9-day breaks and thus save us from the absurd spectacle of unelected judges evaluating (after an evidentiary hearing?) whether an alleged "catastrophe" was sufficiently "urgent" to trigger the recess-appointment power. The majority also says that "political opposition in the Senate would not qualify as an unusual circumstance." So if the Senate should refuse to confirm a nominee whom the President considers highly qualified; or even if it should refuse to confirm any nominee for an office, thinking the office better left vacant for the time being; the President's power would not be triggered during a 4-to-9-day break, no matter how "urgent" the President's perceived need for the officer's assistance. (The majority protests that this "should go without saying—except that Justice Scalia compels us to say it," seemingly forgetting that the appointments at issue in this very case were justified on those grounds and that the Solicitor General has asked us to view the recess-appointment power as a "safety valve" against Senatorial "intransigence." Tr. of Oral Arg.). . . .

If the Constitution's text empowers the President to make appointments during any break in the Senate's proceedings, by what right does the majority subject the President's exercise of that power to vague, court-crafted limitations with no textual basis? The majority claims its temporal guideposts are informed by executive practice, but a President's self-restraint cannot "bind his successors by diminishing their powers." *Free Enterprise Fund.*

An interpretation that calls for this kind of judicial adventurism cannot be correct. Indeed, if the Clause really did use "Recess" in its colloquial sense, then there would be no "judicially discoverable and manageable standard for resolving" whether a particular break was long enough to trigger the recess-appointment power, making that a nonjusticiable political question. *Zivotofsky.*

B. HISTORICAL PRACTICE

For the foregoing reasons, the Constitution's text and structure unambiguously refute the majority's freewheeling interpretation of "the Recess." It is not plausible that the Constitution uses that term in a sense that authorizes the President to make unilateral appointments during *any* break in Senate proceedings, subject only to hazy, atextual limits crafted by this Court centuries after ratification. The majority, however, insists that history "offers strong support" for its interpretation. The historical practice of the political branches is, of course, irrelevant when the Constitution is clear. But even if the Constitution were thought ambiguous on this point, history does not support the majority's interpretation. . . .

Intra-session recess appointments were virtually unheard of for the first 130 years of the Republic, were deemed unconstitutional by the first Attorney General to address them, were not openly defended by the Executive until 1921, were not made in significant numbers until after World War II, and have been repeatedly criticized as unconstitutional by Senators of both parties. It is astonishing for the majority to assert that this history lends "strong support," to its interpretation of the Recess Appointments Clause. And the majority's contention that recent executive practice in this area merits deference because the Senate has not done more to oppose it is utterly divorced from our precedent. "The structural interests protected by the Appointments Clause are not those of any one branch of Government but of the entire Republic," *Freytag*, and the Senate could not give away those protections even if it wanted to.

Moreover, the majority's insistence that the Senate gainsay an executive practice "as a body" in order to prevent the Executive from acquiring power by adverse possession, will systematically favor the expansion of executive power at the expense of Congress. In any controversy between the political branches over a separation-of-powers question, staking out a position and defending it over time is far easier for the Executive Branch than for the Legislative Branch. All Presidents have a high interest in expanding the powers of their office, since the more power the President can wield, the more effectively he can implement his political agenda; whereas individual Senators may have little interest in opposing Presidential encroachment on legislative prerogatives, especially when the encroacher is a President who is the leader of their own party. And when the President wants to assert a power and establish a precedent, he faces neither the collective-action problems nor the procedural inertia inherent in the legislative process. The majority's methodology thus all but guarantees the continuing aggrandizement of the Executive Branch.

III. Pre-Recess Vacancies

The second question presented is whether vacancies that "happen during the Recess of the Senate," which the President is empowered to fill with recess appointments, are (a) vacancies that *arise* during the recess, or (b) all vacancies that *exist* during the recess, regardless of when they arose. I would hold that the recess-appointment power is limited to vacancies that arise during the recess in which they are filled, and I would hold that the appointments at issue here—which undisputedly filled pre-recess vacancies—are invalid for that reason as well as for the reason that they were made during the session. The Court's contrary conclusion is inconsistent with the Constitution's text and structure, and it further undermines the balance the Framers struck between Presidential and Senatorial power. Historical practice also fails to support the majority's conclusion on this issue.

A. Plain Meaning

As the majority concedes, "the most natural meaning of 'happens' as applied to a 'vacancy' . . . is that the vacancy 'happens' when it initially occurs." The majority adds that this meaning is most natural "to a modern ear," but it fails to show that founding-era ears heard it differently. "Happen" meant then, as it does now, "[t]o fall out; to chance; to come to pass." 1 Johnson, Dictionary of the English Language 913. Thus, a vacancy that *happened* during the Recess was most reasonably understood as one that *arose* during the recess. It was, of course, possible in certain contexts for the word "happen" to mean "happen to be" rather than "happen to occur," as in the idiom "it so happens." But that meaning is not at all natural when the subject is a vacancy, a state of affairs that comes into existence at a particular moment in time.[2]

In any event, no reasonable reader would have understood the Recess Appointments Clause to use the word "happen" in the majority's "happen to be" sense, and thus to empower the President to fill all vacancies that might *exist* during a recess, regardless of when they arose. For one thing, the Clause's language would have been a surpassingly odd way of giving the President that power. The Clause easily could have been written to convey that meaning clearly: It could have referred to "all Vacancies that may exist during the Recess," or it could have omitted the qualifying phrase entirely and simply authorized the President to "fill up all Vacancies during the Recess." Given those readily available alternative phrasings, the reasonable reader might have wondered, why would any intelligent drafter intending the majority's reading have inserted the words "that may happen"—words that, as the majority admits, make the majority's desired reading awkward and unnatural, and that must be effectively read out of the Clause to achieve that reading?

For another thing, the majority's reading not only strains the Clause's language but distorts its constitutional role, which was meant to be subordinate. As Hamilton explained, appointment with the advice and consent of the Senate was to be "the general mode of appointing officers of the United States." The Federalist No. 67, at 455. The Senate's check on the President's appointment power was seen as vital because "'manipulation of official appointments' had long been one of the American revolutionary generation's greatest grievances against executive power." *Freytag*. The unilateral power conferred on the President by the Recess Appointments Clause was therefore understood to be "nothing more than a supplement" to the "general method" of advice and consent. The Federalist No. 67.

If, however, the Clause had allowed the President to fill *all* pre-existing vacancies during the recess by granting commissions that would last throughout the following session, it would have been impossible to regard it—as the Framers plainly did—as a mere codicil to the Constitution's principal, power-sharing scheme for filling federal offices. On the majority's reading, the President

2. Despite initially admitting that the text "does not naturally favor" its interpretation, the majority halfheartedly suggests that the "happen to be" reading may be admissible when the subject, like "vacancy," denotes a "continuing state." That suggestion distorts ordinary English usage. It is indeed natural to say that an ongoing activity or event, like a war, a parade, or a financial crisis, is "happening" for as long as it continues. But the same is not true when the subject is a settled state of affairs, like death, marriage, or vacancy, all of which "happen" when they come into being.

would have had no need *ever* to seek the Senate's advice and consent for his appointments: Whenever there was a fair prospect of the Senate's rejecting his preferred nominee, the President could have appointed that individual unilaterally during the recess, allowed the appointment to expire at the end of the next session, renewed the appointment the following day, and so on *ad infinitum.* (Circumvention would have been especially easy if, as the majority also concludes, the President was authorized to make such appointments during any intra-session break of more than a few days.) It is unthinkable that such an obvious means for the Executive to expand its power would have been overlooked during the ratification debates.

The original understanding of the Clause was consistent with what the majority concedes is the text's "most natural meaning." In 1792, Attorney General Edmund Randolph, who had been a leading member of the Constitutional Convention, provided the Executive Branch's first formal interpretation of the Clause. He advised President Washington that the Constitution did not authorize a recess appointment to fill the office of Chief Coiner of the United States Mint, which had been created by Congress on April 2, 1792, during the Senate's session. Randolph wrote: "[I]s it a vacancy which has *happened* during the recess of the Senate? It is now the same and no other vacancy, than that, which existed on the 2nd. of April 1792. It commenced therefore on that day or may be said to have *happened* on that day." Opinion on Recess Appointments (July 7, 1792). Randolph added that his interpretation was the most congruent with the Constitution's structure, which made the recess-appointment power "an exception to the general participation of the Senate."

President John Adams' Attorney General, Charles Lee, was in agreement. See Letter to George Washington (July 7, 1796) (the President may "fill for a limited time an old office *become vacant* during [the] recess" (emphasis added)). . . . The majority, however, relies heavily on a contrary account of the Clause given by Attorney General William Wirt in 1823. Wirt notably began — as does the majority — by acknowledging that his predecessors' reading was "most accordant with the letter of the constitution." But he thought the "most natural" reading had to be rejected because it would interfere with the "substantial purpose of the constitution," namely, "keep[ing] . . . offices filled." He was chiefly concerned that giving the Clause its plain meaning would produce "embarrassing inconveniences" if a distant office were to become vacant during the Senate's session, but news of the vacancy were not to reach the President until the recess. The majority fully embraces Wirt's reasoning.

Wirt's argument is doubly flawed. To begin, the Constitution provides ample means, short of rewriting its text, for dealing with the hypothetical dilemma Wirt posed. Congress can authorize "acting" officers to perform the duties associated with a temporarily vacant office — and has done that, in one form or another, since 1792. . . . More fundamentally, Wirt and the majority are mistaken to say that the Constitution's " 'substantial purpose' " is to " 'keep . . . offices filled.' " The Constitution is not a road map for maximally efficient government, but a system of "carefully crafted restraints" designed to "protect the people from the improvident exercise of power." [*INS v. Chadha* (1983).] Wirt's and the majority's *argumentum ab inconvenienti* thus proves far too much. There are many circumstances other than a vacancy that can produce similar inconveniences if they arise late in the session: For example, a natural disaster might occur to which the Executive cannot respond effectively without a supplemental appropriation. But in those circumstances, the Constitution would not permit the President to appropriate funds himself. See Art. I, §9, cl. 7. Congress must either anticipate such eventualities or be prepared to be haled back into session. The troublesome need to do so is not a bug to be fixed by this Court, but a calculated feature of the constitutional framework. As we have recognized, while the Constitution's government-structuring provisions can seem "clumsy" and "inefficient," they reflect "hard choices . . . consciously made by men who had lived under a form of government that permitted arbitrary governmental acts to go unchecked." *Chadha*.

B. HISTORICAL PRACTICE

For the reasons just given, it is clear that the Constitution authorizes the President to fill unilaterally only those vacancies that arise during a recess, not every vacancy that happens to exist during a recess. Again, however, the majority says "[h]istorical practice" requires the broader interpretation. And again the majority is mistaken. Even if the Constitution were wrongly thought to be ambiguous on this point, a fair recounting of the relevant history does not support the majority's interpretation.

1. 1789 to 1822

The majority correctly admits that there is "no undisputed record of Presidents George Washington, John Adams, or Thomas Jefferson" using a recess appointment to fill a pre-recess vacancy. That is not surprising in light of Randolph's early conclusion that doing so would be unconstitutional. Adams on one occasion contemplated filling pre-recess vacancies but was dissuaded by, among others, Attorney General Lee, who said the Constitution did not permit him to do so. See 1799 McHenry Letter. And the Solicitor General does not allege that even a single appointment made by Adams filled a pre-recess vacancy. Jefferson, too, at one point thought the Clause "susceptible of" the majority's reading, 1802 Jefferson Letter, but his administration, like Adams', appears never to have adopted that reading.

James Madison's administration seems to have rejected the majority's reading as well. In 1814, Madison wanted to appoint Andrew Jackson to a vacant major-generalship in the Army during the Senate's recess, but he accepted, without contradiction or reservation, his Secretary of War's advice that he lacked the power to do so because the post's previous occupant had resigned before the recess. He therefore ordered that Jackson be given a "brevet of Major General," *i.e.*, a warrant conferring the nominal rank without the salary thereof. Letter from John Armstrong to Madison (May 14, 1814); Letter from Madison to Armstrong

(May 17, 1814). In conveying the brevet, Madison's Secretary of War explained to Jackson that "'[t]he vacancy produced by General Hampton's resignation, not having been filled during the late session of the Senate, cannot be supplied constitutionally, during the recess.'" Letter from Armstrong to Jackson (May 22, 1814). A week later, when Madison learned that a different major general had resigned *during* the recess, he thought that development would enable him to appoint Jackson "at once." Letter from Madison to Armstrong (May 24, 1814); see Letter from Armstrong to Madison (May 20, 1814) (reporting the resignation).

The majority discounts that evidence of an occasion when Madison and his advisers actually considered the precise constitutional question presented here. It does so apparently because Madison, in acting on the advice he was given without questioning the interpretation of the recess-appointment power that was offered as the reason for that advice, did not explicitly say "I agree." The majority prefers to focus on five appointments by Madison, unremarked by anyone at the time, that "the evidence suggests" filled pre-recess vacancies. *Ante,* at 27. Even if the majority is correct about those appointments, there is no indication that any thought was given to their constitutionality, either within or outside the Executive Branch. A handful of appointments that appear to contravene the written opinions of Attorneys General Randolph and Lee and the written evidence of Madison's own beliefs about what the Constitution authorized, and that lack any contemporaneous explanation, are not convincing evidence of the Constitution's original meaning.[3]

If Madison or his predecessors made any appointments in reliance on the broader reading, those appointments must have escaped general notice. In 1822, the Senate Committee on Military Affairs declared that the President had "no power to make [appointments] in the recess" where "the vacancies did not *happen* in the recess." 38 Annals of Cong. 500. The Committee believed its construction had been "heretofore observed" and that "no instance ha[d] before occurred . . . where the President ha[d] felt himself authorized to fill such vacancies, without special authority by law." *Ibid.*; see also T. Sergeant, Constitutional Law 373 (2d ed. 1830) ("[I]t seemed distinctly understood to be the sense of the senate, that [it] is only in offices that become vacant during the recess, that the president is authorised to exercise the right of appointing"). . . .

2. 1823 to 1862

The Executive Branch did not openly depart from Randolph and Lee's interpretation until 1823, when Wirt issued the opinion discussed earlier. Even within

---

3. The same can be said of the Solicitor General's claim to have found two recess appointments by Washington and four by Jefferson that filled pre-existing vacancies. Noel Canning disputes that claim, pointing out that Washington told the Senate the offices in question had "fallen vacant during the recess" and arguing that Jefferson may have removed the incumbent officers during the recess. Suffice it to say that if either Washington or Jefferson had adopted the broader reading, against the written advice of Attorneys General Randolph and Lee, one would expect a good deal more evidence of that fact.

that branch, Wirt's view was hotly contested: William Crawford, Monroe's Treasury Secretary, argued "with great pertinacity" that the Clause authorized the President to fill only "vacancies which happen during the recess" and not those "which happen while Congress are in session." Wirt's analysis nonetheless gained ground in the Executive Branch over the next four decades; but it did so slowly and fitfully. . . .

In sum: Washington's and Adams' Attorneys General read the Constitution to restrict recess appointments to vacancies arising during the recess, and there is no evidence that any of the first four Presidents consciously departed from that reading. The contrary reading was first defended by an executive official in 1823, was vehemently rejected by the Senate in 1863, was vigorously resisted by legislation in place from 1863 until 1940, and is arguably inconsistent with legislation in place from 1940 to the present. The Solicitor General has identified only about 100 appointments that have ever been made under the broader reading, and while it seems likely that a good deal more have been made in the last few decades, there is good reason to doubt that many were made before 1940 (since the appointees could not have been compensated). I can conceive of no sane constitutional theory under which this evidence of "historical practice"—which is actually evidence of a long-simmering inter-branch conflict—would require us to defer to the views of the Executive Branch.

IV. Conclusion

What the majority needs to sustain its judgment is an ambiguous text and a clear historical practice. What it has is a clear text and an at-best-ambiguous historical practice. Even if the Executive could accumulate power through adverse possession by engaging in a *consistent* and *unchallenged* practice over a long period of time, the oft-disputed practices at issue here would not meet that standard. Nor have those practices created any justifiable expectations that could be disappointed by enforcing the Constitution's original meaning. There is thus no ground for the majority's deference to the unconstitutional recess-appointment practices of the Executive Branch.

The majority replaces the Constitution's text with a new set of judge-made rules to govern recess appointments. Henceforth, the Senate can avoid triggering the President's now-vast recess-appointment power by the odd contrivance of never adjourning for more than three days without holding a *pro forma* session at which it is understood that no business will be conducted. How this new regime will work in practice remains to be seen. Perhaps it will reduce the prevalence of recess appointments. But perhaps not: Members of the President's party in Congress may be able to prevent the Senate from holding *pro forma* sessions with the necessary frequency, and if the House and Senate disagree, the President may be able to adjourn both "to such Time as he shall think proper." U.S. Const., Art. II, §3. In any event, the limitation upon the President's appointment power is there not for the benefit of the Senate, but for the protection of the people; it should not be dependent on Senate action for its existence.

The real tragedy of today's decision is not simply the abolition of the Constitution's limits on the recess-appointment power and the substitution of a novel framework invented by this Court. It is the damage done to our separation-of-powers jurisprudence more generally. It is not every day that we encounter a proper case or controversy requiring interpretation of the Constitution's structural provisions. Most of the time, the interpretation of those provisions is left to the political branches—which, in deciding how much respect to afford the constitutional text, often take their cues from this Court. We should therefore take every opportunity to affirm the primacy of the Constitution's enduring principles over the politics of the moment. Our failure to do so today will resonate well beyond the particular dispute at hand. Sad, but true: The Court's embrace of the adverse-possession theory of executive power (a characterization the majority resists but does not refute) will be cited in diverse contexts, including those presently unimagined, and will have the effect of aggrandizing the Presidency beyond its constitutional bounds and undermining respect for the separation of powers.

I concur in the judgment only.

Chapter 4

Standing, Ripeness, and Mootness

ASSIGNMENT S-5

Standing

STUDY GUIDE:

- What would have happened if, in addition to refusing to defend DOMA in court, the Department of Justice had also refused to enforce it? Would Windsor have still had standing? Does this raise any concerns?
- Can you identify a fundamental disagreement between Justices Kennedy and Scalia about the source and nature of "the judicial power" that explains their differing stances on standing?

UNITED STATES v. WINDSOR

No. 12-307

Argued Mar. 27, 2013 | Decided June 26, 2013

JUSTICE KENNEDY delivered the opinion of the Court.

Two women then resident in New York were married in a lawful ceremony in Ontario, Canada, in 2007. Edith Windsor and Thea Spyer returned to their home in New York City. When Spyer died in 2009, she left her entire estate to Windsor. Windsor sought to claim the estate tax exemption for surviving spouses. She was barred from doing so, however, by a federal law, the Defense of Marriage Act, which excludes a same-sex partner from the definition of "spouse" as that term is used in federal statutes. Windsor paid the taxes but filed suit to challenge the constitutionality of this provision. The United States District Court and the Court of Appeals ruled that this portion of the statute is unconstitutional and ordered the United States to pay Windsor a refund. This Court granted certiorari and now affirms the judgment in Windsor's favor.

I

. . . While the tax refund suit was pending, the Attorney General of the United States notified the Speaker of the House of Representatives, pursuant to 28

U.S.C. §530D, that the Department of Justice would no longer defend the constitutionality of DOMA's §3. Noting that "the Department has previously defended DOMA against . . . challenges involving legally married same-sex couples," the Attorney General informed Congress that "the President has concluded that given a number of factors, including a documented history of discrimination, classifications based on sexual orientation should be subject to a heightened standard of scrutiny." The Department of Justice has submitted many §530D letters over the years refusing to defend laws it deems unconstitutional, when, for instance, a federal court has rejected the Government's defense of a statute and has issued a judgment against it. This case is unusual, however, because the §530D letter was not preceded by an adverse judgment. The letter instead reflected the Executive's own conclusion, relying on a definition still being debated and considered in the courts, that heightened equal protection scrutiny should apply to laws that classify on the basis of sexual orientation.

Although "the President . . . instructed the Department not to defend the statute in *Windsor,*" he also decided "that Section 3 will continue to be enforced by the Executive Branch" and that the United States had an "interest in providing Congress a full and fair opportunity to participate in the litigation of those cases." The stated rationale for this dual-track procedure (determination of unconstitutionality coupled with ongoing enforcement) was to "recogniz[e] the judiciary as the final arbiter of the constitutional claims raised."

In response to the notice from the Attorney General, the Bipartisan Legal Advisory Group (BLAG) of the House of Representatives voted to intervene in the litigation to defend the constitutionality of §3 of DOMA. The Department of Justice did not oppose limited intervention by BLAG. . . .

On the merits of the tax refund suit, the District Court ruled against the United States. It held that §3 of DOMA is unconstitutional and ordered the Treasury to refund the tax with interest. Both the Justice Department and BLAG filed notices of appeal, and the Solicitor General filed a petition for certiorari before judgment. Before this Court acted on the petition, the Court of Appeals for the Second Circuit affirmed the District Court's judgment. It applied heightened scrutiny to classifications based on sexual orientation, as both the Department and Windsor had urged. The United States has not complied with the judgment. Windsor has not received her refund, and the Executive Branch continues to enforce §3 of DOMA. In granting certiorari on the question of the constitutionality of §3 of DOMA, the Court requested argument on two additional questions: whether the United States' agreement with Windsor's legal position precludes further review and whether BLAG has standing to appeal the case. All parties agree that the Court has jurisdiction to decide this case; and, with the case in that framework, the Court appointed Professor Vicki Jackson as *amicus curiae* to argue the position that the Court lacks jurisdiction to hear the dispute. She has ably discharged her duties. . . .

II

It is appropriate to begin by addressing whether either the Government or BLAG, or both of them, were entitled to appeal to the Court of Appeals and later to seek certiorari and appear as parties here. There is no dispute that when this case was in the District Court it presented a concrete disagreement between opposing parties, a dispute suitable for judicial resolution. "[A] taxpayer has standing to challenge the collection of a specific tax assessment as unconstitutional; being forced to pay such a tax causes a real and immediate economic injury to the individual taxpayer." *Hein v. Freedom From Religion Foundation, Inc.* (2007) (plurality opinion) (emphasis deleted). Windsor suffered a redressable injury when she was required to pay estate taxes from which, in her view, she was exempt but for the alleged invalidity of §3 of DOMA.

The decision of the Executive not to defend the constitutionality of §3 in court while continuing to deny refunds and to assess deficiencies does introduce a complication. Even though the Executive's current position was announced before the District Court entered its judgment, the Government's agreement with Windsor's position would not have deprived the District Court of jurisdiction to entertain and resolve the refund suit; for her injury (failure to obtain a refund allegedly required by law) was concrete, persisting, and unredressed. The Government's position—agreeing with Windsor's legal contention but refusing to give it effect—meant that there was a justiciable controversy between the parties, despite what the claimant would find to be an inconsistency in that stance. Windsor, the Government, BLAG, and the *amicus* appear to agree upon that point. The disagreement is over the standing of the parties, or aspiring parties, to take an appeal in the Court of Appeals and to appear as parties in further proceedings in this Court.

The *amicus*' position is that, given the Government's concession that §3 is unconstitutional, once the District Court ordered the refund the case should have ended; and the *amicus* argues the Court of Appeals should have dismissed the appeal. The *amicus* submits that once the President agreed with Windsor's legal position and the District Court issued its judgment, the parties were no longer adverse. From this standpoint the United States was a prevailing party below, just as Windsor was. Accordingly, the *amicus* reasons, it is inappropriate for this Court to grant certiorari and proceed to rule on the merits; for the United States seeks no redress from the judgment entered against it.

This position, however, elides the distinction between two principles: the jurisdictional requirements of Article III and the prudential limits on its exercise. See *Warth v. Seldin* (1975). The latter are "essentially matters of judicial self-governance." The Court has kept these two strands separate: "Article III standing, which enforces the Constitution's case-or-controversy requirement, see *Lujan v. Defenders of Wildlife* (1992); and prudential standing, which embodies 'judicially self-imposed limits on the exercise of federal jurisdiction,' *Allen* [*v. Wright*] (1984)." *Elk Grove Unified School Dist. v. Newdow* (2004).

The requirements of Article III standing are familiar:

> First, the plaintiff must have suffered an "injury in fact"—an invasion of a legally protected interest which is (a) concrete and particularized, and (b) "actual or imminent, not "conjectural or hypothetical." Second, there must be a causal connection between the injury and the conduct complained of—the injury has to be "fairly . . . trace[able] to the challenged action of the defendant, and not . . . th[e] result [of]

> the independent action of some third party not before the court." Third, it must be "likely," as opposed to merely "speculative," that the injury will be "redressed by a favorable decision." *Lujan.*

Rules of prudential standing, by contrast, are more flexible "rule[s] . . . of federal appellate practice," *Deposit Guaranty Nat. Bank v. Roper* (1980), designed to protect the courts from "decid[ing] abstract questions of wide public significance even [when] other governmental institutions may be more competent to address the questions and even though judicial intervention may be unnecessary to protect individual rights." *Warth.*

In this case the United States retains a stake sufficient to support Article III jurisdiction on appeal and in proceedings before this Court. The judgment in question orders the United States to pay Windsor the refund she seeks. An order directing the Treasury to pay money is "a real and immediate economic injury," *Hein*, indeed as real and immediate as an order directing an individual to pay a tax. That the Executive may welcome this order to pay the refund if it is accompanied by the constitutional ruling it wants does not eliminate the injury to the national Treasury if payment is made, or to the taxpayer if it is not. The judgment orders the United States to pay money that it would not disburse but for the court's order. The Government of the United States has a valid legal argument that it is injured even if the Executive disagrees with §3 of DOMA, which results in Windsor's liability for the tax. Windsor's ongoing claim for funds that the United States refuses to pay thus establishes a controversy sufficient for Article III jurisdiction. It would be a different case if the Executive had taken the further step of paying Windsor the refund to which she was entitled under the District Court's ruling.

This Court confronted a comparable case in *INS v. Chadha* (1983). A statute by its terms allowed one House of Congress to order the Immigration and Naturalization Service (INS) to deport the respondent Chadha. There, as here, the Executive determined that the statute was unconstitutional, and "the INS presented the Executive's views on the constitutionality of the House action to the Court of Appeals." The INS, however, continued to abide by the statute, and "the INS brief to the Court of Appeals did not alter the agency's decision to comply with the House action ordering deportation of Chadha." This Court held "that the INS was sufficiently aggrieved by the Court of Appeals decision prohibiting it from taking action it would otherwise take," regardless of whether the agency welcomed the judgment. The necessity of a "case or controversy" to satisfy Article III was defined as a requirement that the Court's "decision will have real meaning: if we rule for Chadha, he will not be deported; if we uphold [the statute], the INS will execute its order and deport him." This conclusion was not dictum. It was a necessary predicate to the Court's holding that "prior to Congress' intervention, there was adequate Art. III adverseness." The holdings of cases are instructive, and the words of *Chadha* make clear its holding that the refusal of the Executive to provide the relief sought suffices to preserve a justiciable dispute as required by Article III. In short, even where "the Government largely agree[s] with the opposing party on the merits of the controversy," there is sufficient adverseness and an "adequate basis for jurisdiction in the fact that the Government intended to enforce the challenged law against that party."

It is true that "[a] party who receives all that he has sought generally is not aggrieved by the judgment affording the relief and cannot appeal from it." *Roper.* But this rule "does not have its source in the jurisdictional limitations of Art. III. In an appropriate case, appeal may be permitted . . . at the behest of the party who has prevailed on the merits, so long as that party retains a stake in the appeal satisfying the requirements of Art. III." *Roper.*

While these principles suffice to show that this case presents a justiciable controversy under Article III, the prudential problems inherent in the Executive's unusual position require some further discussion. The Executive's agreement with Windsor's legal argument raises the risk that instead of a "real, earnest and vital controversy," the Court faces a "friendly, non-adversary, proceeding . . . [in which] a party beaten in the legislature [seeks to] transfer to the courts an inquiry as to the constitutionality of the legislative act." *Ashwander v. TVA* (1936) (Brandeis, J., concurring). Even when Article III permits the exercise of federal jurisdiction, prudential considerations demand that the Court insist upon "that concrete adverseness which sharpens the presentation of issues upon which the court so largely depends for illumination of difficult constitutional questions." *Baker v. Carr* (1962).

There are, of course, reasons to hear a case and issue a ruling even when one party is reluctant to prevail in its position. Unlike Article III requirements — which must be satisfied by the parties before judicial consideration is appropriate — the relevant prudential factors that counsel against hearing this case are subject to "countervailing considerations [that] may outweigh the concerns underlying the usual reluctance to exert judicial power." *Warth.* One consideration is the extent to which adversarial presentation of the issues is assured by the participation of *amici curiae* prepared to defend with vigor the constitutionality of the legislative act. With respect to this prudential aspect of standing as well, the *Chadha* Court encountered a similar situation. It noted that "there may be prudential, as opposed to Art. III, concerns about sanctioning the adjudication of [this case] in the absence of any participant supporting the validity of [the statute]. The Court of Appeals properly dispelled any such concerns by inviting and accepting briefs from both Houses of Congress." *Chadha* was not an anomaly in this respect. The Court adopts the practice of entertaining arguments made by an *amicus* when the Solicitor General confesses error with respect to a judgment below, even if the confession is in effect an admission that an Act of Congress is unconstitutional.

In the case now before the Court the attorneys for BLAG present a substantial argument for the constitutionality of §3 of DOMA. BLAG's sharp adversarial presentation of the issues satisfies the prudential concerns that otherwise might counsel against hearing an appeal from a decision with which the principal parties agree. Were this Court to hold that prudential rules require it to dismiss the case, and, in consequence, that the Court of Appeals erred in failing to dismiss it as well, extensive litigation would ensue. The district courts in 94 districts throughout the Nation would be without precedential guidance not only in tax refund suits but also in cases involving the whole of DOMA's sweep involving over 1,000 federal statutes and a myriad of federal regulations. For instance, the opinion of the Court of Appeals for the First Circuit, addressing the validity of DOMA in a case involving regulations of the Department of Health and Human Services, likely would be vacated with instructions to dismiss, its ruling and guidance also then erased. Rights and privileges of hundreds of thousands of persons would be adversely affected, pending a case in which all prudential concerns about justiciability are absent. That numerical prediction may not be certain, but it is certain that the cost in judicial resources and expense of litigation for all persons adversely affected would be immense. True, the very extent of DOMA's mandate means that at some point a case likely would arise without the prudential concerns raised here; but the costs, uncertainties, and alleged harm and injuries likely would continue for a time measured in years before the issue is resolved. In these unusual and urgent circumstances, the very term "prudential" counsels that it is a proper exercise of the Court's responsibility to take jurisdiction. For these reasons, the prudential and Article III requirements are met here. . . .

The Court's conclusion that this petition may be heard on the merits does not imply that no difficulties would ensue if this were a common practice in ordinary cases. The Executive's failure to defend the constitutionality of an Act of Congress based on a constitutional theory not yet established in judicial decisions has created a procedural dilemma. On the one hand, as noted, the Government's agreement with Windsor raises questions about the propriety of entertaining a suit in which it seeks affirmance of an order invalidating a federal law and ordering the United States to pay money. On the other hand, if the Executive's agreement with a plaintiff that a law is unconstitutional is enough to preclude judicial review, then the Supreme Court's primary role in determining the constitutionality of a law that has inflicted real injury on a plaintiff who has brought a justiciable legal claim would become only secondary to the President's. This would undermine the clear dictate of the separation-of-powers principle that when an Act of Congress is alleged to conflict with the Constitution, "[i]t is emphatically the province and duty of the judicial department to say what the law is." *Marbury v. Madison* (1803). Similarly, with respect to the legislative power, when Congress has passed a statute and a President has signed it, it poses grave challenges to the separation of powers for the Executive at a particular moment to be able to nullify Congress' enactment solely on its own initiative and without any determination from the Court.

The Court's jurisdictional holding, it must be underscored, does not mean the arguments for dismissing this dispute on prudential grounds lack substance. Yet the difficulty the Executive faces should be acknowledged. When the Executive makes a principled determination that a statute is unconstitutional, it faces a difficult choice. Still, there is no suggestion here that it is appropriate for the Executive as a matter of course to challenge statutes in the judicial forum rather than making the case to Congress for their amendment or repeal. The integrity of the political process would be at risk if difficult constitutional issues were simply referred to the Court as a routine exercise. But this case is not routine. And the capable defense of the law by BLAG ensures that these prudential issues do not cloud the merits question, which is one of immediate importance to the Federal Government and to hundreds of thousands of persons. These circumstances support the Court's decision to proceed to the merits.

JUSTICE SCALIA, with whom JUSTICE THOMAS joins, and with whom THE CHIEF JUSTICE joins as to Part I, dissenting. . . .

This case is about power in several respects. It is about the power of our people to govern themselves, and the power of this Court to pronounce the law. Today's opinion aggrandizes the latter, with the predictable consequence of diminishing the former. We have no power to decide this case. And even if we did, we have no power under the Constitution to invalidate this democratically adopted legislation. The Court's errors on both points spring forth from the same diseased root: an exalted conception of the role of this institution in America.

I

A

The Court is eager—*hungry*—to tell everyone its view of the legal question at the heart of this case. Standing in the way is an obstacle, a technicality of little interest to anyone but the people of We the People, who created it as a barrier against judges' intrusion into their lives. They gave judges, in Article III, only the "judicial Power," a power to decide not abstract questions but real, concrete "Cases" and "Controversies." Yet the plaintiff and the Government agree entirely on what should happen in this lawsuit. They agree that the court below got it right; and they agreed in the court below that the court below that one got it right as well. What, then, are we *doing* here? The answer lies at the heart of the jurisdictional portion of today's opinion, where a single sentence lays bare the majority's vision of our role. The Court says that we have the power to decide this case because if we did not, then our "primary role in determining the constitutionality of a law" (at least one that "has inflicted real injury on a plaintiff") would "become only secondary to the President's." But wait, the reader wonders—Windsor won below, and so *cured* her injury, and the President was glad to see it. True, says the majority, but judicial review must march on regardless, lest we "undermine the clear dictate of the separation-of-powers principle that when an Act of Congress is alleged to conflict with the Constitution, it is emphatically the province and duty of the judicial department to say what the law is."

That is jaw-dropping. It is an assertion of judicial supremacy over the people's Representatives in Congress and the Executive. It envisions a Supreme Court standing (or rather enthroned) at the apex of government, empowered to decide all constitutional questions, always and everywhere "primary" in its role.

This image of the Court would have been unrecognizable to those who wrote and ratified our national charter. They knew well the dangers of "primary" power, and so created branches of government that would be "perfectly co-ordinate by the terms of their common commission," none of which branches could "pretend to an exclusive or superior right of settling the boundaries between their respective powers." The Federalist, No. 49 (J. Madison). The people did this to protect themselves. They did it to guard their right to self-rule against the black-robed supremacy that today's majority finds so attractive. So it was that Madison could confidently state, with no fear of contradiction, that there was nothing of "greater intrinsic value" or "stamped with the authority of more enlightened patrons of liberty" than a government of separate and coordinate powers. *Id.*, No. 47.

For this reason we are quite forbidden to say what the law is whenever (as today's opinion asserts) "an Act of Congress is alleged to conflict with the Constitution." We can do so only when that allegation will determine the outcome of a lawsuit, and is contradicted by the other party. The "judicial Power" is not, as the majority believes, the power "to say what the law is," giving the Supreme Court the "primary role in determining the constitutionality of laws." The majority must have in mind one of the foreign constitutions that pronounces such primacy for its constitutional court and allows that primacy to be exercised in contexts other than a lawsuit. See, *e.g.*, Basic Law for the Federal Republic of Germany, Art. 93. The judicial power as Americans have understood it (and their English ancestors before them) is the power to adjudicate, with conclusive effect, disputed government claims (civil or criminal) against private persons, and disputed claims by private persons against the government or other private persons. Sometimes (though not always) the parties before the court disagree not with regard to the facts of their case (or not *only* with regard to the facts) but with regard to the applicable law—in which event (and *only* in which event) it becomes the "province and duty of the judicial department to say what the law is."

In other words, declaring the compatibility of state or federal laws with the Constitution is not only not the "primary role" of this Court, it is not a separate, free-standing role *at all.* We perform that role incidentally—by accident, as it were—when that is necessary to resolve the dispute before us. Then, and only then, does it become "the province and duty of the judicial department to say what the law is." That is why, in 1793, we politely declined the Washington Administration's request to "say what the law is" on a particular treaty matter that was not the subject of a concrete legal controversy. And that is why, as our opinions have said, some questions of law will *never* be presented to this Court, because there will never be anyone with standing to bring a lawsuit. See *Schlesinger v. Reservists Comm. to Stop the War* (1974); *United States v. Richardson* (1974). As Justice Brandeis put it, we cannot "pass upon the constitutionality of legislation in a friendly, non-adversary, proceeding"; absent a "real, earnest and vital controversy between individuals," we have neither any work to do nor any power to do it. *Ashwander v. TVA* (1936) (concurring opinion). Our authority begins and ends with the need to adjudge the rights of an injured party who stands before us seeking redress. *Lujan v. Defenders of Wildlife* (1992). That is completely absent here. Windsor's injury was cured by the judgment in her favor. And while, in ordinary circumstances, the United States is injured by a directive to pay a tax refund, this suit is far from ordinary. Whatever injury the

United States has suffered will surely not be redressed by the action that it, as a litigant, asks us to take. The final sentence of the Solicitor General's brief on the merits reads: "For the foregoing reasons, the judgment of the court of appeals *should be affirmed*." That will not cure the Government's injury, but carve it into stone. One could spend many fruitless afternoons ransacking our library for any other petitioner's brief seeking an affirmance of the judgment against it. What the petitioner United States asks us to do in the case before us is exactly what the respondent Windsor asks us to do: not to provide relief from the judgment below but to say that that judgment was correct. And the same was true in the Court of Appeals: Neither party sought to undo the judgment for Windsor, and so that court should have dismissed the appeal (just as we should dismiss) for lack of jurisdiction. Since both parties agreed with the judgment of the District Court for the Southern District of New York, the suit should have ended there. The further proceedings have been a contrivance, having no object in mind except to elevate a District Court judgment that has no precedential effect in other courts, to one that has precedential effect throughout the Second Circuit, and then (in this Court) precedential effect throughout the United States.

We have never before agreed to speak—to "say what the law is"—where there is no controversy before us. In the more than two centuries that this Court has existed as an institution, we have never suggested that we have the power to decide a question when every party agrees with both its nominal opponent *and the court below* on that question's answer. The United States reluctantly conceded that at oral argument. See Tr. of Oral Arg. 19-20.

The closest we have ever come to what the Court blesses today was our opinion in *INS v. Chadha* (1983). But in that case, two parties to the litigation disagreed with the position of the United States and with the court below: the House and Senate, which had intervened in the case. Because *Chadha* concerned the validity of a mode of congressional action—the one-house legislative veto—the House and Senate were threatened with destruction of what they claimed to be one of their institutional powers. The Executive choosing not to defend that power,[1] we permitted the House and Senate to intervene. Nothing like that is present here.

To be sure, the Court in *Chadha* said that statutory aggrieved-party status was "not altered by the fact that the Executive may agree with the holding that the statute in question is unconstitutional." But in a footnote to that statement, the Court acknowledged Article III's separate requirement of a "justiciable case or controversy," and stated that *this* requirement was satisfied "because of the presence of the two Houses of Congress as adverse parties." . . . When a private

---

1. There the Justice Department's refusal to defend the legislation was in accord with its longstanding (and entirely reasonable) practice of declining to defend legislation that in its view infringes upon Presidential powers. There is no justification for the Justice Department's abandoning the law in the present case. The majority opinion makes a point of scolding the President for his "failure to defend the constitutionality of an Act of Congress based on a constitutional theory not yet established in judicial decisions." But the rebuke is tongue-in-cheek, for the majority gladly gives the President what he wants. Contrary to all precedent, it decides this case (and even decides it the way the President wishes) *despite* his abandonment of the defense and the consequent absence of a case or controversy.

party has a judicial decree safely in hand to prevent his injury, additional judicial action requires that a party injured by the decree *seek to undo it*. In *Chadha*, the intervening House and Senate fulfilled that requirement. Here no one does.

The majority's discussion of the requirements of Article III bears no resemblance to our jurisprudence. It accuses the *amicus* (appointed to argue against our jurisdiction) of "elid[ing] the distinction between . . . the jurisdictional requirements of Article III and the prudential limits on its exercise." It then proceeds to call the requirement of adverseness a "prudential" aspect of standing. *Of standing*. That is incomprehensible. A plaintiff (or appellant) can have all the standing in the world—satisfying all three standing requirements of *Lujan* that the majority so carefully quotes—and yet no Article III controversy may be before the court. Article III requires not just a plaintiff (or appellant) who has standing to complain but *an opposing party* who denies the validity of the complaint. It is not the *amicus* that has done the eliding of distinctions, but the majority, calling the quite separate Article III requirement of adverseness between the parties an element (which it then pronounces a "prudential" element) of standing. The question here is not whether, as the majority puts it, "the United States retains a stake sufficient to support Article III jurisdiction," the question is whether there is any controversy (which requires *contradiction*) between the United States and Ms. Windsor. There is not.

I find it wryly amusing that the majority seeks to dismiss the requirement of party-adverseness as nothing more than a "prudential" aspect of the sole Article III requirement of standing. (Relegating a jurisdictional requirement to "prudential" status is a wondrous device, enabling courts to ignore the requirement whenever they believe it "prudent"—which is to say, a good idea.) Half a century ago, a Court similarly bent upon announcing its view regarding the constitutionality of a federal statute achieved that goal by effecting a remarkably similar *but completely opposite* distortion of the principles limiting our jurisdiction. The Court's notorious opinion in *Flast v. Cohen* (1968), held that *standing* was merely an element (which it pronounced to be a "prudential" element) of the sole Article III requirement of *adverseness*. We have been living with the chaos created by that power-grabbing decision ever since, see *Hein v. Freedom From Religion Foundation, Inc.* (2007), as we will have to live with the chaos created by this one. . . .

It may be argued that if what we say is true some Presidential determinations that statutes are unconstitutional will not be subject to our review. That is as it should be, when both the President and the plaintiff agree that the statute is unconstitutional. Where the Executive is enforcing an unconstitutional law, suit will of course lie; but if, in that suit, the Executive admits the unconstitutionality of the law, the litigation should end in an order or a consent decree enjoining enforcement. This suit saw the light of day only because the President enforced the Act (and thus gave Windsor standing to sue) even though he believed it unconstitutional. He could have equally chosen (more appropriately, some would say) neither to enforce nor to defend the statute he believed to be unconstitutional, see Presidential Authority to Decline to Execute Unconstitutional Statutes, 18 Op. Off. Legal Counsel 199 (Nov. 2, 1994)—in which event Windsor would not have been injured, the District Court could not have refereed this friendly scrimmage, and the Executive's determination of unconstitutionality would have escaped this Court's desire to blurt out its view of the law. The matter would have been left, as so many matters ought to be left, to a tug of war between the President and the Congress, which has innumerable means (up to and including impeachment) of compelling the President to enforce the laws it has written. Or the President could have evaded presentation of the constitutional issue to this Court simply by declining to appeal the District Court and Court of Appeals dispositions he agreed with. Be sure of this much: If a President wants to insulate his judgment of unconstitutionality from our review, he can. What the views urged in this dissent produce is not insulation from judicial review but insulation from Executive contrivance.

The majority brandishes the famous sentence from *Marbury v. Madison* (1803) that "[i]t is emphatically the province and duty of the judicial department to say what the law is." But that sentence neither says nor implies that it is *always* the province and duty of the Court to say what the law is — much less that its responsibility in that regard is a "primary" one. The very next sentence of Chief Justice Marshall's opinion makes the crucial qualification that today's majority ignores: "*Those who apply the rule to particular cases,* must of necessity expound and interpret that rule." (emphasis added). Only when a "particular case" is before us — that is, a controversy that it is our business to resolve under Article III — do we have the province and duty to pronounce the law. For the views of our early Court more precisely addressing the question before us here, the majority ought instead to have consulted the opinion of Chief Justice Taney in *Lord v. Veazie* (1850):

> The objection in the case before us is . . . that the plaintiff and defendant have the same interest, and that interest adverse and in conflict with the interest of third persons, whose rights would be seriously affected if the question of law was decided in the manner that both of the parties to this suit desire it to be. A judgment entered under such circumstances, and for such purposes, is a mere form. The whole proceeding was in contempt of the court, and highly reprehensible. . . . A judgment in form, thus procured, in the eye of the law is no judgment of the court. It is a nullity, and no writ of error will lie upon it. This writ is, therefore, dismissed.

There is, in the words of *Marbury,* no "necessity [to] expound and interpret" the law in this case; just a desire to place this Court at the center of the Nation's life. . . .

B

A few words in response to the theory of jurisdiction set forth in Justice Alito's dissent: Though less far reaching in its consequences than the majority's conversion of constitutionally required adverseness into a discretionary element of standing, the theory of that dissent similarly elevates the Court to the "primary" determiner of constitutional questions involving the separation of powers, and, to boot, increases the power of the most dangerous branch: the "legislative department," which by its nature "draw[s] all power into its impetuous vortex." The Federalist, No. 48, at 309 (J. Madison). Heretofore in our national history, the President's failure to "take Care that the Laws be faithfully executed," U.S. Const., Art. II, §3, could only be brought before a judicial tribunal by someone whose concrete interests were harmed by that alleged failure. Justice Alito would create a system in which Congress can hale the Executive before the courts not only to vindicate its own institutional powers to act, but to correct a perceived inadequacy in the execution of its laws.[2] This would lay to rest Tocqueville's praise of our judicial system as one which "intimately bind[s] the case made for the law with the case made for one man," one in which legislation is "no longer exposed to the daily aggression of the parties," and in which "[t]he political question that [the judge] must resolve is linked to the interest" of private litigants. A. de Tocqueville, Democracy in America 97 (H. Mansfield & D. Winthrop eds. 2000). That would be replaced by a system in which Congress and the Executive can pop immediately into court, in their institutional capacity, whenever the President refuses to implement a statute he believes to be unconstitutional, and whenever he implements a law in a manner that is not to Congress's liking.

Justice Alito's notion of standing will likewise enormously shrink the area to which "judicial censure, exercised by the courts on legislation, cannot extend." *ibid.* For example, a bare majority of both Houses could bring into court the assertion that the Executive's implementation of welfare programs is too generous — a failure that no other litigant would have standing to complain about. . . .

To be sure, if Congress cannot invoke our authority in the way that Justice Alito proposes, then its only recourse is to confront the President directly. Unimaginable evil this is not. Our system is *designed* for confrontation. That is what "[a]mbition . . . counteract[ing] ambition," The Federalist, No. 51, at 322 (J. Madison), is all about. If majorities in both Houses of Congress care enough about the matter, they have available innumerable ways to compel executive action without a lawsuit — from refusing to confirm Presidential appointees to the elimination of funding. (Nothing says "enforce the Act" quite like ". . . or you will have money for little else.") But the condition is crucial; Congress must care enough to act against the President itself, not merely enough to instruct its lawyers to ask *us* to do so. Placing the Constitution's entirely anticipated

2. Justice Alito attempts to limit his argument by claiming that Congress is injured (and can therefore appeal) when its statute is held unconstitutional without Presidential defense, but is *not* injured when its statute is held unconstitutional *despite* Presidential defense. I do not understand that line. The injury to Congress is the same whether the President has defended the statute or not. And if the injury is threatened, why should Congress not be able to participate in the suit from the beginning, just as the President can? And if having a statute declared unconstitutional (and therefore inoperative) by a court is an injury, why is it not an injury when a statute is declared unconstitutional by the President and rendered inoperative by his consequent failure to enforce it? Or when the President simply declines to enforce it without opining on its constitutionality? If it is the *inoperativeness* that constitutes the injury — the "impairment of [the legislative] function," as Justice Alito puts it — it should make no difference which of the other two branches inflicts it, and whether the Constitution is the pretext. A principled and predictable system of jurisprudence cannot rest upon a shifting concept of injury, designed to support standing when we would like it. . . .

political arm wrestling into permanent judicial receivership does not do the system a favor. And by the way, if the President loses the lawsuit but does not faithfully implement the Court's decree, just as he did not faithfully implement Congress's statute, what then? Only Congress can bring him to heel by . . . what do you think? Yes: a direct confrontation with the President.

JUSTICE ALITO . . . dissenting. . . .

In my view, the United States clearly is not a proper petitioner in this case. The United States does not ask us to overturn the judgment of the court below or to alter that judgment in any way. Quite to the contrary, the United States argues emphatically in favor of the correctness of that judgment. We have never before reviewed a decision at the sole behest of a party that took such a position, and to do so would be to render an advisory opinion, in violation of Article III's dictates. For the reasons given in Justice Scalia's dissent, I do not find the Court's arguments to the contrary to be persuasive. Whether the Bipartisan Legal Advisory Group of the House of Representatives (BLAG) has standing to petition is a much more difficult question. It is also a significantly closer question than whether the intervenors in *Hollingsworth v. Perry,* which the Court also decides today—have standing to appeal. It is remarkable that the Court has simultaneously decided that the United States, which "receive[d] all that [it] ha[d] sought" below, *Deposit Guaranty Nat. Bank v. Roper* (1980), is a proper petitioner in this case but that the intervenors in *Hollingsworth,* who represent the party that lost in the lower court, are not. In my view, both the *Hollingsworth* intervenors and BLAG have standing. . . .

A party invoking the Court's authority has a sufficient stake to permit it to appeal when it has "'suffered an injury in fact' that is caused by 'the conduct complained of' and that 'will be redressed by a favorable decision.'" *Camreta v. Greene* (2011) (quoting *Lujan v. Defenders of Wildlife* (1992)). In the present case, the House of Representatives, which has authorized BLAG to represent its interests in this matter, suffered just such an injury. In *INS v. Chadha* (1983), the Court held that the two Houses of Congress were "proper parties" to file a petition in defense of the constitutionality of the one-house veto statute. Accordingly, the Court granted and decided petitions by both the Senate and the House, in addition to the Executive's petition. That the two Houses had standing to petition is not surprising: The Court of Appeals' decision in *Chadha,* by holding the one-house veto to be unconstitutional, had limited Congress' power to legislate. In discussing Article III standing, the Court suggested that Congress suffered a similar injury whenever federal legislation it had passed was struck down, noting that it had "long held that Congress is the proper party to defend the validity of a statute when an agency of government, as a defendant charged with enforcing the statute, agrees with plaintiffs that the statute is inapplicable or unconstitutional."

The United States attempts to distinguish *Chadha* on the ground that it "involved an unusual statute that vested the House and the Senate themselves each with special procedural rights—namely, the right effectively to veto

Executive action." But that is a distinction without a difference: just as the Court of Appeals decision that the *Chadha* Court affirmed impaired Congress' power by striking down the one-house veto, so the Second Circuit's decision here impairs Congress' legislative power by striking down an Act of Congress. The United States has not explained why the fact that the impairment at issue in *Chadha* was "special" or "procedural" has any relevance to whether Congress suffered an injury. Indeed, because legislating is Congress' central function, any impairment of that function is a more grievous injury than the impairment of a procedural add-on. . . .

Both the United States and the Court-appointed *amicus* err in arguing that *Raines v. Byrd* (1997), is to the contrary. . . . *Raines* dealt with individual Members of Congress and specifically pointed to the individual Members' lack of institutional endorsement as a sign of their standing problem: "We attach some importance to the fact that appellees have not been authorized to represent their respective Houses of Congress in this action, and indeed both Houses actively oppose their suit." . . . Here, by contrast, passage by the House was needed for DOMA to become law. U.S. Const., Art. I, §7 (bicameralism and presentment requirements for legislation).

I appreciate the argument that the Constitution confers on the President alone the authority to defend federal law in litigation, but in my view, as I have explained, that argument is contrary to the Court's holding in *Chadha,* and it is certainly contrary to the *Chadha* Court's endorsement of the principle that "Congress is the proper party to defend the validity of a statute" when the Executive refuses to do so on constitutional grounds. Accordingly, in the narrow category of cases in which a court strikes down an Act of Congress and the Executive declines to defend the Act, Congress both has standing to defend the undefended statute and is a proper party to do so. . . .

Study Guide:

- In the next case, Justices Kennedy and Alito argued in favor of standing as they had in *Windsor*. Chief Justice Roberts and Justice Scalia argued against standing in both cases. By contrast, Justices Breyer, Sotomayor, and Kagan switched from standing in *Windsor* to no standing here, while Justice Thomas switched from no standing in *Windsor* to standing here. Can these shifts in the line-ups be explained by differing philosophies on the doctrine of standing, as opposed to a desire to reach different outcomes in each case?
- If an initiative's proponents lack standing to defend it from constitutional challenge when the government refuses to do so, does this undermine the popular check on government that is supposed to be provided by popular initiatives? Should doctrine of federal standing reflect this difficulty?
- Is there any way for states with initiatives to fix this problem consistent with Chief Justice Roberts' opinion?
- Can you see the continuing relevance of the differing concepts of sovereignty we have seen discussed in previous chapters?

HOLLINGSWORTH v. PERRY

No. 12-144

Argued Mar. 26, 2013 | Decided June 26, 2013

Chief Justice Roberts delivered the opinion of the Court.

The public is currently engaged in an active political debate over whether same-sex couples should be allowed to marry. That question has also given rise to litigation. In this case, petitioners, who oppose same-sex marriage, ask us to decide whether the Equal Protection Clause "prohibits the State of California from defining marriage as the union of a man and a woman." Pet. for Cert. i. Respondents, same-sex couples who wish to marry, view the issue in somewhat different terms: For them, it is whether California—having previously recognized the right of same-sex couples to marry—may reverse that decision through a referendum. Federal courts have authority under the Constitution to answer such questions only if necessary to do so in the course of deciding an actual "case" or "controversy." As used in the Constitution, those words do not include every sort of dispute, but only those "historically viewed as capable of resolution through the judicial process." *Flast v. Cohen* (1968). This is an essential limit on our power: It ensures that we act *as judges,* and do not engage in policymaking properly left to elected representatives.

For there to be such a case or controversy, it is not enough that the party invoking the power of the court have a keen interest in the issue. That party must also have "standing," which requires, among other things, that it have suffered a concrete and particularized injury. Because we find that petitioners do not have standing, we have no authority to decide this case on the merits, and neither did the Ninth Circuit.

I

In 2008, the California Supreme Court held that limiting the official designation of marriage to opposite-sex couples violated the equal protection clause of the California Constitution. *In re Marriage Cases* (Cal. 2008) Later that year, California voters passed the ballot initiative at the center of this dispute, known as Proposition 8. That proposition amended the California Constitution to provide that "[o]nly marriage between a man and a woman is valid or recognized in California." Cal. Const., Art. I, §7.5. Shortly thereafter, the California Supreme Court rejected a procedural challenge to the amendment, and held that the Proposition was properly enacted under California law. *Strauss v. Horton* (Cal. 2009). According to the California Supreme Court, Proposition 8 created a "narrow and limited exception" to the state constitutional rights otherwise guaranteed to same-sex couples. Under California law, same-sex couples have a right to enter into relationships recognized by the State as "domestic partnerships," which carry "the same rights, protections, and benefits, and shall be subject to the same responsibilities, obligations, and duties under law . . . as are granted to and imposed upon spouses." Cal. Fam. Code Ann. §297.5(a) (2004). In *In re*

Marriage Cases, the California Supreme Court concluded that the California Constitution further guarantees same-sex couples "all of the constitutionally based incidents of marriage," including the right to have that marriage "officially recognized" as such by the State. Proposition 8, the court explained in *Strauss,* left those rights largely undisturbed, reserving only "the official *designation* of the term 'marriage' for the union of opposite-sex couples as a matter of state constitutional law."

Respondents, two same-sex couples who wish to marry, filed suit in federal court, challenging Proposition 8 under the Due Process and Equal Protection Clauses of the Fourteenth Amendment to the Federal Constitution. The complaint named as defendants California's Governor, attorney general, and various other state and local officials responsible for enforcing California's marriage laws. Those officials refused to defend the law, although they have continued to enforce it throughout this litigation. The District Court allowed petitioners — the official proponents of the initiative — to intervene to defend it. After a 12-day bench trial, the District Court declared Proposition 8 unconstitutional, permanently enjoining the California officials named as defendants from enforcing the law, and "directing the official defendants that all persons under their control or supervision" shall not enforce it. *Perry v. Schwarzenegger* (N.D. Cal. 2010). Those officials elected not to appeal the District Court order. When petitioners did, the Ninth Circuit asked them to address "why this appeal should not be dismissed for lack of Article III standing." *Perry v. Schwarzenegger* (CA9, Aug. 16, 2010). After briefing and argument, the Ninth Circuit certified a question to the California Supreme Court:

> Whether under Article II, Section 8 of the California Constitution, or otherwise under California law, the official proponents of an initiative measure possess either a particularized interest in the initiative's validity or the authority to assert the State's interest in the initiative's validity, which would enable them to defend the constitutionality of the initiative upon its adoption or appeal a judgment invalidating the initiative, when the public officials charged with that duty refuse to do so.

The California Supreme Court agreed to decide the certified question, and answered in the affirmative. Without addressing whether the proponents have a particularized interest of their own in an initiative's validity, the court concluded that "[i]n a postelection challenge to a voter-approved initiative measure, the official proponents of the initiative are authorized under California law to appear and assert the state's interest in the initiative's validity and to appeal a judgment invalidating the measure when the public officials who ordinarily defend the measure or appeal such a judgment decline to do so." *Perry v. Brown* (CA9, 2011).

Relying on that answer, the Ninth Circuit concluded that petitioners had standing under federal law to defend the constitutionality of Proposition 8. California, it reasoned, "'has standing to defend the constitutionality of its [laws],'" and States have the "prerogative, as independent sovereigns, to decide for themselves who may assert their interests." *Perry v. Brown* (CA9, 2012). "All a federal court need determine is that the state has suffered a harm sufficient to confer standing and that the party seeking to invoke the jurisdiction of the court is authorized by the state to represent its interest in remedying that harm."

On the merits, the Ninth Circuit affirmed the District Court. The court held the Proposition unconstitutional under the rationale of our decision in *Romer v. Evans* (1996). In the Ninth Circuit's view, *Romer* stands for the proposition that "the Equal Protection Clause requires the state to have a legitimate reason for withdrawing a right or benefit *from one group but not others,* whether or not it was required to confer that right or benefit in the first place." The Ninth Circuit concluded that "taking away the official designation" of "marriage" from same-sex couples, while continuing to afford those couples all the rights and obligations of marriage, did not further any legitimate interest of the State. Proposition 8, in the court's view, violated the Equal Protection Clause because it served no purpose "but to impose on gays and lesbians, through the public law, a majority's private disapproval of them and their relationships."

We granted certiorari to review that determination, and directed that the parties also brief and argue "Whether petitioners have standing under Article III, §2, of the Constitution in this case."

II

Article III of the Constitution confines the judicial power of federal courts to deciding actual "Cases" or "Controversies." §2. One essential aspect of this requirement is that any person invoking the power of a federal court must demonstrate standing to do so. This requires the litigant to prove that he has suffered a concrete and particularized injury that is fairly traceable to the challenged conduct, and is likely to be redressed by a favorable judicial decision. *Lujan v. Defenders of Wildlife* (1992). In other words, for a federal court to have authority under the Constitution to settle a dispute, the party before it must seek a remedy for a personal and tangible harm. "The presence of a disagreement, however sharp and acrimonious it may be, is insufficient by itself to meet Art. III's requirements." [*Diamond v. Charles* (1986).] The doctrine of standing, we recently explained, "serves to prevent the judicial process from being used to usurp the powers of the political branches." *Clapper v. Amnesty Int'l USA* (2013). In light of this "overriding and time-honored concern about keeping the Judiciary's power within its proper constitutional sphere, we must put aside the natural urge to proceed directly to the merits of [an] important dispute and to 'settle' it for the sake of convenience and efficiency." *Raines v. Byrd* (1997).

Most standing cases consider whether a plaintiff has satisfied the requirement when filing suit, but Article III demands that an "actual controversy" persist throughout all stages of litigation. *Already, LLC v. Nike, Inc.* (2013) (internal quotation marks omitted). That means that standing "must be met by persons seeking appellate review, just as it must be met by persons appearing in courts of first instance." *Arizonans for Official English v. Arizona* (1997). We therefore must decide whether petitioners had standing to appeal the District Court's order.

Respondents initiated this case in the District Court against the California officials responsible for enforcing Proposition 8. The parties do not contest that respondents had Article III standing to do so. Each couple expressed a desire to marry and obtain "official sanction" from the State, which was unavailable to them given the declaration in Proposition 8 that "marriage" in California is solely between a man and a woman.

After the District Court declared Proposition 8 unconstitutional and enjoined the state officials named as defendants from enforcing it, however, the inquiry under Article III changed. Respondents no longer had any injury to redress—they had won—and the state officials chose not to appeal.

The only individuals who sought to appeal that order were petitioners, who had intervened in the District Court. But the District Court had not ordered them to do or refrain from doing anything. To have standing, a litigant must seek relief for an injury that affects him in a "personal and individual way." *Defenders of Wildlife*. He must possess a "direct stake in the outcome" of the case. *Arizonans for Official English*. Here, however, petitioners had no "direct stake" in the outcome of their appeal. Their only interest in having the District Court order reversed was to vindicate the constitutional validity of a generally applicable California law.

We have repeatedly held that such a "generalized grievance," no matter how sincere, is insufficient to confer standing. A litigant "raising only a generally available grievance about government—claiming only harm to his and every citizen's interest in proper application of the Constitution and laws, and seeking relief that no more directly and tangibly benefits him than it does the public at large—does not state an Article III case or controversy." *Defenders of Wildlife*.

Petitioners argue that the California Constitution and its election laws give them a "'unique,' 'special,' and 'distinct' role in the initiative process—one 'involving both authority and responsibilities that differ from other supporters of the measure.'" True enough—but only when it comes to the process of enacting the law. Upon submitting the proposed initiative to the attorney general, petitioners became the official "proponents" of Proposition 8. As such, they were responsible for collecting the signatures required to qualify the measure for the ballot. After those signatures were collected, the proponents alone had the right to file the measure with election officials to put it on the ballot. Petitioners also possessed control over the arguments in favor of the initiative that would appear in California's ballot pamphlets.

But once Proposition 8 was approved by the voters, the measure became "a duly enacted constitutional amendment or statute." *Perry*. Petitioners have no role—special or otherwise—in the enforcement of Proposition 8. See *id.* (petitioners do not "possess any official authority . . . to directly enforce the initiative measure in question"). They therefore have no "personal stake" in defending its enforcement that is distinguishable from the general interest of every citizen of California. *Defenders of Wildlife*.

Article III standing "is not to be placed in the hands of 'concerned bystanders,' who will use it simply as a 'vehicle for the vindication of value interests.'" *Diamond*. No matter how deeply committed petitioners may be to upholding

Proposition 8 or how "zealous [their] advocacy," (Kennedy, J., dissenting), that is not a "particularized" interest sufficient to create a case or controversy under Article III.

III

A

Without a judicially cognizable interest of their own, petitioners attempt to invoke that of someone else. They assert that even if *they* have no cognizable interest in appealing the District Court's judgment, the State of California does, and they may assert that interest on the State's behalf. It is, however, a "fundamental restriction on our authority" that "[i]n the ordinary course, a litigant must assert his or her own legal rights and interests, and cannot rest a claim to relief on the legal rights or interests of third parties." *Powers v. Ohio* (1991). There are "certain, limited exceptions" to that rule. But even when we have allowed litigants to assert the interests of others, the litigants themselves still "must have suffered an injury in fact, thus giving [them] a sufficiently concrete interest in the outcome of the issue in dispute." In *Diamond v. Charles,* for example, we refused to allow Diamond, a pediatrician engaged in private practice in Illinois, to defend the constitutionality of the State's abortion law. In that case, a group of physicians filed a constitutional challenge to the Illinois statute in federal court. The State initially defended the law, and Diamond, a professed "conscientious object[or] to abortions," intervened to defend it alongside the State.

After the Seventh Circuit affirmed a permanent injunction against enforcing several provisions of the law, the State chose not to pursue an appeal to this Court. But when Diamond did, the state attorney general filed a "letter of interest," explaining that the State's interest in the proceeding was "essentially coterminous with the position on the issues set forth by [Diamond]." That was not enough, we held, to allow the appeal to proceed. As the Court explained, "[e]ven if there were circumstances in which a private party would have standing to defend the constitutionality of a challenged statute, this [was] not one of them," because Diamond was not able to assert an injury in fact of his own. And without "any judicially cognizable interest," Diamond could not "maintain the litigation abandoned by the State."

For the reasons we have explained, petitioners have likewise not suffered an injury in fact, and therefore would ordinarily have no standing to assert the State's interests.

B

Petitioners contend that this case is different, because the California Supreme Court has determined that they are "authorized under California law to appear and assert the state's interest" in the validity of Proposition 8. The court below agreed: "All a federal court need determine is that the state has suffered a harm sufficient to confer standing and that the party seeking to invoke the jurisdiction of the court is authorized by the state to represent its interest in remedying that harm." As petitioners put it, they "need no more show a personal injury, separate from the State's indisputable interest in the validity of its law, than would California's Attorney General or did the legislative leaders held to have standing in *Karcher v. May* (1987)." In *Karcher,* we held that two New Jersey state legislators—Speaker of the General Assembly Alan Karcher and President of the Senate Carmen Orechio—could intervene in a suit against the State to defend the constitutionality of a New Jersey law, after the New Jersey attorney general had declined to do so. "Since the New Jersey Legislature had authority under state law to represent the State's interests in both the District Court and the Court of Appeals," we held that the Speaker and the President, in their official capacities, could vindicate that interest in federal court on the legislature's behalf.

Far from supporting petitioners' standing, however, *Karcher* is compelling precedent against it. The legislators in that case intervened in their official capacities as Speaker and President of the legislature. No one doubts that a State has a cognizable interest "in the continued enforceability" of its laws that is harmed by a judicial decision declaring a state law unconstitutional. To vindicate that interest or any other, a State must be able to designate agents to represent it in federal court. See *Poindexter v. Greenhow* (1885) ("The State is a political corporate body [that] can act only through agents"). That agent is typically the State's attorney general. But state law may provide for other officials to speak for the State in federal court, as New Jersey law did for the State's presiding legislative officers in *Karcher.*

What is significant about *Karcher* is what happened after the Court of Appeals decision in that case. Karcher and Orechio lost their positions as Speaker and President, but nevertheless sought to appeal to this Court. We held that they could not do so. We explained that while they were able to participate in the lawsuit in their official capacities as presiding officers of the incumbent legislature, "since they no longer hold those offices, they lack authority to pursue this appeal."

The point of *Karcher* is not that a State could authorize *private parties* to represent its interests; Karcher and Orechio were permitted to proceed only because they were state officers, acting in an official capacity. As soon as they lost that capacity, they lost standing. Petitioners here hold no office and have always participated in this litigation solely as private parties. . . .

C

Both petitioners and respondents seek support from dicta in *Arizonans for Official English v. Arizona*. The plaintiff in *Arizonans for Official English* filed a constitutional challenge to an Arizona ballot initiative declaring English "the official language of the State of Arizona." After the District Court declared the initiative unconstitutional, Arizona's Governor announced that she would not pursue an appeal. Instead, the principal sponsor of the ballot initiative—the Arizonans for Official English Committee—sought to defend the measure in the Ninth Circuit. Analogizing the sponsors to the Arizona Legislature, the Ninth Circuit held that the Committee was "qualified to defend [the initiative] on appeal," and affirmed the District Court. Before finding the case mooted by other events, this Court expressed "grave doubts" about the Ninth Circuit's standing analysis. We reiterated that "[s]tanding to defend on appeal in the place of an original defendant . . . demands that the litigant possess 'a direct stake in the outcome.'" (quoting *Diamond*). We recognized that a legislator authorized by state law to represent the State's interest may satisfy standing requirements, as in *Karcher*, but noted that the Arizona committee and its members were "not elected representatives, and we [we]re aware of no Arizona law appointing initiative sponsors as agents of the people of Arizona to defend, in lieu of public officials, the constitutionality of initiatives made law of the State." *Arizonans for Official English.*

Petitioners argue that, by virtue of the California Supreme Court's decision, they *are* authorized to act " 'as agents of the people' of California." But that Court never described petitioners as "agents of the people," or of anyone else. Nor did the Ninth Circuit. The Ninth Circuit asked—and the California Supreme Court answered—only whether petitioners had "the authority to assert the State's interest in the initiative's validity." All that the California Supreme Court decision stands for is that, so far as California is concerned, petitioners may argue in defense of Proposition 8. This "does not mean that the proponents become de facto public officials"; the authority they enjoy is "simply the authority to participate as parties in a court action and to assert legal arguments in defense of the state's interest in the validity of the initiative measure." That interest is by definition a generalized one, and it is precisely because proponents assert such an interest that they lack standing under our precedents.

And petitioners are plainly not agents of the State—"formal" or otherwise. . . . [T]he point, the most basic features of an agency relationship are missing here. Agency requires more than mere authorization to assert a particular interest. "An essential element of agency is the principal's right to control the agent's actions." 1 Restatement (Third) of Agency §1.01, Comment *f* (2005) (hereinafter Restatement). Yet petitioners answer to no one; they decide for themselves, with no review, what arguments to make and how to make them. Unlike California's attorney general, they are not elected at regular intervals—or elected at all. No provision provides for their removal. As one *amicus* explains, "the proponents apparently have an unelected appointment for an unspecified period of time as defenders of the initiative, however and to whatever extent they choose to defend it." Brief for Walter Dellinger. "If the relationship between two persons is one of agency . . . , the agent owes a fiduciary obligation to the principal." 1 Restatement §1.01, Comment *e*. But petitioners owe nothing of the sort to the people of California. Unlike California's elected officials, they have taken no oath of office. As the California Supreme Court explained, petitioners are bound simply by "the same ethical constraints that apply to all other parties in a legal proceeding." They are free to pursue a purely ideological commitment to the law's constitutionality without the need to take cognizance of resource constraints, changes in public opinion, or potential ramifications for other state priorities. . . .

Neither the California Supreme Court nor the Ninth Circuit ever described the proponents as agents of the State, and they plainly do not qualify as such.

IV

The dissent eloquently recounts the California Supreme Court's reasons for deciding that state law authorizes petitioners to defend Proposition 8. . . . We do not "disrespect[ ]" or "disparage[ ]" those reasons. Nor do we question California's sovereign right to maintain an initiative process, or the right of initiative proponents to defend their initiatives in California courts, where Article III does not apply. But as the dissent acknowledges, standing in federal court is a question of federal law, not state law. And no matter its reasons, the fact that a State thinks a private party should have standing to seek relief for a generalized grievance cannot override our settled law to the contrary. The Article III requirement that a party invoking the jurisdiction of a federal court seek relief for a personal, particularized injury serves vital interests going to the role of the Judiciary in our system of separated powers. "Refusing to entertain generalized grievances ensures that . . . courts exercise power that is judicial in nature," *Lance*, and ensures that the Federal Judiciary respects "the proper—and properly limited—role of the courts in a democratic society," *DaimlerChrysler Corp. v. Cuno* (2006). States cannot alter that role simply by issuing to private parties who otherwise lack standing a ticket to the federal courthouse.

* * *

We have never before upheld the standing of a private party to defend the constitutionality of a state statute when state officials have chosen not to. We decline to do so for the first time here. Because petitioners have not satisfied their burden to demonstrate standing to appeal the judgment of the District Court, the Ninth Circuit was without jurisdiction to consider the appeal. The judgment of the Ninth Circuit is vacated, and the case is remanded with instructions to dismiss the appeal for lack of jurisdiction. It is so ordered.

JUSTICE KENNEDY, with whom JUSTICE THOMAS, JUSTICE ALITO, and JUSTICE SOTOMAYOR join, dissenting. . . .

In my view Article III does not require California, when deciding who may appear in court to defend an initiative on its behalf, to comply with the Restatement of Agency or with this Court's view of how a State should make its laws or structure its government. The Court's reasoning does not take into account the fundamental principles or the practical dynamics of the initiative system in California, which uses this mechanism to control and to bypass public officials—the same officials who would not defend the initiative, an injury the Court now leaves unremedied. The Court's decision also has implications for the 26 other States that use an initiative or popular referendum system and which, like California, may choose to have initiative proponents stand in for the State when public officials decline to defend an initiative in litigation. In my submission, the Article III requirement for a justiciable case or controversy does not prevent proponents from having their day in court.

These are the premises for this respectful dissent.

I

As the Court explains, the State of California sustained a concrete injury, sufficient to satisfy the requirements of Article III, when a United States District Court nullified a portion of its State Constitution. To determine whether justiciability continues in appellate proceedings after the State Executive acquiesced in the District Court's adverse judgment, it is necessary to ascertain what persons, if any, have "authority under state law to represent the State's interests" in federal court. *Karcher v. May* (1987). . . .

This Court, in determining the substance of state law, is "bound by a state court's construction of a state statute." *Wisconsin v. Mitchell* (1993). And the Supreme Court of California, in response to the certified question submitted to it in this case, has determined that State Elections Code provisions directed to initiative proponents do inform and instruct state law respecting the rights and status of proponents in post election judicial proceedings. Here, in reliance on these statutes and the California Constitution, the State Supreme Court has held that proponents do have authority "under California law to appear and assert the state's interest in the initiative's validity and appeal a judgment invalidating the measure when the public officials who ordinarily defend the measure or appeal such a judgment decline to do so." *Perry v. Brown* (Cal. 2011).

The reasons the Supreme Court of California gave for its holding have special relevance in the context of determining whether proponents have the authority to seek a federal-court remedy for the State's concrete, substantial, and continuing injury. As a class, official proponents are a small, identifiable group. Because many of their decisions must be unanimous, they are necessarily few in number. Their identities are public. Their commitment is substantial [including obtaining petition signatures, paying monetary fee, and drafting arguments for official ballot pamphlet]. They know and understand the purpose and operation of the proposed law, an important requisite in defending initiatives on complex matters such as taxation and insurance. Having gone to great lengths to convince voters to enact an initiative, they have a stake in the outcome and the necessary commitment to provide zealous advocacy.

Thus, in California, proponents play a "unique role . . . in the initiative process." They "have a unique relationship to the voter-approved measure that makes them especially likely to be reliable and vigorous advocates for the measure and to be so viewed by those whose votes secured the initiative's enactment into law." See also *id.* (because of "their special relationship to the initiative measure," proponents are "the most obvious and logical private individuals to ably and vigorously defend the validity of the challenged measure on behalf of the interests of the voters who adopted the initiative into law"). Proponents' authority under state law is not a contrivance. It is not a fictional construct. It is the product of the California Constitution and the California Elections Code. There is no basis for this Court to set aside the California Supreme Court's determination of state law. . . .

For these and other reasons, the Supreme Court of California held that the California Elections Code and Article II, §8, of the California Constitution afford proponents "the authority . . . to assert the state's interest in the validity of the initiative" when State officials decline to do so. The court repeated this unanimous holding more than a half-dozen times and in no uncertain terms. That should suffice to resolve the central issue on which the federal question turns.

II

A

The Court concludes that proponents lack sufficient ties to the state government. It notes that they "are not elected," "answer to no one," and lack "a fiduciary obligation" to the State (quoting 1 Restatement (Third) of Agency §1.01, Comments *e, f* (2005)). But what the Court deems deficiencies in the proponents' connection to the State government, the State Supreme Court saw as essential qualifications to defend the initiative system. The very object of the initiative system is to establish a lawmaking process that does not depend upon state officials. In California, the popular initiative is necessary to implement "the theory that all power of government ultimately resides in the people." The right to adopt initiatives has been described by the California courts as "one of the most precious rights of [the State's] democratic process." That historic role for the initiative system "grew out of dissatisfaction with the then governing public officials and a widespread belief that the people had lost control of the political process." The initiative's "primary purpose," then, "was to afford the people the ability to propose and to adopt constitutional amendments or statutory provisions that their elected public officials had refused or declined to adopt." The California Supreme Court has determined that this purpose is undermined if the very officials the initiative process seeks to circumvent are the only parties who can defend an enacted initiative when it is challenged in a legal proceeding. Giving the Governor and attorney general this *de facto* veto will erode one of the cornerstones of the State's governmental structure. And in light of the frequency with which initiatives' opponents resort to litigation, the impact of that veto could be substantial. As a consequence, California finds it necessary to vest the responsibility and right to defend a voter-approved initiative in the initiative's proponents when the State Executive declines to do so.

Yet today the Court demands that the State follow the Restatement of Agency. There are reasons, however, why California might conclude that a conventional agency relationship is inconsistent with the history, design, and purpose of the initiative process. The State may not wish to associate itself with proponents or their views outside of the "extremely narrow and limited" context of this litigation, or to bear the cost of proponents' legal fees. The State may also wish to avoid the odd conflict of having a formal agent of the State (the initiative's proponent) arguing in favor of a law's validity while state officials (*e.g.*, the attorney general) contend in the same proceeding that it should be found invalid.

Furthermore, it is not clear who the principal in an agency relationship would be. It would make little sense if it were the Governor or attorney general, for that would frustrate the initiative system's purpose of circumventing elected officials who fail or refuse to effect the public will. If there is to be a principal, then, it must be the people of California, as the ultimate sovereign in the State. See [Cal. Const., Art. II, §1] ("All political power is inherent in the people.") But the Restatement may offer no workable example of an agent representing a principal composed of nearly 40 million residents of a State. Cf. 1 Restatement (Second) of Agency, p. 2, Scope Note (1957) (noting that the Restatement "does not state the special rules applicable to public officers").

And if the Court's concern is that the proponents are unaccountable, that fear is neither well founded nor sufficient to overcome the contrary judgment of the State Supreme Court. It must be remembered that both elected officials and initiative proponents receive their authority to speak for the State of California directly from the people. The Court apparently believes that elected officials are acceptable "agents" of the State, but they are no more subject to ongoing supervision of their principal—*i.e.*, the people of the State—than are initiative proponents. At most, a Governor or attorney general can be recalled or voted out of office in a subsequent election, but proponents, too, can have their authority terminated or their initiative overridden by a subsequent ballot measure. Finally, proponents and their attorneys, like all other litigants and counsel who appear before a federal court, are subject to duties of candor, decorum, and respect for the tribunal and co-parties alike, all of which guard against the possibility that initiative proponents will somehow fall short of the appropriate standards for federal litigation.

B

Contrary to the Court's suggestion, this Court's precedents do not indicate that a formal agency relationship is necessary. In *Karcher v. May* (1987), the Speaker of the New Jersey Assembly (Karcher) and President of the New Jersey Senate (Orechio) intervened in support of a school moment-of-silence law that the State's Governor and attorney general declined to defend in court. In considering the question of standing, the Court looked to New Jersey law to determine whether Karcher and Orechio "had authority under state law to represent the State's interest in both the District Court and Court of Appeals." The Court concluded that they did. Because the "New Jersey Supreme Court ha[d] granted applications of the Speaker of the General Assembly and the President of the Senate to intervene as parties-respondent on behalf of the legislature in defense of a legislative enactment," the *Karcher* Court held that standing had been proper in the District Court and Court of Appeals. By the time the case arrived in this

Court, Karcher and Orechio had lost their presiding legislative offices, without which they lacked the authority to represent the State under New Jersey law. This, the Court held, deprived them of standing. Here, by contrast, proponents' authority under California law is not contingent on officeholder status, so their standing is unaffected by the fact that they "hold no office" in California's Government. *Arizonans for Official English v. Arizona* (1997) is consistent with the premises of this dissent, not with the rationale of the Court's opinion. There, the Court noted its serious doubts as to the aspiring defenders' standing because there was "no Arizona law appointing initiative sponsors as agents of the people of Arizona to defend, in lieu of public officials, the constitutionality of initiatives made law of the State." The Court did use the word "agents"; but, read in context, it is evident that the Court's intention was not to demand a formal agency relationship in compliance with the Restatement. Rather, the Court used the term as shorthand for a party whom "state law authorizes" to "represent the State's interests" in court. . . .

III

There is much irony in the Court's approach to justiciability in this case. A prime purpose of justiciability is to ensure vigorous advocacy, yet the Court insists upon litigation conducted by state officials whose preference is to lose the case. The doctrine is meant to ensure that courts are responsible and constrained in their power, but the Court's opinion today means that a single district court can make a decision with far-reaching effects that cannot be reviewed. And rather than honor the principle that justiciability exists to allow disputes of public policy to be resolved by the political process rather than the courts, see, *e.g.*, *Allen v. Wright* (1984), here the Court refuses to allow a State's authorized representatives to defend the outcome of a democratic election. The Court's opinion disrespects and disparages both the political process in California and the well-stated opinion of the California Supreme Court in this case. The California Supreme Court, not this Court, expresses concern for vigorous representation; the California Supreme Court, not this Court, recognizes the necessity to avoid conflicts of interest; the California Supreme Court, not this Court, comprehends the real interest at stake in this litigation and identifies the most proper party to defend that interest. The California Supreme Court's opinion reflects a better understanding of the dynamics and principles of Article III than does this Court's opinion. . . .

* * *

In the end, what the Court fails to grasp or accept is the basic premise of the initiative process. And it is this. The essence of democracy is that the right to make law rests in the people and flows to the government, not the other way around. Freedom resides first in the people without need of a grant from government. The California initiative process embodies these principles and has done so for over a century. . . . In California and the 26 other States that permit initiatives and popular referendums, the people have exercised their own inherent sovereign right to govern themselves. The Court today frustrates that choice by nullifying, for failure to comply with the Restatement of Agency, a State Supreme Court decision holding that state law authorizes an enacted initiative's proponents to defend the law if and when the State's usual legal advocates decline to do so. The Court's opinion fails to abide by precedent and misapplies basic principles of justiciability. Those errors necessitate this respectful dissent.

Chapter 5

The Equal Protection of the Law: Racial Discrimination

ASSIGNMENT S-6

"Reverse" Racial Discrimination

Admission to School

FISHER v. UNIVERSITY OF TEXAS AT AUSTIN
No. 11-345
Argued Oct. 10, 2012 | Decided June 24, 2013

KENNEDY, J., delivered the opinion of the Court, in which ROBERTS, C.J., and SCALIA, THOMAS, BREYER, ALITO, and SOTOMAYOR, JJ., joined. SCALIA, J., and THOMAS, J., filed concurring opinions. GINSBURG, J., filed a dissenting opinion. KAGAN, J., took no part in the consideration or decision of the case.

JUSTICE KENNEDY delivered the opinion of the Court.

The University of Texas at Austin considers race as one of various factors in its undergraduate admissions process. Race is not itself assigned a numerical value for each applicant, but the University has committed itself to increasing racial minority enrollment on campus. It refers to this goal as a "critical mass." Petitioner, who is Caucasian, sued the University after her application was rejected. She contends that the University's use of race in the admissions process violated the Equal Protection Clause of the Fourteenth Amendment.

The parties asked the Court to review whether the judgment below was consistent with "this Court's decisions interpreting the Equal Protection Clause of the Fourteenth Amendment, including Grutter v. Bollinger (2003)." Pet. for Cert. i. The Court concludes that the Court of Appeals did not hold the University to the demanding burden of strict scrutiny articulated in *Grutter* and *Regents of Univ. of Cal. v. Bakke* (1978) (opinion of Powell, J.). Because the Court of Appeals did not apply the correct standard of strict scrutiny, its decision affirming the District Court's grant of summary judgment to the University was incorrect. That decision is vacated, and the case is remanded for further proceedings.

I

A

Located in Austin, Texas, on the most renowned campus of the Texas state university system, the University is one of the leading institutions of higher education in the Nation. Admission is prized and competitive. In 2008, when petitioner sought admission to the University's entering class, she was 1 of 29,501 applicants. From this group 12,843 were admitted, and 6,715 accepted and enrolled. Petitioner was denied admission.

In recent years the University has used three different programs to evaluate candidates for admission. The first is the program it used for some years before 1997, when the University considered two factors: a numerical score reflecting an applicant's test scores and academic performance in high school (Academic Index or AI), and the applicant's race. In 1996, this system was held unconstitutional by the United States Court of Appeals for the Fifth Circuit. It ruled the University's consideration of race violated the Equal Protection Clause because it did not further any compelling government interest. *Hopwood v. Texas* (1996).

The second program was adopted to comply with the *Hopwood* decision. The University stopped considering race in admissions and substituted instead a new holistic metric of a candidate's potential contribution to the University, to be used in conjunction with the Academic Index. This "Personal Achievement Index" (PAI) measures a student's leadership and work experience, awards, extracurricular activities, community service, and other special circumstances that give insight into a student's background. These included growing up in a single-parent home, speaking a language other than English at home, significant family responsibilities assumed by the applicant, and the general socioeconomic condition of the student's family. Seeking to address the decline in minority enrollment after *Hopwood*, the University also expanded its outreach programs.

The Texas State Legislature also responded to the *Hopwood* decision. It enacted a measure known as the Top Ten Percent Law (West 2009). Also referred to as H. B. 588, the Top Ten Percent Law grants automatic admission to any public state college, including the University, to all students in the top 10% of their class at high schools in Texas that comply with certain standards.

The University's revised admissions process, coupled with the operation of the Top Ten Percent Law, resulted in a more racially diverse environment at the University. Before the admissions program at issue in this case, in the last year under the post-*Hopwood* AI/PAI system that did not consider race, the entering class was 4.5% African-American and 16.9% Hispanic. This is in contrast with the 1996 pre-*Hopwood* and Top Ten Percent regime, when race was explicitly considered, and the University's entering freshman class was 4.1% African-American and 14.5% Hispanic.

Following this Court's decisions in *Grutter v. Bollinger* and *Gratz v. Bollinger* (2003), the University adopted a third admissions program, the 2004 program in which the University reverted to explicit consideration of race. This is the program here at issue. In *Grutter*, the Court upheld the use of race as one of many "plus factors" in an admissions program that considered the overall individual contribution of each candidate. In *Gratz*, by contrast, the Court held unconstitutional Michigan's undergraduate admissions program, which automatically awarded points to applicants from certain racial minorities.

The University's plan to resume race-conscious admissions was given formal expression in June 2004 in an internal document entitled *Proposal to Consider Race and Ethnicity in Admissions* (Proposal). The Proposal relied in substantial part on a study of a subset of undergraduate classes containing between 5 and 24 students. It showed that few of these classes had significant enrollment by members of racial minorities. In addition the Proposal relied on what it called "anecdotal" reports from students regarding their "interaction in the classroom." The Proposal concluded that the University lacked a "critical mass" of minority students and that to remedy the deficiency it was necessary to give explicit consideration to race in the undergraduate admissions program.

To implement the Proposal the University included a student's race as a component of the PAI score, beginning with applicants in the fall of 2004. The University asks students to classify themselves from among five predefined racial categories on the application. Race is not assigned an explicit numerical value, but it is undisputed that race is a meaningful factor.

Once applications have been scored, they are plotted on a grid with the Academic Index on the x-axis and the Personal Achievement Index on the y-axis. On that grid students are assigned to so-called cells based on their individual scores. All students in the cells falling above a certain line are admitted. All students below the line are not. Each college—such as Liberal Arts or Engineering—admits students separately. So a student is considered initially for her first-choice college, then for her second choice, and finally for general admission as an undeclared major. . . .

The District Court granted summary judgment to the University. The United States Court of Appeals for the Fifth Circuit affirmed. It held that *Grutter* required courts to give substantial deference to the University, both in the definition of the compelling interest in diversity's benefits and in deciding whether its specific plan was narrowly tailored to achieve its stated goal. Applying that standard, the court upheld the University's admissions plan. . . .

B

Among the Court's cases involving racial classifications in education, there are three decisions that directly address the question of considering racial minority status as a positive or favorable factor in a university's admissions process, with the goal of achieving the educational benefits of a more diverse student body: *Bakke*, *Gratz*, and *Grutter*. We take those cases as given for purposes of deciding this case. We begin with the principal opinion authored by Justice Powell in *Bakke*. In *Bakke*, the Court considered a system used by the medical school of the University of California at Davis. From an entering class of 100 students the school had set aside 16 seats for minority applicants. In holding this program impermissible under the Equal Protection Clause Justice Powell's opinion stated certain basic premises. First, "decisions based on race or ethnic origin by faculties and administrations of state universities are reviewable under the Fourteenth Amendment." The principle of equal protection admits no "artificial line of a 'two-class theory'" that "permits the recognition of special wards entitled to a degree of protection greater than that accorded others." It is therefore irrelevant that a system of racial preferences in admissions may seem benign. Any racial classification must meet strict scrutiny, for when government decisions "touch upon an individual's race or ethnic background, he is entitled to a judicial determination that the burden he is asked to bear on that basis is precisely tailored to serve a compelling governmental interest."

Next, Justice Powell identified one compelling interest that could justify the consideration of race: the interest in the educational benefits that flow from a diverse student body. Redressing past discrimination could not serve as a compelling interest, because a university's "broad mission [of] education" is incompatible with making the "judicial, legislative, or administrative findings of constitutional or statutory violations" necessary to justify remedial racial classification.

The attainment of a diverse student body, by contrast, serves values beyond race alone, including enhanced classroom dialogue and the lessening of racial isolation and stereotypes. . . . Justice Powell's central point, however, was that this interest in securing diversity's benefits, although a permissible objective, is complex. "It is not an interest in simple ethnic diversity, in which a specified percentage of the student body is in effect guaranteed to be members of selected ethnic groups, with the remaining percentage an undifferentiated aggregation of students. The diversity that furthers a compelling state interest encompasses a far broader array of qualifications and characteristics of which racial or ethnic origin is but a single though important element."

In *Gratz* and *Grutter*, the Court endorsed the precepts stated by Justice Powell. In *Grutter*, the Court reaffirmed his conclusion that obtaining the educational benefits of "student body diversity is a compelling state interest that can justify the use of race in university admissions."

As *Gratz* and *Grutter* observed, however, this follows only if a clear precondition is met: The particular admissions process used for this objective is subject to judicial review. Race may not be considered unless the admissions process can withstand strict scrutiny. "Nothing in Justice Powell's opinion in *Bakke* signaled that a university may employ whatever means it desires to achieve the stated goal of diversity without regard to the limits imposed by our strict scrutiny analysis." *Gratz*. "To be narrowly tailored, a race-conscious admissions program cannot use a quota system," *Grutter*, but instead must "remain flexible enough to ensure that each applicant is evaluated as an individual and not in a way that makes an applicant's race or ethnicity the defining feature of his or her application." Strict scrutiny requires the university to demonstrate with clarity that its "purpose or interest is both constitutionally permissible and substantial, and that its use of the classification is necessary . . . to the accomplishment of its purpose." *Bakke* (opinion of Powell, J.).

While these are the cases that most specifically address the central issue in this case, additional guidance may be found in the Court's broader equal protection jurisprudence which applies in this context. "Distinctions between citizens solely because of their ancestry are by their very nature odious to a free people," *Rice v. Cayetano* (2000) (internal quotation marks omitted), and therefore "are contrary to our traditions and hence constitutionally suspect," *Bolling v. Sharpe* (1954). " '[B]ecause racial characteristics so seldom provide a relevant basis for disparate treatment,' " *Richmond v. J. A. Croson Co.* (1989), "the Equal Protection Clause demands that racial classifications . . . be subjected to the 'most rigid scrutiny.' " *Loving v. Virginia* (1967).

To implement these canons, judicial review must begin from the position that "any official action that treats a person differently on account of his race or ethnic origin is inherently suspect." *Fullilove* [*v. Klutznick* (1980)] (Stewart, J., dissenting). Strict scrutiny is a searching examination, and it is the government that bears the burden to prove " 'that the reasons for any [racial] classification [are] clearly identified and unquestionably legitimate,' " *Croson*.

II

Grutter made clear that racial "classifications are constitutional only if they are narrowly tailored to further compelling governmental interests." And *Grutter* endorsed Justice Powell's conclusion in *Bakke* that "the attainment of a diverse student body . . . is a constitutionally permissible goal for an institution of higher education." Thus, under *Grutter*, strict scrutiny must be applied to any admissions program using racial categories or classifications.

According to *Grutter*, a university's "educational judgment that such diversity is essential to its educational mission is one to which we defer." *Grutter* concluded that the decision to pursue "the educational benefits that flow from student body diversity," that the University deems integral to its mission is, in substantial measure, an academic judgment to which some, but not complete, judicial deference is proper under *Grutter*. A court, of course, should ensure that there is a reasoned, principled explanation for the academic decision. On this point, the District Court and Court of Appeals were correct in finding that *Grutter* calls for deference to the University's conclusion, " 'based on its experience and expertise,' " that a diverse student body would serve its educational goals. There is disagreement about whether *Grutter* was consistent with the principles of equal protection in approving this compelling interest in diversity. But the parties here do not ask the Court to revisit that aspect of *Grutter*'s holding.

A university is not permitted to define diversity as "some specified percentage of a particular group merely because of its race or ethnic origin." *Bakke*, "That would amount to outright racial balancing, which is patently unconstitutional." *Grutter*. "Racial balancing is not transformed from 'patently unconstitutional' to a compelling state interest simply by relabeling it 'racial diversity.' " *Parents Involved in Community Schools v. Seattle School Dist. No. 1* (2007).

Once the University has established that its goal of diversity is consistent with strict scrutiny, however, there must still be a further judicial determination that the admissions process meets strict scrutiny in its implementation. The

University must prove that the means chosen by the University to attain diversity are narrowly tailored to that goal. On this point, the University receives no deference. *Grutter* made clear that it is for the courts, not for university administrators, to ensure that "[t]he means chosen to accomplish the [government's] asserted purpose must be specifically and narrowly framed to accomplish that purpose." True, a court can take account of a university's experience and expertise in adopting or rejecting certain admissions processes. But, as the Court said in *Grutter*, it remains at all times the University's obligation to demonstrate, and the Judiciary's obligation to determine, that admissions processes "ensure that each applicant is evaluated as an individual and not in a way that makes an applicant's race or ethnicity the defining feature of his or her application."

Narrow tailoring also requires that the reviewing court verify that it is "necessary" for a university to use race to achieve the educational benefits of diversity. *Bakke*. This involves a careful judicial inquiry into whether a university could achieve sufficient diversity without using racial classifications. Although "[n]arrow tailoring does not require exhaustion of every *conceivable* race-neutral alternative," strict scrutiny does require a court to examine with care, and not defer to, a university's "serious, good faith consideration of workable race-neutral alternatives." See *Grutter* (emphasis added). Consideration by the university is of course necessary, but it is not sufficient to satisfy strict scrutiny: The reviewing court must ultimately be satisfied that no workable race-neutral alternatives would produce the educational benefits of diversity. If " 'a nonracial approach . . . could promote the substantial interest about as well and at tolerable administrative expense,' " *Wygant v. Jackson Bd. of Ed.* (1986) (quoting Greenawalt, Judicial Scrutiny of "Benign" Racial Preference in Law School Admissions, 75 Colum. L. Rev. 559, 578-579 (1975)), then the university may not consider race. A plaintiff, of course, bears the burden of placing the validity of a university's adoption of an affirmative action plan in issue. But strict scrutiny imposes on the university the ultimate burden of demonstrating, before turning to racial classifications, that available, workable race-neutral alternatives do not suffice.

Rather than perform this searching examination, however, the Court of Appeals held petitioner could challenge only "whether [the University's] decision to reintroduce race as a factor in admissions was made in good faith." And in considering such a challenge, the court would "presume the University acted in good faith" and place on petitioner the burden of rebutting that presumption. The Court of Appeals held that to "second-guess the merits" of this aspect of the University's decision was a task it was "ill-equipped to perform" and that it would attempt only to "ensure that [the University's] decision to adopt a race-conscious admissions policy followed from [a process of] good faith consideration." The Court of Appeals thus concluded that "the narrow-tailoring inquiry—like the compelling-interest inquiry—is undertaken with a degree of deference to the Universit[y]." Because "the efforts of the University have been studied, serious, and of high purpose," the Court of Appeals held that the use of race in the admissions program fell within "a constitutionally protected zone of discretion."

These expressions of the controlling standard are at odds with *Grutter*'s command that "all racial classifications imposed by government 'must be analyzed by a reviewing court under strict scrutiny.' " (quoting *Adarand Constructors, Inc. v. Peña* (1995)). In *Grutter*, the Court approved the plan at issue upon concluding that it was not a quota, was sufficiently flexible, was limited in time, and followed "serious, good faith consideration of workable race-neutral alternatives." As noted above, the parties do not challenge, and the Court therefore does not consider, the correctness of that determination.

Grutter did not hold that good faith would forgive an impermissible consideration of race. It must be remembered that "the mere recitation of a 'benign' or legitimate purpose for a racial classification is entitled to little or no weight." *Croson*. Strict scrutiny does not permit a court to accept a school's assertion that its admissions process uses race in a permissible way without a court giving close analysis to the evidence of how the process works in practice.

The higher education dynamic does not change the narrow tailoring analysis of strict scrutiny applicable in other contexts. . . . The District Court and Court of Appeals confined the strict scrutiny inquiry in too narrow a way by deferring to the University's good faith in its use of racial classifications and affirming the grant of summary judgment on that basis. The Court vacates that judgment, but fairness to the litigants and the courts that heard the case requires that it be remanded so that the admissions process can be considered and judged under a correct analysis. Unlike *Grutter*, which was decided after trial, this case arises from cross-motions for summary judgment. In this case, as in similar cases, in determining whether summary judgment in favor of the University would be appropriate, the Court of Appeals must assess whether the University has offered sufficient evidence that would prove that its admissions program is narrowly tailored to obtain the educational benefits of diversity. Whether this record—and not "simple . . . assurances of good intention," *Croson*—is sufficient is a question for the Court of Appeals in the first instance.

* * *

Strict scrutiny must not be " 'strict in theory, but fatal in fact,' " *Adarand*. But the opposite is also true. Strict scrutiny must not be strict in theory but feeble in fact. In order for judicial review to be meaningful, a university must make a showing that its plan is narrowly tailored to achieve the only interest that this Court has approved in this context: the benefits of a student body diversity that "encompasses a . . . broa[d] array of qualifications and characteristics of which racial or ethnic origin is but a single though important element." *Bakke*. The judgment of the Court of Appeals is vacated, and the case is remanded for further proceedings consistent with this opinion.

It is so ordered.

JUSTICE KAGAN took no part in the consideration or decision of this case.

JUSTICE SCALIA, concurring.

I adhere to the view I expressed in *Grutter v. Bollinger*: "The Constitution proscribes government discrimination on the basis of race, and state-provided education is no exception." (opinion concurring in part and dissenting in part). The petitioner in this case did not ask us to overrule *Grutter*'s holding that a "compelling interest" in the educational benefits of diversity can justify racial preferences in university admissions. I therefore join the Court's opinion in full.

JUSTICE THOMAS, concurring.

I join the Court's opinion because I agree that the Court of Appeals did not apply strict scrutiny to the University of Texas at Austin's (University) use of racial discrimination in admissions decisions. I write separately to explain that I would overrule *Grutter v. Bollinger* (2003), and hold that a State's use of race in higher education admissions decisions is categorically prohibited by the Equal Protection Clause. . . .

I

A

The Fourteenth Amendment provides that no State shall "deny to any person . . . the equal protection of the laws." The Equal Protection Clause guarantees every person the right to be treated equally by the State, without regard to race. "At the heart of this [guarantee] lies the principle that the government must treat citizens as individuals, and not as members of racial, ethnic, or religious groups." *Missouri v. Jenkins* (1995) (Thomas, J., concurring). "It is for this reason that we must subject all racial classifications to the strictest of scrutiny." *Id.*, at 121.

Under strict scrutiny, all racial classifications are categorically prohibited unless they are " 'necessary to further a compelling governmental interest' " and "narrowly tailored to that end." *Johnson v. California* (2005) (quoting *Grutter*). This most exacting standard "has proven automatically fatal" in almost every case. *Jenkins* (Thomas, J., concurring). And rightly so. "Purchased at the price of immeasurable human suffering, the equal protection principle reflects our Nation's understanding that [racial] classifications ultimately have a destructive impact on the individual and our society." *Adarand Constructors, Inc. v. Peña* (1995) (Thomas, J., concurring in part and concurring in judgment). "The Constitution abhors classifications based on race" because "every time the government places citizens on racial registers and makes race relevant to the provision of burdens or benefits, it demeans us all." *Grutter* (Thomas, J., concurring in part and dissenting in part). . . .

B

2

Grutter was a radical departure from our strict-scrutiny precedents. In *Grutter*, the University of Michigan Law School (Law School) claimed that it had a compelling reason to discriminate based on race. The reason it advanced did not concern protecting national security or remedying its own past discrimination. Instead, the Law School argued that it needed to discriminate in admissions decisions in order to obtain the "educational benefits that flow from a diverse student body." Contrary to the very meaning of strict scrutiny, the Court deferred to the Law School's determination that this interest was sufficiently compelling to justify racial discrimination. I dissented from that part of the Court's decision. I explained that "only those measures the State must take to provide a bulwark against anarchy, or to prevent violence, will constitute a 'pressing public necessity'" sufficient to satisfy strict scrutiny. I adhere to that view today. As should be obvious, there is nothing "pressing" or "necessary" about obtaining whatever educational benefits may flow from racial diversity. . . .

III

While I find the theory advanced by the University to justify racial discrimination facially inadequate, I also believe that its use of race has little to do with the alleged educational benefits of diversity. I suspect that the University's program is instead based on the benighted notion that it is possible to tell when discrimination helps, rather than hurts, racial minorities. See post, at 3 (Ginsburg, J., dissenting) ("[G]overnment actors, including state universities, need not be blind to the lingering effects of 'an overtly discriminatory past,' the legacy of 'centuries of law-sanctioned inequality'"). But "[h]istory should teach greater humility." *Metro Broadcasting, Inc. v. FCC* (1990) (O'Connor, J., dissenting). The worst forms of racial discrimination in this Nation have always been accompanied by straight-faced representations that discrimination helped minorities.

A

Slaveholders argued that slavery was a "positive good" that civilized blacks and elevated them in every dimension of life. See, e.g., Calhoun, Speech in the U.S. Senate, 1837, in P. Finkelman, *Defending Slavery* (2003) ("Never before has the black race of Central Africa, from the dawn of history to the present day, attained a condition so civilized and so improved, not only physically, but morally and intellectually. . . . [T]he relation now existing in the slaveholding States between the two [races], is, instead of an evil, a good—a positive good"); Harper, Memoir on Slavery, in The Ideology of Slavery (D. Faust ed. 1981) ("Slavery, as it is said in an eloquent article published in a Southern periodical work . . . 'has done more to elevate a degraded race in the scale of humanity; to tame the savage; to civilize the barbarous; to soften the ferocious; to enlighten the ignorant, and to spread the blessings of [C]hristianity among the heathen, than all the missionaries that philanthropy and religion have ever sent forth'"); Hammond, The Mudsill Speech, 1858, in Defending Slavery ("They are elevated from the condition in which God first created them, by being made our slaves").

A century later, segregationists similarly asserted that segregation was not only benign, but good for black students. They argued, for example, that separate schools protected black children from racist white students and teachers. See, e.g., Brief for Appellees in *Briggs* ("'I have repeatedly seen wise and loving colored parents take infinite pains to force their little children into schools where the white children, white teachers, and white parents despised and resented the dark child, made mock of it, neglected or bullied it, and literally rendered its life a living hell. Such parents want their child to "fight" this thing out,—but, dear God, at what a cost! . . . We shall get a finer, better balance of spirit; an infinitely more capable and rounded personality by putting children in schools where they are wanted, and where they are happy and inspired, than in thrusting them into hells where they are ridiculed and hated'" (quoting DuBois, Does the Negro Need Separate Schools? 4 J. of Negro Educ. 328 (1935))); Tr. of Oral Arg. in *Bolling v. Sharpe*, 1952 ("There was behind these [a]cts a kindly feeling [and] an intention to help these people who had been in bondage. And there was and there still is an intention by the Congress to see that these children shall be educated in a healthful atmosphere, in a wholesome atmosphere, in a place where they are wanted, in a place where they will not be looked upon with hostility, in a place where there will be a receptive atmosphere for learning for both races without the hostility that undoubtedly Congress thought might creep into these situations"). And they even appealed to the fact that many blacks agreed that separate schools were in the "best interests" of both races. See, e.g., Brief for Appellees in *Davis* ("'It has been my experience, in working with the people of Virginia, including both white and Negro, that the customs and the habits and the traditions of Virginia citizens are such that they believe for the best interests of both the white and the Negro that the separate school is best'").

Following in these inauspicious footsteps, the University would have us believe that its discrimination is likewise benign. I think the lesson of history is clear enough: Racial discrimination is never benign. "'[B]enign' carries with it no independent meaning, but reflects only acceptance of the current generation's conclusion that a politically acceptable burden, imposed on particular citizens on the basis of race, is reasonable." See *Metro Broadcasting* (O'Connor, J., dissenting). It is for this reason that the Court has repeatedly held that strict scrutiny applies to all racial classifications, regardless of whether the government has benevolent motives. The University's professed good intentions cannot excuse its outright racial discrimination any more than such intentions justified the now denounced arguments of slaveholders and segregationists.

B

While it does not, for constitutional purposes, matter whether the University's racial discrimination is benign, I note that racial engineering does in fact have insidious consequences. There can be no doubt that the University's discrimination injures white and Asian applicants who are denied admission because of their race. But I believe the injury to those admitted under the University's discriminatory admissions program is even more harmful. Blacks and Hispanics admitted to the University as a result of racial discrimination are, on average, far less prepared than their white and Asian classmates. In the University's entering class of 2009, for example, among the students admitted outside the Top Ten

Percent plan, blacks scored at the 52d percentile of 2009 SAT takers nationwide, while Asians scored at the 93d percentile. Brief for Richard Sander et al. as Amici Curiae 3-4, and n. 4. Blacks had a mean GPA of 2.57 and a mean SAT score of 1524; Hispanics had a mean GPA of 2.83 and a mean SAT score of 1794; whites had a mean GPA of 3.04 and a mean SAT score of 1914; and Asians had a mean GPA of 3.07 and a mean SAT score of 1991.[1]

Tellingly, neither the University nor any of the 73 amici briefs in support of racial discrimination has presented a shred of evidence that black and Hispanic students are able to close this substantial gap during their time at the University. There is no reason to believe this is not the case at the University. The University and its dozens of amici are deafeningly silent on this point.

Furthermore, the University's discrimination does nothing to increase the number of blacks and Hispanics who have access to a college education generally. Instead, the University's discrimination has a pervasive shifting effect. See T. Sowell, Affirmative Action Around the World 145-146 (2004). The University admits minorities who otherwise would have attended less selective colleges where they would have been more evenly matched. But, as a result of the mismatching, many blacks and Hispanics who likely would have excelled at less elite schools are placed in a position where underperformance is all but inevitable because they are less academically prepared than the white and Asian students with whom they must compete. Setting aside the damage wreaked upon the self confidence of these overmatched students, there is no evidence that they learn more at the University than they would have learned at other schools for which they were better prepared. Indeed, they may learn less. . . .

Moreover, the University's discrimination "stamp[s] [blacks and Hispanics] with a badge of inferiority." *Adarand* (opinion of Thomas, J.). It taints the accomplishments of all those who are admitted as a result of racial discrimination. Cf. J. McWhorter, Losing the Race: Self-Sabotage in Black America 248 (2000) ("I was never able to be as proud of getting into Stanford as my classmates could be. . . . [H]ow much of an achievement can I truly say it was to have been a good enough black person to be admitted, while my colleagues had been considered good enough people to be admitted"). And, it taints the accomplishments of all those who are the same race as those admitted as a result of racial discrimination. In this case, for example, most blacks and Hispanics attending the University were admitted without discrimination under the Top Ten Percent plan, but no one can distinguish those students from the ones whose race played a role in their admission. "When blacks [and Hispanics] take positions in the highest places of government, industry, or academia, it is an open question . . . whether their skin color played a part in their advancement." See *Grutter* (opinion of Thomas, J.). "The question itself is the stigma—because either racial discrimination did play a role, in which case the person may be deemed 'otherwise unqualified,' or it did not, in which case asking the question itself unfairly marks those . . . who would

1. The lowest possible score on the SAT is 600, and the highest possible score is 2400.

succeed without discrimination." Ibid. Although cloaked in good intentions, the University's racial tinkering harms the very people it claims to be helping.

* * *

For the foregoing reasons, I would overrule *Grutter*. However, because the Court correctly concludes that the Court of Appeals did not apply strict scrutiny, I join its opinion.

JUSTICE GINSBURG, dissenting.

The University of Texas at Austin (University) is candid about what it is endeavoring to do: It seeks to achieve student-body diversity through an admissions policy patterned after the Harvard plan referenced as exemplary in Justice Powell's opinion in *Regents of Univ. of Cal. v. Bakke* (1978). The University has steered clear of a quota system like the one struck down in *Bakke*, which excluded all nonminority candidates from competition for a fixed number of seats. And, like so many educational institutions across the Nation, the University has taken care to follow the model approved by the Court in *Grutter v. Bollinger* (2003).

Texas' percentage plan was adopted with racially segregated neighborhoods and schools front and center stage. It is race consciousness, not blindness to race, that drives such plans. As for holistic review, if universities cannot explicitly include race as a factor, many may "resort to camouflage" to "maintain their minority enrollment." *Gratz* (Ginsburg, J., dissenting). I have several times explained why government actors, including state universities, need not be blind to the lingering effects of "an overtly discriminatory past," the legacy of "centuries of law-sanctioned inequality." *Id.* (dissenting opinion). Among constitutionally permissible options, I remain convinced, "those that candidly disclose their consideration of race [are] preferable to those that conceal it." *Gratz* (dissenting opinion).

Accordingly, I would not return this case for a second look. As the thorough opinions below show, the University's admissions policy flexibly considers race only as a "factor of a factor of a factor of a factor" in the calculus; followed a year long review through which the University reached the reasonable, good-faith judgment that supposedly race-neutral initiatives were insufficient to achieve, in appropriate measure, the educational benefits of student body diversity; and is subject to periodic review to ensure that the consideration of race remains necessary and proper to achieve the University's educational objectives. Justice Powell's opinion in *Bakke* and the Court's decision in *Grutter* require no further determinations.

The Court rightly declines to cast off the equal protection framework settled in *Grutter*. Yet it stops short of reaching the conclusion that framework warrants. Instead, the Court vacates the Court of Appeals' judgment and remands for the Court of Appeals to "assess whether the University has offered sufficient evidence [to] prove that its admissions program is narrowly tailored to obtain the educational benefits of diversity." *Ante*. As I see it, the Court of Appeals has already completed that inquiry, and its judgment, trained on this Court's *Bakke* and *Grutter* pathmarkers, merits our approbation.

For the reasons stated, I would affirm the judgment of the Court of Appeals.

ASSIGNMENT S-7

Can Race-Based "Affirmative Action" Be Barred by the Electorate?

Study Guide:

- The next case concerned not whether race-based "affirmative action" remedies are permissible, but instead whether it constitutes a violation of the Equal Protection Clause for the voters of Michigan to prohibit their use.
- Even the dissent, however, did not contend that such a policy was mandated by the Equal Protection Clause. Instead, the issue was whether barring government officials from using this practice by state referendum violated the so-called political process doctrine.

SCHUETTE v. COALITION TO DEFEND AFFIRMATIVE ACTION, INTEGRATION AND IMMIGRANT RIGHTS AND FIGHT FOR EQUALITY BY ANY MEANS NECESSARY (BAMN)

No. 12-682

Argued Oct. 15, 2013 | Decided Apr. 22, 2014

Justice Kennedy announced the judgment of the Court and delivered an opinion, in which The Chief Justice and Justice Alito join.

The Court in this case must determine whether an amendment to the Constitution of the State of Michigan, approved and enacted by its voters, is invalid under the Equal Protection Clause of the Fourteenth Amendment to the Constitution of the United States.

In 2003 the Court reviewed the constitutionality of two admissions systems at the University of Michigan, one for its undergraduate class and one for its law school. The undergraduate admissions plan was addressed in *Gratz v. Bollinger* (2003). The law school admission plan was addressed in *Grutter v. Bollinger* (2003). Each admissions process permitted the explicit consideration of an applicant's race. In *Gratz,* the Court invalidated the undergraduate plan as a violation of the Equal Protection Clause. In *Grutter,* the Court found no constitutional flaw in the law school admission plan's more limited use of race-based preferences.

In response to the Court's decision in *Gratz,* the university revised its undergraduate admissions process, but the revision still allowed limited use of race-based preferences. After a statewide debate on the question of racial preferences in the context of governmental decisionmaking, the voters, in 2006, adopted an amendment to the State Constitution prohibiting state and other governmental entities in Michigan from granting certain preferences, including race-based preferences, in a wide range of actions and decisions. Under the terms of the amendment, race-based preferences cannot be part of the admissions process for state universities. That particular prohibition is central to the instant case.

The ballot proposal was called Proposal 2 and, after it passed by a margin of 58 percent to 42 percent, the resulting enactment became Article I, §26, of the Michigan Constitution. . . .

> "(1) The University of Michigan, Michigan State University, Wayne State University, and any other public college or university, community college, or school district shall not discriminate against, or grant preferential treatment to, any individual or group on the basis of race, sex, color, ethnicity, or national origin in the operation of public employment, public education, or public contracting.
>
> "(2) The state shall not discriminate against, or grant preferential treatment to, any individual or group on the basis of race, sex, color, ethnicity, or national origin in the operation of public employment, public education, or public contracting.
>
> "(3) For the purposes of this section 'state' includes, but is not necessarily limited to, the state itself, any city, county, any public college, university, or community college, school district, or other political subdivision or governmental instrumentality of or within the State of Michigan not included in sub-section 1." . . .

A panel of the United States Court of Appeals for the Sixth Circuit . . . held that Proposal 2 had violated the principles elaborated by this Court in *Washington v. Seattle School Dist. No. 1* (1982) [and *Hunter v. Erickson* (1969)]. In *Hunter*, the Court for the first time elaborated what the Court of Appeals here styled the "political process" doctrine. There, the Akron City Council found that the citizens of Akron consisted of "people of different race[s], . . . many of whom live in circumscribed and segregated areas, under sub-standard unhealthful, unsafe, unsanitary and overcrowded conditions, because of discrimination in the sale, lease, rental and financing of housing." To address the problem, Akron enacted a fair housing ordinance to prohibit that sort of discrimination. In response, voters amended the city charter to overturn the ordinance and to require that any additional antidiscrimination housing ordinance be approved by referendum. But most other ordinances "regulating the real property market" were not subject to those threshold requirements. . . . *Hunter* rests on the unremarkable principle that the State may not alter the procedures of government to target racial minorities. The facts in *Hunter* established that invidious discrimination would be the necessary result of the procedural restructuring. Thus, in . . . *Hunter*, there was a demonstrated injury on the basis of race that, by reasons of state encouragement or participation, became more aggravated.

[In *Seattle*,] the school board adopted a mandatory busing program to alleviate racial isolation of minority students in local schools. Voters who opposed the school board's busing plan passed a state initiative that barred busing to desegregate. . . . *Seattle* is best understood as a case in which the state action in question (the bar on busing enacted by the State's voters) had the serious risk, if not purpose, of causing specific injuries on account of race. . . . *Seattle* involved a state initiative that "was carefully tailored to interfere only with desegregative busing." The *Seattle* Court . . . found that the State's disapproval of the school board's busing remedy was an aggravation of the very racial injury in which the State itself was complicit.

The broad language used in *Seattle,* however, went well beyond the analysis needed to resolve the case. . . . *Seattle* stated that where a government policy "inures primarily to the benefit of the minority" and "minorities . . . consider" the policy to be "in their interest," then any state action that "place[s] effective decisionmaking authority over" that policy "at a different level of government" must be reviewed under strict scrutiny. In essence, according to the broad reading of *Seattle*, any state action with a "racial focus" that makes it "more difficult for certain racial minorities than for other groups" to "achieve legislation that is in their interest" is subject to strict scrutiny. It is this reading of *Seattle* that the Court of Appeals found to be controlling here. And that reading must be rejected. . . . The expansive reading of *Seattle* has no principled limitation and raises serious questions of compatibility with the Court's settled equal protection jurisprudence. To the extent *Seattle* is read to require the Court to determine and declare which political policies serve the "interest" of a group defined in racial terms, that rationale was unnecessary to the decision in *Seattle*; it has no support in precedent; and it raises serious constitutional concerns. That expansive language does not provide a proper guide for decisions and should not be deemed authoritative or controlling. . . . There would be no apparent limiting standards defining what public policies should be included in what *Seattle* called policies that "inur[e] primarily to the benefit of the minority" and that "minorities . . . consider" to be "in their interest." Those who seek to represent the interests of particular racial groups could attempt to advance those aims by demanding an equal protection ruling that any number of matters be foreclosed from voter review or participation. In a nation in which governmental policies are wide ranging, those who seek to limit voter participation might be tempted, were this Court to adopt the *Seattle* formulation, to urge that a group they choose to define by race or racial stereotypes are advantaged or disadvantaged by any number of laws or decisions. Tax policy, housing subsidies, wage regulations, and even the naming of public schools, highways, and monuments are just a few examples of what could become a list of subjects that some organizations could insist should be beyond the power of voters to decide, or beyond the power of a legislature to decide when enacting limits on the power of local authorities or other governmental entities to address certain subjects. Racial division would be validated, not discouraged, were the *Seattle* formulation, and the reasoning of the Court of Appeals in this case, to remain in force. . . .

Perhaps, when enacting policies as an exercise of democratic self-government, voters will determine that race-based preferences should be adopted. The constitutional validity of some of those choices regarding racial preferences is not at issue here. The holding in the instant case is simply that the courts may not disempower the voters from choosing which path to follow. In the realm of policy discussions the regular give-and-take of debate ought to be a context in which rancor or discord based on race are avoided, not invited. And if these factors are to be interjected, surely it ought not to be at the invitation or insistence of the courts. . . .

By approving Proposal 2 and thereby adding §26 to their State Constitution, the Michigan voters exercised their privilege to enact laws as a basic exercise of their democratic power. In the federal system States "respond, through the enactment of positive law, to the initiative of those who seek a voice in shaping the destiny of their own times." [*Bond v. United States* (2011).] Michigan voters used the initiative system to bypass public officials who were deemed not responsive to the concerns of a majority of the voters with respect to a policy of granting race-based preferences that raises difficult and delicate issues.

The freedom secured by the Constitution consists, in one of its essential dimensions, of the right of the individual not to be injured by the unlawful exercise of governmental power. The mandate for segregated schools, *Brown v. Board of Education* (1954); a wrongful invasion of the home, *Silverman v. United States* (1961); or punishing a protester whose views offend others, *Texas v. Johnson* (1989); and scores of other examples teach that individual liberty has constitutional protection, and that liberty's full extent and meaning may remain yet to be discovered and affirmed. Yet freedom does not stop with individual rights. Our constitutional system embraces, too, the right of citizens to debate so they can learn and decide and then, through the political process, act in concert to try to shape the course of their own times and the course of a nation that must strive always to make freedom ever greater and more secure. Here Michigan voters acted in concert and statewide to seek consensus and adopt a policy on a difficult subject against a historical background of race in America that has been a source of tragedy and persisting injustice. That history demands that we continue to learn, to listen, and to remain open to new approaches if we are to aspire always to a constitutional order in which all persons are treated with fairness and equal dignity. Were the Court to rule that the question addressed by Michigan voters is too sensitive or complex to be within the grasp of the electorate; or that the policies at issue remain too delicate to be resolved save by university officials or faculties, acting at some remove from immediate public scrutiny and control; or that these matters are so arcane that the electorate's power must be limited because the people cannot prudently exercise that power even after a full debate, that holding would be an unprecedented restriction on the exercise of a fundamental right held not just by one person but by all in common. It is the right to speak and debate and learn and then, as a matter of political will, to act through a lawful electoral process.

The respondents in this case insist that a difficult question of public policy must be taken from the reach of the voters, and thus removed from the realm of public discussion, dialogue, and debate in an election campaign. Quite in addition to the serious First Amendment implications of that position with respect to any particular election, it is inconsistent with the underlying premises of a responsible, functioning democracy. One of those premises is that a democracy has the capacity—and the duty—to learn from its past mistakes; to discover and confront persisting biases; and by respectful, rationale deliberation to rise above those flaws and injustices. That process is impeded, not advanced, by court decrees based on the proposition that the public cannot have the requisite repose to discuss certain issues. It is demeaning to the democratic process to presume that the voters are not capable of deciding an issue of this sensitivity on decent and rational grounds. The process of public discourse and political debate should not be foreclosed even if there is a risk that during a public campaign there will be those, on both sides, who seek to use racial division and discord to their own political advantage. An informed public can, and must, rise above this. The idea of democracy is that it can, and must, mature. Freedom embraces the right, indeed the duty, to engage in a rational, civic discourse in order to determine how best to form a consensus to shape the destiny of the Nation and its people. These First Amendment dynamics would be disserved if this Court were to say that the question here at issue is beyond the capacity of the voters to debate and then to determine. . . .

Mulkey, Hunter, and *Seattle* are not precedents that stand for the conclusion that Michigan's voters must be disempowered from acting. Those cases were ones in which the political restriction in question was designed to be used, or was likely to be used, to encourage infliction of injury by reason of race. What is at stake here is not whether injury will be inflicted but whether government can be instructed not to follow a course that entails, first, the definition of racial categories and, second, the grant of favored status to persons in some racial categories and not others. The electorate's instruction to governmental entities not to embark upon the course of race-defined and race-based preferences was adopted, we must assume, because the voters deemed a preference system to be unwise, on account of what voters may deem its latent potential to become itself a source of the very resentments and hostilities based on race that this Nation seeks to put behind it. Whether those adverse results would follow is, and should be, the subject of debate. Voters might likewise consider, after debate and reflection, that programs designed to increase diversity—consistent with the Constitution—are a necessary part of progress to transcend the stigma of past racism.

This case is not about how the debate about racial preferences should be resolved. It is about who may resolve it. There is no authority in the Constitution of the United States or in this Court's precedents for the Judiciary to set aside Michigan laws that commit this policy determination to the voters. Deliberative debate on sensitive issues such as racial preferences all too often may shade into rancor. But that does not justify removing certain court-determined issues from the voters' reach. Democracy does not presume that some subjects are either too divisive or too profound for public debate.

The judgment of the Court of Appeals for the Sixth Circuit is reversed.

It is so ordered.

JUSTICE KAGAN took no part in the consideration or decision of this case.

CHIEF JUSTICE ROBERTS, concurring.

The dissent devotes 11 pages to expounding its own policy preferences in favor of taking race into account in college admissions, while nonetheless concluding that it "do[es] not mean to suggest that the virtues of adopting race-sensitive admissions policies should inform the legal question before the Court." *Post* (opinion of Sotomayor, J.). The dissent concedes that the governing boards of the State's various universities could have implemented a policy making it illegal to "discriminate against, or grant preferential treatment to," any individual on the basis of race. On the dissent's view, if the governing boards conclude that drawing racial distinctions in university admissions is undesirable or counterproductive, they are permissibly exercising their policymaking authority. But others who might reach the same conclusion are failing to take race seriously.

The dissent states that "[t]he way to stop discrimination on the basis of race is to speak openly and candidly on the subject of race." And it urges that "[r]ace matters because of the slights, the snickers, the silent judgments that reinforce that most crippling of thoughts: 'I do not belong here.'" But it is not "out of touch with reality" to conclude that racial preferences may themselves have the debilitating effect of reinforcing precisely that doubt, and—if so—that the preferences do more harm than good. To disagree with the dissent's views on the costs and benefits of racial preferences is not to "wish away, rather than confront" racial inequality. People can disagree in good faith on this issue, but it similarly does more harm than good to question the openness and candor of those on either side of the debate.

JUSTICE SCALIA, with whom JUSTICE THOMAS joins, concurring in the judgment.

It has come to this. Called upon to explore the jurisprudential twilight zone between two errant lines of precedent, we confront a frighteningly bizarre question: Does the Equal Protection Clause of the Fourteenth Amendment *forbid* what its text plainly *requires*? Needless to say (except that this case obliges us to say it), the question answers itself. "The Constitution proscribes government discrimination on the basis of race, and state-provided education is no exception." *Grutter v. Bollinger* (2003) (Scalia, J., concurring in part and dissenting in part). It is precisely this understanding—the correct understanding—of the federal Equal Protection Clause that the people of the State of Michigan have adopted for their own fundamental law. By adopting it, they did not simultaneously *offend* it. . . .

But the battleground for this case is not the constitutionality of race-based admissions—at least, not quite. Rather, it is the so-called political-process doctrine, derived from this Court's opinions in *Washington v. Seattle School Dist. No. 1* (1982), and *Hunter v. Erickson* (1969). I agree with those parts of the plurality opinion that repudiate this doctrine. But I do not agree with its reinterpretation of *Seattle* and *Hunter*, which makes them stand in part for the cloudy and doctrinally anomalous proposition that whenever state action poses "the serious risk . . . of causing specific injuries on account of race," it denies equal protection. I would instead reaffirm that the "ordinary principles of our law [and] of our democratic heritage" require "plaintiffs alleging equal protection violations" stemming from facially neutral acts to "prove intent and causation and not merely the existence of racial disparity." *Freeman v. Pitts* (1992) (Scalia, J., concurring) (citing *Washington v. Davis* (1976)). I would further hold that a law directing state actors to provide equal protection is (to say the least) facially neutral, and cannot violate the Constitution. Section 26 of the Michigan Constitution (formerly Proposal 2) rightly stands. . . .

Generally, "a State is afforded wide leeway when experimenting with the appropriate allocation of state legislative power" and may create "political subdivisions such as cities and counties . . . 'as convenient agencies for exercising such of the governmental powers of the state as may be entrusted to them.'" *Holt Civic Club v. Tuscaloosa* (1978). Accordingly, States have "absolute discretion" to determine the "number, nature and duration of the powers conferred upon [municipal] corporations and the territory over which they shall be exercised." *Holt.* So it would seem to go without saying that a State may give certain powers to cities, later assign the same powers to counties, and even reclaim them for itself. . . .

I part ways with *Hunter, Seattle,* and (I think) the plurality for an additional reason: Each endorses a version of the proposition that a facially neutral law may deny equal protection solely because it has a disparate racial impact. Few equal-protection theories have been so squarely and soundly rejected. . . . Notwithstanding our dozens of cases confirming the exceptionless nature of the *Washington v. Davis* rule, the plurality opinion leaves ajar an effects-test escape hatch modeled after *Hunter* and *Seattle*, suggesting that state action denies equal protection when it "ha[s] the *serious risk,* if not purpose, of causing specific injuries on account of race," or is either "designed to be used, or . . . *likely to be used*, to encourage infliction of injury by reason of race." *Ante* (emphasis added). Since these formulations enable a determination of an equal-protection violation where there is no discriminatory intent, they are inconsistent with the long *Washington v. Davis* line of cases. . . .

Thus, the question in this case, as in every case in which neutral state action is said to deny equal protection on account of race, is whether the action reflects a racially discriminatory purpose. *Seattle* stresses that "singling out the political processes affecting racial issues for uniquely disadvantageous treatment inevitably raises dangers of impermissible motivation." True enough, but that motivation must be proved. And respondents do not have a prayer of proving it here. . . . In my view, any law expressly requiring state actors to afford all persons equal protection of the laws . . . does not—*cannot*—deny "to any person . . . equal protection of the laws," U.S. Const., Amdt. 14, §1, regardless of whatever evidence of seemingly foul purposes plaintiffs may cook up in the trial court.

* * *

As Justice Harlan observed over a century ago, "[o]ur Constitution is color-blind, and neither knows nor tolerates classes among citizens." *Plessy v. Ferguson* (1896) (dissenting opinion). The people of Michigan wish the same for their governing charter. It would be shameful for us to stand in their way.

JUSTICE BREYER, concurring in the judgment. . . .

I continue to believe that the Constitution permits, though it does not require, the use of the kind of race-conscious programs that are now barred by the Michigan Constitution. The serious educational problems that faced Americans at the time this Court decided *Grutter* endure. And low educational achievement continues to be correlated with income and race.

The Constitution allows local, state, and national communities to adopt narrowly tailored race-conscious programs designed to bring about greater inclusion and diversity. But the Constitution foresees the ballot box, not the courts, as the normal instrument for resolving differences and debates about the merits of these programs. . . .

Hunter and *Seattle* involved efforts to manipulate the political process in a way not here at issue. Both cases involved a restructuring of the political process that changed the political level at which policies were enacted. In *Hunter*, decisionmaking was moved from the elected city council to the local electorate at large. And in *Seattle*, decisionmaking by an elected school board was replaced with decisionmaking by the state legislature and electorate at large.

This case, in contrast, does not involve a reordering of the *political* process; it does not in fact involve the movement of decisionmaking from one political level to another. Rather, here, Michigan law delegated broad policymaking authority to elected university boards, see Mich. Const., Art. VIII, §5, but those boards delegated admissions-related decisionmaking authority to unelected university faculty members and administrators. . . . Thus, unelected faculty members and administrators, not voters or their elected representatives, adopted the race-conscious admissions programs affected by Michigan's constitutional amendment. The amendment took decisionmaking authority away from these unelected actors and placed it in the hands of the voters. . . .

[T]o extend the holding of *Hunter* and *Seattle* to reach situations in which decisionmaking authority is moved from an administrative body to a political one would pose significant difficulties. The administrative process encompasses vast numbers of decisionmakers answering numerous policy questions in hosts of different fields. Administrative bodies modify programs in detail, and decisionmaking authority within the administrative process frequently moves around—due to amendments to statutes, new administrative rules, and evolving agency practice. It is thus particularly difficult in this context for judges to determine when a change in the locus of decisionmaking authority places a comparative structural burden on a racial minority. And to apply *Hunter* and *Seattle* to the administrative process would, by tending to hinder change, risk discouraging experimentation, interfering with efforts to see when and how race-conscious policies work.

Finally, the principle that underlies *Hunter* and *Seattle* runs up against a competing principle. . . . This competing principle favors decisionmaking though the democratic process. Just as this principle strongly supports the right of the people, or their elected representatives, to adopt race-conscious policies for reasons of inclusion, so must it give them the right to vote not to do so. . . .

Therefore, I concur in the judgment of the Court.

JUSTICE SOTOMAYOR, with whom JUSTICE GINSBURG joins, dissenting.

We are fortunate to live in a democratic society. But without checks, democratically approved legislation can oppress minority groups. For that reason, our Constitution places limits on what a majority of the people may do. This case implicates one such limit: the guarantee of equal protection of the laws. Although that guarantee is traditionally understood to prohibit intentional discrimination under existing laws, equal protection does not end there. Another fundamental strand of our equal protection jurisprudence focuses on process, securing to all citizens the right to participate meaningfully and equally in self-government. That right is the bedrock of our democracy, for it preserves all other rights. . . .

A majority of the Michigan electorate changed the basic rules of the political process in that State in a manner that uniquely disadvantaged racial minorities. Prior to the enactment of the constitutional initiative at issue here, all of the admissions policies of Michigan's public colleges and universities—including race-sensitive admissions policies—were in the hands of each institution's governing board. The members of those boards are nominated by political parties and elected by the citizenry in statewide elections. After over a century of being shut out of Michigan's institutions of higher education, racial minorities in Michigan had succeeded in persuading the elected board representatives to adopt admissions policies that took into account the benefits of racial diversity. And this Court twice blessed such efforts—first in *Regents of Univ. of Cal.* and again in *Grutter,* a case that itself concerned a Michigan admissions policy.

In the wake of *Grutter,* some voters in Michigan set out to eliminate the use of race-sensitive admissions policies. Those voters were of course free to pursue this end in any number of ways. For example, they could have persuaded existing board members to change their minds through individual or grassroots lobbying efforts, or through general public awareness campaigns. Or they could have mobilized efforts to vote uncooperative board members out of office, replacing them with members who would share their desire to abolish race-sensitive admissions policies. When this Court holds that the Constitution permits a particular policy, nothing prevents a majority of a State's voters from choosing not to adopt that policy. Our system of government encourages—and indeed, depends on—that type of democratic action.

But instead, the majority of Michigan voters changed the rules in the middle of the game, reconfiguring the existing political process in Michigan in a manner that burdened racial minorities. They did so in the 2006 election by amending the Michigan Constitution to enact Art. I, §26, which provides in relevant part that Michigan's public universities "shall not discriminate against, or grant preferential treatment to, any individual or group on the basis of race, sex, color, ethnicity, or national origin in the operation of public employment, public education, or public contracting."

As a result of §26, there are now two very different processes through which a Michigan citizen is permitted to influence the admissions policies of the State's universities: one for persons interested in race-sensitive admissions policies and one for everyone else. A citizen who is a University of Michigan alumnus, for instance, can advocate for an admissions policy that considers an applicant's legacy status by meeting individually with members of the Board of Regents to convince them of her views, by joining with other legacy parents to lobby the Board, or by voting for and supporting Board candidates who share her position. The same options are available to a citizen who wants the Board to adopt admissions policies that consider athleticism, geography, area of study, and so on. The one and only policy a Michigan citizen may not seek through this long-established process is a race-sensitive admissions policy that considers race in an individualized manner when it is clear that race-neutral alternatives are not adequate to achieve diversity. For that policy alone, the citizens of Michigan must undertake the daunting task of amending the State Constitution.

Our precedents do not permit political restructurings that create one process for racial minorities and a separate, less burdensome process for everyone else. This Court has held that the Fourteenth Amendment does not tolerate "a political structure that treats all individuals as equals, yet more subtly distorts governmental processes in such a way as to place special burdens on the ability of minority groups to achieve beneficial legislation." *Seattle*. Such restructuring, the Court explained, "is no more permissible than denying [the minority] the [right to] vote, on an equal basis with others." *Hunter*. In those cases—*Hunter* and *Seattle*—the Court recognized what is now known as the "political-process doctrine": When the majority reconfigures the political process in a manner that burdens only a racial minority, that alteration triggers strict judicial scrutiny.

Today, disregarding *stare decisis*, a majority of the Court effectively discards those precedents. The plurality does so, it tells us, because the freedom actually secured by the Constitution is the freedom of self-government—because the majority of Michigan citizens "exercised their privilege to enact laws as a basic exercise of their democratic power." It would be "demeaning to the democratic process," the plurality concludes, to disturb that decision in any way. This logic embraces majority rule without an important constitutional limit.

The plurality's decision fundamentally misunderstands the nature of the injustice worked by §26. This case is not, as the plurality imagines, about "who may resolve" the debate over the use of race in higher education admissions. I agree wholeheartedly that nothing vests the resolution of that debate exclusively in the courts or requires that we remove it from the reach of the electorate. Rather, this case is about *how* the debate over the use of race-sensitive admissions policies may be resolved—that is, it must be resolved in constitutionally permissible ways. While our Constitution does not guarantee minority groups victory in the political process, it does guarantee them meaningful and equal access to that process. It guarantees that the majority may not win by stacking the political process against minority groups permanently, forcing the minority alone to surmount unique obstacles in pursuit of its goals—here, educational diversity that cannot reasonably be accomplished through race-neutral measures. Today, by permitting a majority of the voters in Michigan to do what our Constitution forbids, the Court ends the debate over race-sensitive admissions policies in Michigan in a manner that contravenes constitutional protections long recognized in our precedents.

Like the plurality, I have faith that our citizenry will continue to learn from this Nation's regrettable history; that it will strive to move beyond those injustices towards a future of equality. And I, too, believe in the importance of public discourse on matters of public policy. But I part ways with the plurality when it suggests that judicial intervention in this case "impede[s]" rather than "advance[s]" the democratic process and the ultimate hope of equality. I firmly believe that our role as judges includes policing the process of self-government and stepping in when necessary to secure the constitutional guarantee of equal protection. Because I would do so here, I respectfully dissent. . . .

My colleagues are of the view that we should leave race out of the picture entirely and let the voters sort it out. We have seen this reasoning before. See *Parents Involved* ("The way to stop discrimination on the basis of race is to stop discriminating on the basis of race"). It is a sentiment out of touch with reality, one not required by our Constitution, and one that has properly been rejected as "not sufficient" to resolve cases of this nature. While "[t]he enduring hope is that race should not matter[,] the reality is that too often it does." *Parents Involved.*

Race matters. Race matters in part because of the long history of racial minorities' being denied access to the political process. And although we have made great strides, "voting discrimination still exists; no one doubts that." *Shelby County [v. Holder* (2013).]

Race also matters because of persistent racial inequality in society — inequality that cannot be ignored and that has produced stark socioeconomic disparities. See *Gratz* (Ginsburg, J., dissenting) (cataloging the many ways in which "the effects of centuries of law-sanctioned inequality remain painfully evident in our communities and schools," in areas like employment, poverty, access to health care, housing, consumer transactions, and education).

And race matters for reasons that really are only skin deep, that cannot be discussed any other way, and that cannot be wished away. Race matters to a young man's view of society when he spends his teenage years watching others tense up as he passes, no matter the neighborhood where he grew up. Race matters to a young woman's sense of self when she states her hometown, and then is pressed, "No, where are you *really* from?", regardless of how many generations her family has been in the country. Race matters to a young person addressed by a stranger in a foreign language, which he does not understand because only English was spoken at home. Race matters because of the slights, the snickers, the silent judgments that reinforce that most crippling of thoughts: "I do not belong here."

In my colleagues' view, examining the racial impact of legislation only perpetuates racial discrimination. This refusal to accept the stark reality that race matters is regrettable. The way to stop discrimination on the basis of race is to speak openly and candidly on the subject of race, and to apply the Constitution with eyes open to the unfortunate effects of centuries of racial discrimination. As members of the judiciary tasked with intervening to carry out the guarantee of equal protection, we ought not sit back and wish away, rather than confront, the racial inequality that exists in our society. It is this view that works harm, by perpetuating the facile notion that what makes race matter is acknowledging the simple truth that race *does* matter. . . .

For over a century, racial minorities in Michigan fought to bring diversity to their State's public colleges and universities. Before the advent of race-sensitive admissions policies, those institutions, like others around the country, were essentially segregated. In 1868, two black students were admitted to the University of Michigan, the first of their race. In 1935, over six decades later, there were still only 35 black students at the University. By 1954, this number had risen to slightly below 200. And by 1966, to around 400, among a total student population of roughly 32,500—barely over 1 percent. The numbers at the University of Michigan Law School are even more telling. During the 1960's, the Law School produced 9 black graduates among a total of 3,041—less than three-tenths of 1 percent.

The housing and extracurricular policies at these institutions also perpetuated open segregation. For instance, incoming students were permitted to opt out of rooming with black students. And some fraternities and sororities excluded black students from membership.

In 1966, the Defense Department conducted an investigation into the University's compliance with Title VI of the Civil Rights Act, and made 25 recommendations for increasing opportunities for minority students. In 1970, a student group launched a number of protests, including a strike, demanding that the University increase its minority enrollment. The University's Board of Regents responded, adopting a goal of 10 percent black admissions by the fall of 1973.

During the 1970's, the University continued to improve its admissions policies, encouraged by this Court's 1978 decision in *Bakke*. In that case, the Court told our Nation's colleges and universities that they could consider race in admissions as part of a broader goal to create a diverse student body, in which students of different backgrounds would learn together, and thereby learn to live together. A little more than a decade ago, in *Grutter,* the Court reaffirmed this understanding. In upholding the admissions policy of the Law School, the Court laid to rest any doubt whether student body diversity is a compelling interest that may justify the use of race.

Race-sensitive admissions policies are now a thing of the past in Michigan after §26, even though—as experts agree and as research shows—those policies were making a difference in achieving educational diversity. . . . The Board of Regents of the University of Michigan and the Board of Trustees of Michigan State University inform us that those institutions cannot achieve the benefits of a diverse student body without race-sensitive admissions plans. During proceedings before the lower courts, several university officials testified that §26 would depress minority enrollment at Michigan's public universities. The Director of Undergraduate Admissions at the University of Michigan "expressed doubts over the ability to maintain minority enrollment through the use of a proxy, like socioeconomic status." He explained that university officials in States with laws similar to §26 had not " 'achieve[d] the same sort of racial and ethnic diversity that they had prior to such measures . . . without considering race.' " Similarly, the Law School's Dean of Admissions testified that she expected "a decline in minority admissions because, in her view, it is impossible 'to get a critical mass of underrepresented minorities . . . without considering race.' " And the Dean of Wayne State University Law School stated that "although some creative approaches might mitigate the effects of [§26], he 'did not think that any one of these proposals or any combination of these proposals was reasonably likely to result in the admission of a class that had the same or similar or higher numbers of African Americans, Latinos and Native Americans as the prior policy.' " . . .

Section 26 has already led to decreased minority enrollment at Michigan's public colleges and universities. In 2006 (before §26 took effect), underrepresented minorities made up 12.15 percent of the University of Michigan's freshman class, compared to 9.54 percent in 2012—a roughly 25 percent decline. . . . The elimination of race-sensitive admissions policies in California has been especially harmful to black students. In 2006, for example, there were fewer than 100 black students in UCLA's incoming class of roughly 5,000, the lowest number since at least 1973. . . .

As in Michigan, the declines in minority representation at the University of California have come even as the minority population in California has increased. At UCLA, for example, the proportion of Hispanic freshmen among those enrolled declined from 23 percent in 1995 to 17 percent in 2011, even though the proportion of Hispanic college-aged persons in California increased from 41 percent to 49 percent during that same period. . . .

To be clear, I do not mean to suggest that the virtues of adopting race-sensitive admissions policies should inform the legal question before the Court today regarding the constitutionality of §26. But I cannot ignore the unfortunate outcome of today's decision: Short of amending the State Constitution, a Herculean task, racial minorities in Michigan are deprived of even an opportunity to convince Michigan's public colleges and universities to consider race in their admissions plans when other attempts to achieve racial diversity have proved unworkable, and those institutions are unnecessarily hobbled in their pursuit of a diverse student body.

* * *

The Constitution does not protect racial minorities from political defeat. But neither does it give the majority free rein to erect selective barriers against racial minorities. The political-process doctrine polices the channels of change to ensure that the majority, when it wins, does so without rigging the rules of the game to ensure its success. Today, the Court discards that doctrine without good reason.

In doing so, it permits the decision of a majority of the voters in Michigan to strip Michigan's elected university boards of their authority to make decisions with respect to constitutionally permissible race-sensitive admissions policies, while preserving the boards' plenary authority to make all other educational decisions. "In a most direct sense, this implicates the judiciary's special role in safeguarding the interests of those groups that are relegated to such a position of political powerlessness as to command extraordinary protection from the majoritarian political process." *Seattle*. The Court abdicates that role, permitting the majority to use its numerical advantage to change the rules mid-contest and forever stack the deck against racial minorities in Michigan. The result is that Michigan's public colleges and universities are less equipped to do their part in ensuring that students of all races are "better prepare[d] . . . for an increasingly diverse workforce and society. . . ." *Grutter.*

Today's decision eviscerates an important strand of our equal protection jurisprudence. For members of historically marginalized groups, which rely on the federal courts to protect their constitutional rights, the decision can hardly bolster hope for a vision of democracy that preserves for all the right to participate meaningfully and equally in self-government.

I respectfully dissent.

Chapter 6

Modern Substantive Due Process

ASSIGNMENT S-8

Protecting "Liberty"

STUDY GUIDE:

- If, as Justice Kennedy wrote, "it is unnecessary to decide whether this federal intrusion on state power is a violation of the Constitution because it disrupts the federal balance," why does he persist in discussing such federalism issues throughout his opinion?
- How does the federal government defining marriage *for purposes of its own laws* interfere with, or infringe upon, the states' traditional power to define marriage?
- Can you articulate the *structure* of Justice Kennedy's analysis? How does it compare with the doctrines governing equal protection and due process described in the cases we have read? In particular, what does he say justifies heightened scrutiny in this case? (Hint: How does his analysis square with Justice Alito's description of the modern doctrines of substantive due process and equal protection?)
- Does this case represent either a rejection of or an alternative to the Court's approach to substantive due process in *Glucksburg*?
- Is this a "substantive due process" or "equal protection" decision, or both? How do the two theories relate to each other here?
- Justice Scalia asks, "Even after the opinion has formally disclaimed reliance upon principles of federalism, mentions of 'the usual tradition of recognizing and accepting state definitions of marriage' continue. What to make of this?" What do you make of it? Has "federalism" now become relevant to a due process inquiry and, if so, how?
- Could Justice Kennedy's approach be adapted to protect the "right to use marijuana for medical purposes" that the Ninth Circuit denied in *Raich*?
- Does the majority provide arguments to support constitutional challenges to *state* laws restricting marriage to opposite sex couples? If so, what do you make of the majority's emphasis on federalism? Do you think that the "community's considered perspective" on the scope of marriage will be allowed by the Court to cut both ways?

UNITED STATES v. WINDSOR

No. 12-307

Argued Mar. 27, 2013 | Decided June 26, 2013

JUSTICE KENNEDY delivered the opinion of the Court. . . .

I

In 1996, as some States were beginning to consider the concept of same-sex marriage, and before any State had acted to permit it, Congress enacted the Defense of Marriage Act (DOMA). DOMA contains two operative sections: Section 2, which has not been challenged here, allows States to refuse to recognize same-sex marriages performed under the laws of other States. Section 3 is at issue here. It amends the Dictionary Act in Title 1, §7, of the United States Code to provide a federal definition of "marriage" and "spouse." Section 3 of DOMA provides as follows:

> In determining the meaning of any Act of Congress, or of any ruling, regulation, or interpretation of the various administrative bureaus and agencies of the United States, the word "marriage" means only a legal union between one man and one woman as husband and wife, and the word "spouse" refers only to a person of the opposite sex who is a husband or a wife.

The definitional provision does not by its terms forbid States from enacting laws permitting same-sex marriages or civil unions or providing state benefits to residents in that status. The enactment's comprehensive definition of marriage for purposes of all federal statutes and other regulations or directives covered by its terms, however, does control over 1,000 federal laws in which marital or spousal status is addressed as a matter of federal law.

Edith Windsor and Thea Spyer met in New York City in 1963 and began a long-term relationship. Windsor and Spyer registered as domestic partners when New York City gave that right to same-sex couples in 1993. Concerned about Spyer's health, the couple made the 2007 trip to Canada for their marriage, but they continued to reside in New York City. The State of New York deems their Ontario marriage to be a valid one.

Spyer died in February 2009, and left her entire estate to Windsor. Because DOMA denies federal recognition to same-sex spouses, Windsor did not qualify for the marital exemption from the federal estate tax, which excludes from taxation "any interest in property which passes or has passed from the decedent to his surviving spouse." Windsor paid $363,053 in estate taxes and sought a refund. The Internal Revenue Service denied the refund, concluding that, under DOMA, Windsor was not a "surviving spouse." Windsor commenced this refund suit in the United States District Court for the Southern District of New York. She contended that DOMA violates the guarantee of equal protection, as applied to the Federal Government through the Fifth Amendment. . . .

III

When at first Windsor and Spyer longed to marry, neither New York nor any other State granted them that right. After waiting some years, in 2007 they traveled to Ontario to be married there. It seems fair to conclude that, until recent years, many citizens had not even considered the possibility that two persons of the same sex might aspire to occupy the same status and dignity as that of a man and woman in lawful marriage. For marriage between a man and a woman no doubt had been thought of by most people as essential to the very definition of that term and to its role and function throughout the history of civilization. That belief, for many who long have held it, became even more urgent, more cherished when challenged. For others, however, came the beginnings of a new perspective, a new insight. Accordingly some States concluded that same-sex marriage ought to be given recognition and validity in the law for those same-sex couples who wish to define themselves by their commitment to each other. The limitation of lawful marriage to heterosexual couples, which for centuries had been deemed both necessary and fundamental, came to be seen in New York and certain other States as an unjust exclusion. Slowly at first and then in rapid course, the laws of New York came to acknowledge the urgency of this issue for same-sex couples who wanted to affirm their commitment to one another before their children, their family, their friends, and their community. And so New York recognized same-sex marriages performed elsewhere; and then it later amended its own marriage laws to permit same-sex marriage. New York, in common with, as of this writing, 11 other States and the District of Columbia, decided that same-sex couples should have the right to marry and so live with pride in themselves and their union and in a status of equality with all other married persons. After a statewide deliberative process that enabled its citizens to discuss and weigh arguments for and against same-sex marriage, New York acted to enlarge the definition of marriage to correct what its citizens and elected representatives perceived to be an injustice that they had not earlier known or understood.

Against this background of lawful same-sex marriage in some States, the design, purpose, and effect of DOMA should be considered as the beginning point in deciding whether it is valid under the Constitution. By history and tradition the definition and regulation of marriage, as will be discussed in more detail, has been treated as being within the authority and realm of the separate States. Yet it is further established that Congress, in enacting discrete statutes, can make determinations that bear on marital rights and privileges. . . . [W]hen the Federal Government acts in the exercise of its own proper authority, it has a wide choice of the mechanisms and means to adopt. See *McCulloch v. Maryland* (1819). Congress has the power both to ensure efficiency in the administration of its programs and to choose what larger goals and policies to pursue. Other precedents involving congressional statutes which affect marriages and family status further illustrate this point. In addressing the interaction of state domestic relations and federal immigration law Congress determined that marriages "entered into for the purpose of procuring an alien's admission [to the United States] as an immigrant" will not qualify the noncitizen for that status, even if the noncitizen's marriage is valid and proper for state-law purposes. And in establishing income-based criteria for Social Security benefits, Congress decided that although state law would determine in general who qualifies as an applicant's spouse, common-law marriages also should be recognized, regardless of any particular State's view on these relationships.

Though these discrete examples establish the constitutionality of limited federal laws that regulate the meaning of marriage in order to further federal policy, DOMA has a far greater reach; for it enacts a directive applicable to over 1,000 federal statutes and the whole realm of federal regulations. And its operation is directed to a class of persons that the laws of New York, and of 11 other States, have sought to protect.

In order to assess the validity of that intervention it is necessary to discuss the extent of the state power and authority over marriage as a matter of history and tradition. State laws defining and regulating marriage, of course, must respect the constitutional rights of persons, see, *e.g., Loving v. Virginia* (1967); but, subject to those guarantees, "regulation of domestic relations" is "an area that has long been regarded as a virtually exclusive province of the States." *Sosna v. Iowa* (1975).

The recognition of civil marriages is central to state domestic relations law applicable to its residents and citizens. See *Williams v. North Carolina* (1942) ("Each state as a sovereign has a rightful and legitimate concern in the marital status of persons domiciled within its borders"). The definition of marriage is the foundation of the State's broader authority to regulate the subject of domestic relations with respect to the "[p]rotection of offspring, property interests, and the enforcement of marital responsibilities." *Ibid.* "[T]he states, at the time of the adoption of the Constitution, possessed full power over the subject of marriage and divorce . . . [and] the Constitution delegated no authority to the Government of the United States on the subject of marriage and divorce." *Haddock v. Haddock* (1906); see also *In re Burrus* (1890) ("The whole subject of the domestic relations of husband and wife, parent and child, belongs to the laws of the States and not to the laws of the United States").

Consistent with this allocation of authority, the Federal Government, through our history, has deferred to state-law policy decisions with respect to domestic relations. In *De Sylva v. Ballentine* (1956), for example, the Court held that, "[t]o decide who is the widow or widower of a deceased author, or who are his executors or next of kin," under the Copyright Act "requires a reference to the law of the State which created those legal relationships" because "there is no federal law of domestic relations." In order to respect this principle, the federal courts, as a general rule, do not adjudicate issues of marital status even when there might otherwise be a basis for federal jurisdiction. See *Ankenbrandt v. Richards* (1992). Federal courts will not hear divorce and custody cases even if they arise in diversity because of "the virtually exclusive primacy . . . of the States in the regulation of domestic relations." *Id.* (Blackmun, J., concurring in judgment).

The significance of state responsibilities for the definition and regulation of marriage dates to the Nation's beginning; for "when the Constitution was adopted the common understanding was that the domestic relations of husband and wife and parent and child were matters reserved to the States." *Ohio ex rel. Popovici v. Agler* (1930). Marriage laws vary in some respects from State to State. For example, the required minimum age is 16 in Vermont, but only 13 in New Hampshire. Likewise the permissible degree of consanguinity can vary (most States permit first cousins to marry, but a handful—such as Iowa and Washington—prohibit the practice). But these rules are in every event consistent within each State.

Against this background DOMA rejects the long-established precept that the incidents, benefits, and obligations of marriage are uniform for all married couples within each State, though they may vary, subject to constitutional guarantees, from one State to the next. Despite these considerations, it is unnecessary to decide whether this federal intrusion on state power is a violation of the Constitution because it disrupts the federal balance. The State's power in defining the marital relation is of central relevance in this case quite apart from principles of federalism. Here the State's decision to give this class of persons the right to marry conferred upon them a dignity and status of immense import. When the State used its historic and essential authority to define the marital relation in this way, its role and its power in making the decision enhanced the recognition, dignity, and protection of the class in their own community. DOMA, because of its reach and extent, departs from this history and tradition of reliance on state law to define marriage. " '[D]iscriminations of an unusual character especially suggest careful consideration to determine whether they are obnoxious to the constitutional provision.' " *Romer v. Evans* (1996) (quoting *Louisville Gas & Elec. Co. v. Coleman* (1928)).

The Federal Government uses this state-defined class for the opposite purpose—to impose restrictions and disabilities. That result requires this Court now to address whether the resulting injury and indignity is a deprivation of an essential part of the liberty protected by the Fifth Amendment. What the State of New York treats as alike the federal law deems unlike by a law designed to injure the same class the State seeks to protect.

In acting first to recognize and then to allow same-sex marriages, New York was responding "to the initiative of those who [sought] a voice in shaping the destiny of their own times." *Bond v. United States* (2011). These actions were without doubt a proper exercise of its sovereign authority within our federal system, all in the way that the Framers of the Constitution intended. The dynamics of state government in the federal system are to allow the formation of consensus respecting the way the members of a discrete community treat each other in their daily contact and constant interaction with each other.

The States' interest in defining and regulating the marital relation, subject to constitutional guarantees, stems from the understanding that marriage is more than a routine classification for purposes of certain statutory benefits. Private, consensual sexual intimacy between two adult persons of the same sex may not be punished by the State, and it can form "but one element in a personal bond that is more enduring." *Lawrence v. Texas* (2003). By its recognition of the validity of same-sex marriages performed in other jurisdictions and then by authorizing same-sex unions and same-sex marriages, New York sought to give further protection and dignity to that bond. For same-sex couples who wished to be married, the State acted to give their lawful conduct a lawful status. This status is a far-reaching legal acknowledgment of the intimate relationship between two people, a relationship deemed by the State worthy of dignity in the community equal with all other marriages. It reflects both the community's considered perspective on the historical roots of the institution of marriage and its evolving understanding of the meaning of equality.

IV

DOMA seeks to injure the very class New York seeks to protect. By doing so it violates basic due process and equal protection principles applicable to the Federal Government. See U.S. Const., Amdt. 5; *Bolling v. Sharpe* (1954). The Constitution's guarantee of equality "must at the very least mean that a bare congressional desire to harm a politically unpopular group cannot" justify disparate treatment of that group. *Department of Agriculture v. Moreno* (1973). In determining whether a law is motived by an improper animus or purpose, "[d]iscriminations of an unusual character" especially require careful consideration. *Romer*. DOMA cannot survive under these principles. The responsibility of the States for the regulation of domestic relations is an important indicator of the substantial societal impact the State's classifications have in the daily lives and customs of its people. DOMA's unusual deviation from the usual tradition of recognizing and accepting state definitions of marriage here operates to deprive same-sex couples of the benefits and responsibilities that come with the federal recognition of their marriages. This is strong evidence of a law having the purpose and effect of disapproval of that class. The avowed purpose and practical effect of the law here in question are to impose a disadvantage, a separate status, and so a stigma upon all who enter into same-sex marriages made lawful by the unquestioned authority of the States. The history of DOMA's enactment and its own text demonstrate that interference with the equal dignity of same-sex marriages, a dignity conferred by the States in the exercise of their sovereign power, was more than an incidental effect of the federal statute. It was its essence. The House Report announced its conclusion that "it is both appropriate and necessary for Congress to do what it can to defend the institution of traditional heterosexual marriage. . . . H.R. 3396 is appropriately entitled the 'Defense of Marriage Act.' The effort to redefine 'marriage' to extend to homosexual couples is a truly radical proposal that would fundamentally alter the institution of marriage." H.R. Rep. No. 104-664 (1996). The House concluded that DOMA expresses "both moral disapproval of homosexuality, and a moral conviction that heterosexuality better comports with traditional (especially Judeo-Christian) morality." The stated purpose of the law was to promote an "interest in protecting the traditional moral teachings reflected in heterosexual-only marriage laws." Were there any doubt of this far-reaching purpose, the title of the Act confirms it: The Defense of Marriage.

The arguments put forward by [the Bipartisan Legal Advisory Group (BLAG) of the House of Representatives] are just as candid about the congressional purpose to influence or interfere with state sovereign choices about who may be married. As the title and dynamics of the bill indicate, its purpose is to discourage enactment of state same-sex marriage laws and to restrict the freedom and choice of couples married under those laws if they are enacted. The congressional goal was "to put a thumb on the scales and influence a state's decision as to how to shape its own marriage laws." [*Massachusetts v. United States Dept. of Health and Human Servs.* (C.A.1 2012).] The Act's demonstrated purpose is to ensure that if any State decides to recognize same-sex marriages, those unions will be treated as second-class marriages for purposes of federal law. This raises a most serious question under the Constitution's Fifth Amendment.

DOMA's operation in practice confirms this purpose. When New York adopted a law to permit same-sex marriage, it sought to eliminate inequality; but DOMA frustrates that objective through a system-wide enactment with no identified connection to any particular area of federal law. DOMA writes inequality into the entire United States Code. The particular case at hand concerns the estate tax, but DOMA is more than a simple determination of what should or should not be allowed as an estate tax refund. Among the over 1,000 statutes and numerous federal regulations that DOMA controls are laws pertaining to Social Security, housing, taxes, criminal sanctions, copyright, and veterans' benefits.

DOMA's principal effect is to identify a subset of state-sanctioned marriages and make them unequal. The principal purpose is to impose inequality, not for other reasons like governmental efficiency. Responsibilities, as well as rights, enhance the dignity and integrity of the person. And DOMA contrives to deprive some couples married under the laws of their State, but not other couples, of both rights and responsibilities. By creating two contradictory marriage regimes within the same State, DOMA forces same-sex couples to live as married for the purpose of state law but unmarried for the purpose of federal law, thus diminishing the stability and predictability of basic personal relations the State has found it proper to acknowledge and protect. By this dynamic DOMA undermines both the public and private significance of state-sanctioned same-sex marriages; for it tells those couples, and all the world, that their otherwise valid marriages are unworthy of federal recognition. This places same-sex couples in an unstable position of being in a second-tier marriage. The differentiation demeans the couple, whose moral and sexual choices the Constitution protects, see *Lawrence,* and whose relationship the State has sought to dignify. And it humiliates tens of thousands of children now being raised by same-sex couples. The law in question makes it even more difficult for the children to understand the integrity and closeness of their own family and its concord with other families in their community and in their daily lives.

Under DOMA, same-sex married couples have their lives burdened, by reason of government decree, in visible and public ways. By its great reach, DOMA touches many aspects of married and family life, from the mundane to the profound. It prevents same-sex married couples from obtaining government healthcare benefits they would otherwise receive. It deprives them of the Bankruptcy

Code's special protections for domestic-support obligations. It forces them to follow a complicated procedure to file their state and federal taxes jointly. Brief for Federalism Scholars as *Amici Curiae*. It prohibits them from being buried together in veterans' cemeteries. For certain married couples, DOMA's unequal effects are even more serious. The federal penal code makes it a crime to "assaul[t], kidna[p], or murde[r] . . . a member of the immediate family" of "a United States official, a United States judge, [or] a Federal law enforcement officer," with the intent to influence or retaliate against that official. Although a "spouse" qualifies as a member of the officer's "immediate family," DOMA makes this protection inapplicable to same-sex spouses.

DOMA also brings financial harm to children of same-sex couples. It raises the cost of health care for families by taxing health benefits provided by employers to their workers' same-sex spouses. And it denies or reduces benefits allowed to families upon the loss of a spouse and parent, benefits that are an integral part of family security.

DOMA divests married same-sex couples of the duties and responsibilities that are an essential part of married life and that they in most cases would be honored to accept were DOMA not in force. For instance, because it is expected that spouses will support each other as they pursue educational opportunities, federal law takes into consideration a spouse's income in calculating a student's federal financial aid eligibility. Same-sex married couples are exempt from this requirement. The same is true with respect to federal ethics rules. Federal executive and agency officials are prohibited from "participat[ing] personally and substantially" in matters as to which they or their spouses have a financial interest. A similar statute prohibits Senators, Senate employees, and their spouses from accepting high-value gifts from certain sources, and another mandates detailed financial disclosures by numerous high-ranking officials and their spouses. Under DOMA, however, these Government-integrity rules do not apply to same-sex spouses.

* * *

The power the Constitution grants it also restrains. And though Congress has great authority to design laws to fit its own conception of sound national policy, it cannot deny the liberty protected by the Due Process Clause of the Fifth Amendment. What has been explained to this point should more than suffice to establish that the principal purpose and the necessary effect of this law are to demean those persons who are in a lawful same-sex marriage. This requires the Court to hold, as it now does, that DOMA is unconstitutional as a deprivation of the liberty of the person protected by the Fifth Amendment of the Constitution.

The liberty protected by the Fifth Amendment's Due Process Clause contains within it the prohibition against denying to any person the equal protection of the laws. See *Bolling*; *Adarand Constructors, Inc. v. Peña* (1995). While the Fifth Amendment itself withdraws from Government the power to degrade or demean in the way this law does, the equal protection guarantee of the Fourteenth Amendment makes that Fifth Amendment right all the more specific and all the better understood and preserved.

The class to which DOMA directs its restrictions and restraints are those persons who are joined in same-sex marriages made lawful by the State. DOMA singles out a class of persons deemed by a State entitled to recognition and protection to enhance their own liberty. It imposes a disability on the class by refusing to acknowledge a status the State finds to be dignified and proper. DOMA instructs all federal officials, and indeed all persons with whom same-sex couples interact, including their own children, that their marriage is less worthy than the marriages of others. The federal statute is invalid, for no legitimate purpose overcomes the purpose and effect to disparage and to injure those whom the State, by its marriage laws, sought to protect in personhood and dignity. By seeking to displace this protection and treating those persons as living in marriages less respected than others, the federal statute is in violation of the Fifth Amendment. This opinion and its holding are confined to those lawful marriages.

The judgment of the Court of Appeals for the Second Circuit is affirmed.

It is so ordered.

CHIEF JUSTICE ROBERTS, dissenting. . . .

[W]hile I disagree with the result to which the majority's analysis leads it in this case, I think it more important to point out that its analysis leads no further. The Court does not have before it, and the logic of its opinion does not decide, the distinct question whether the States, in the exercise of their "historic and essential authority to define the marital relation," may continue to utilize the traditional definition of marriage.

The majority goes out of its way to make this explicit in the penultimate sentence of its opinion. It states that "[t]his opinion and its holding are confined to those lawful marriages,"—referring to same-sex marriages that a State has already recognized as a result of the local "community's considered perspective on the historical roots of the institution of marriage and its evolving understanding of the meaning of equality." Justice Scalia believes this is a "bald, unreasoned disclaime[r]." In my view, though, the disclaimer is a logical and necessary consequence of the argument the majority has chosen to adopt. The dominant theme of the majority opinion is that the Federal Government's intrusion into an area "central to state domestic relations law applicable to its residents and citizens" is sufficiently "unusual" to set off alarm bells. I think the majority goes off course, as I have said, but it is undeniable that its judgment is based on federalism.

The majority extensively chronicles DOMA's departure from the normal allocation of responsibility between State and Federal Governments, emphasizing that DOMA "rejects the long-established precept that the incidents, benefits, and obligations of marriage are uniform for all married couples within each State." But there is no such departure when one State adopts or keeps a definition of marriage that differs from that of its neighbor, for it is entirely expected that state definitions would "vary, subject to constitutional guarantees, from one State to the next." Thus, while "[t]he State's power in defining the marital relation is of central relevance" to the majority's decision to strike down DOMA here, that power will come into play on the other side of the board in future cases about the constitutionality of state marriage definitions. So too will the concerns for state diversity and sovereignty that weigh against DOMA's constitutionality in this case. It is not just this central feature of the majority's analysis that is unique to DOMA, but many considerations on the periphery as well. For example, the majority focuses on the legislative history and title of this particular Act; those statute-specific considerations will, of course, be irrelevant in future cases about different statutes. The majority emphasizes that DOMA was a "systemwide enactment with no identified connection to any particular area of federal law," but a State's definition of marriage "is the foundation of the State's broader authority to regulate the subject of domestic relations with respect to the '[p]rotection of offspring, property interests, and the enforcement of marital responsibilities.'" And the federal decision undermined (in the majority's view) the "dignity [already] conferred by the States in the exercise of their sovereign power," whereas a State's decision whether to expand the definition of marriage from its traditional contours involves no similar concern.

We may in the future have to resolve challenges to state marriage definitions affecting same-sex couples. That issue, however, is not before us in this case. . . . I write only to highlight the limits of the majority's holding and reasoning today, lest its opinion be taken to resolve not only a question that I believe is not properly before us—DOMA's constitutionality—but also a question that all agree, and the Court explicitly acknowledges, is not at issue.

JUSTICE SCALIA, with whom JUSTICE THOMAS joins. . . .

This case is about power in several respects. It is about the power of our people to govern themselves, and the power of this Court to pronounce the law. Today's opinion aggrandizes the latter, with the predictable consequence of diminishing the former. . . .

II

[Because of the absence of standing,] I think that this Court has, and the Court of Appeals had, no power to decide this suit. We should vacate the decision below and remand to the Court of Appeals for the Second Circuit, with instructions to dismiss the appeal. Given that the majority has volunteered its view of the merits, however, I proceed to discuss that as well.

A

There are many remarkable things about the majority's merits holding. The first is how rootless and shifting its justifications are. For example, the opinion starts with seven full pages about the traditional power of States to define domestic relations—initially fooling many readers, I am sure, into thinking that this is a federalism opinion. But we are eventually told that "it is unnecessary to decide whether this federal intrusion on state power is a violation of the Constitution," and that "[t]he State's power in defining the marital relation is of central relevance in this case quite apart from principles of federalism" because "the State's decision to give this class of persons the right to marry conferred upon them a dignity and status of immense import." But no one questions the power of the States to define marriage (with the concomitant conferral of dignity and status), so what is the point of devoting seven pages to describing how long and well established that power is? Even after the opinion has formally disclaimed reliance upon principles of federalism, mentions of "the usual tradition of recognizing and accepting state definitions of marriage" continue. What to make of this? The opinion never explains. My guess is that the majority, while reluctant to suggest that defining the meaning of "marriage" in federal statutes is unsupported by any of the Federal Government's enumerated powers,[1] nonetheless needs some rhetorical basis to support its pretense that today's prohibition of laws excluding same-sex marriage is confined to the Federal Government (leaving the second, state-law shoe to be dropped later, maybe next Term). But I am only guessing.

Equally perplexing are the opinion's references to "the Constitution's guarantee of equality." Near the end of the opinion, we are told that although the "equal protection guarantee of the Fourteenth Amendment makes [the] Fifth Amendment [due process] right all the more specific and all the better understood and preserved"—what can *that* mean?— "the Fifth Amendment itself withdraws from Government the power to degrade or demean in the way this law does." The only possible interpretation of this statement is that the Equal Protection Clause, even the Equal Protection Clause as incorporated in the Due Process Clause, is not the basis for today's holding. But the portion of the majority opinion that explains why DOMA is unconstitutional (Part IV) begins by citing *Bolling v. Sharpe* (1954), *Department of Agriculture v. Moreno* (1973), and *Romer v. Evans* (1996)—*all* of which are equal-protection cases.[2] And those three cases are the *only* authorities that the Court cites in Part IV about the Constitution's meaning, except for its citation of *Lawrence v. Texas* (2003) (not an equal-protection case) to support its passing assertion that the Constitution protects the "moral and sexual choices" of same-sex couples.

Moreover, if this is meant to be an equal-protection opinion, it is a confusing one. The opinion does not resolve and indeed does not even mention what had been the central question in this litigation: whether, under the Equal Protection Clause, laws restricting marriage to a man and a woman are reviewed for more than mere rationality. That is the issue that divided the parties and the court below. In accord with my previously expressed skepticism about the Court's

---

1. Such a suggestion would be impossible, given the Federal Government's long history of making pronouncements regarding marriage—for example, conditioning Utah's entry into the Union upon its prohibition of polygamy. See Act of July 16, 1894 ("The constitution [of Utah]" must provide "perfect toleration of religious sentiment," "*Provided,* That polygamous or plural marriages are forever prohibited").

2. Since the Equal Protection Clause technically applies only against the States, *Bolling* and *Moreno*, dealing with federal action, relied upon "the equal protection component of the Due Process Clause of the Fifth Amendment," *Moreno*.

"tiers of scrutiny" approach, I would review this classification only for its rationality. See *United States v. Virginia* (1996) (Scalia, J., dissenting). As nearly as I can tell, the Court agrees with that; its opinion does not apply strict scrutiny, and its central propositions are taken from rational-basis cases like *Moreno*. But the Court certainly does not *apply* anything that resembles that deferential framework. See *Heller v. Doe* (1993) (a classification "must be upheld . . . if there is any reasonably conceivable state of facts" that could justify it).

The majority opinion need not get into the strict-vs.-rational-basis scrutiny question, and need not justify its holding under either, because it says that DOMA is unconstitutional as "a deprivation of the liberty of the person protected by the Fifth Amendment of the Constitution"; that it violates "basic due process" principles; and that it inflicts an "injury and indignity" of a kind that denies "an essential part of the liberty protected by the Fifth Amendment." The majority never utters the dread words "substantive due process," perhaps sensing the disrepute into which that doctrine has fallen, but that is what those statements mean. Yet the opinion does not argue that same-sex marriage is "deeply rooted in this Nation's history and tradition," *Washington v. Glucksberg* (1997), a claim that would of course be quite absurd. So would the further suggestion (also necessary, under our substantive-due-process precedents) that a world in which DOMA exists is one bereft of "ordered liberty." *Id.* (quoting *Palko v. Connecticut* (1937)).

Some might conclude that this loaf could have used a while longer in the oven. But that would be wrong; it is already overcooked. The most expert care in preparation cannot redeem a bad recipe. The sum of all the Court's nonspecific hand-waving is that this law is invalid (maybe on equal-protection grounds, maybe on substantive-due-process grounds, and perhaps with some amorphous federalism component playing a role) because it is motivated by a "bare . . . desire to harm" couples in same-sex marriages. It is this proposition with which I will therefore engage.

B

As I have observed before, the Constitution does not forbid the government to enforce traditional moral and sexual norms. See *Lawrence v. Texas* (2003) (Scalia, J., dissenting). I will not swell the U.S. Reports with restatements of that point. It is enough to say that the Constitution neither requires nor forbids our society to approve of same-sex marriage, much as it neither requires nor forbids us to approve of no-fault divorce, polygamy, or the consumption of alcohol. However, even setting aside traditional moral disapproval of same-sex marriage (or indeed same-sex sex), there are many perfectly valid—indeed, downright boring—justifying rationales for this legislation. Their existence ought to be the end of this case. For they give the lie to the Court's conclusion that only those with hateful hearts could have voted "aye" on this Act. And more importantly, they serve to make the contents of the legislators' hearts quite irrelevant: "It is a familiar principle of constitutional law that this Court will not strike down an otherwise constitutional statute on the basis of an alleged illicit legislative motive." *United States v. O'Brien* (1968). Or at least it *was* a familiar principle. By holding to the contrary, the majority has declared open season on any law that (in the opinion of the law's opponents and any panel of like-minded federal judges) can be characterized as mean-spirited.

The majority concludes that the only motive for this Act was the "bare . . . desire to harm a politically unpopular group." Bear in mind that the object of this condemnation is not the legislature of some once-Confederate Southern state (familiar objects of the Court's scorn), but our respected coordinate branches, the Congress and Presidency of the United States. Laying such a charge against them should require the most extraordinary evidence, and I would have thought that every attempt would be made to indulge a more anodyne explanation for the statute. The majority does the opposite—affirmatively concealing from the reader the arguments that exist in justification. It makes only a passing mention of the "arguments put forward" by the Act's defenders, and does not even trouble to paraphrase or describe them. I imagine that this is because it is harder to maintain the illusion of the Act's supporters as unhinged members of a wild-eyed lynch mob when one first describes their views as *they* see them.

To choose just one of these defenders' arguments, DOMA avoids difficult choice-of-law issues that will now arise absent a uniform federal definition of marriage. See, *e.g.*, Baude, Beyond DOMA: Choice of State Law in Federal Statutes, 64 Stan. L. Rev. 1371 (2012). Imagine a pair of women who marry in Albany and then move to Alabama, which does not "recognize as valid any marriage of parties of the same sex." When the couple files their next federal tax return, may it be a joint one? Which State's law controls, for federal-law purposes: their State of celebration (which recognizes the marriage) or their State of domicile (which does not)? (Does the answer depend on whether they were just visiting in Albany?) Are these questions to be answered as a matter of federal common law, or perhaps by borrowing a State's choice-of-law rules? If so, *which* State's? And what about States where the status of an out-of-state same-sex marriage is an unsettled question under local law? DOMA avoided all of this uncertainty by specifying which marriages would be recognized for federal purposes. That is a classic purpose for a definitional provision.

Further, DOMA preserves the intended effects of prior legislation against then-unforeseen changes in circumstance. When Congress provided (for example) that a special estate-tax exemption would exist for spouses, this exemption reached only *opposite-sex* spouses—those being the only sort that were recognized in *any* State at the time of DOMA's passage. When it became clear that changes in state law might one day alter that balance, DOMA's definitional section was enacted to ensure that state-level experimentation did not automatically alter the basic operation of federal law, unless and until Congress made the further judgment to do so on its own. That is not animus—just stabilizing prudence. Congress has hardly demonstrated itself unwilling to make such further, revising judgments upon due deliberation. See, *e.g.*, Don't Ask, Don't Tell Repeal Act of 2010.

The Court mentions none of this. Instead, it accuses the Congress that enacted this law and the President who signed it of something much worse than, for example, having acted in excess of enumerated federal powers — or even having drawn distinctions that prove to be irrational. Those legal errors may be made in good faith, errors though they are. But the majority says that the supporters of this Act acted with *malice* — with *the "purpose"* "to disparage and to injure" same-sex couples. It says that the motivation for DOMA was to "demean," to "impose inequality," to "impose . . . a stigma," to deny people "equal dignity," to brand gay people as "unworthy," and to "*humiliat*[*e*]" their children (emphasis added).

I am sure these accusations are quite untrue. To be sure (as the majority points out), the legislation is called the Defense of Marriage Act. But to defend traditional marriage is not to condemn, demean, or humiliate those who would prefer other arrangements, any more than to defend the Constitution of the United States is to condemn, demean, or humiliate other constitutions. To hurl such accusations so casually demeans *this institution*. In the majority's judgment, any resistance to its holding is beyond the pale of reasoned disagreement. To question its high-handed invalidation of a presumptively valid statute is to act (the majority is sure) with *the purpose* to "disparage," "injure," "degrade," "demean," and "humiliate" our fellow human beings, our fellow citizens, who are homosexual. All that, simply for supporting an Act that did no more than codify an aspect of marriage that had been unquestioned in our society for most of its existence — indeed, had been unquestioned in virtually all societies for virtually all of human history. It is one thing for a society to elect change; it is another for a court of law to impose change by adjudging those who oppose it *hostes humani generis,* enemies of the human race.

* * *

The penultimate sentence of the majority's opinion is a naked declaration that "[t]his opinion and its holding are confined" to those couples "joined in same-sex marriages made lawful by the State." I have heard such "bald, unreasoned disclaimer[s]" before. *Lawrence*. When the Court declared a constitutional right to homosexual sodomy, we were assured that the case had nothing, nothing at all to do with "whether the government must give formal recognition to any relationship that homosexual persons seek to enter." Now we are told that DOMA is invalid because it "demeans the couple, whose moral and sexual choices the Constitution protects," — with an accompanying citation of *Lawrence*. It takes real cheek for today's majority to assure us, as it is going out the door, that a constitutional requirement to give formal recognition to same-sex marriage is not at issue here — when what has preceded that assurance is a lecture on how superior the majority's moral judgment in favor of same-sex marriage is to the Congress's hateful moral judgment against it. I promise you this: The only thing that will "confine" the Court's holding is its sense of what it can get away with. I do not mean to suggest disagreement with The Chief Justice's view that lower federal courts and state courts can distinguish today's case when the issue before them is state denial of marital status to same-sex couples — or even that this Court could *theoretically* do so. Lord, an opinion with such scatter-shot rationales as this one (federalism noises among them) can be distinguished in many ways. And deserves to be. State and lower federal courts should take the Court at its word and distinguish away.

In my opinion, however, the view that *this* Court will take of state prohibition of same-sex marriage is indicated beyond mistaking by today's opinion. As I have said, the real rationale of today's opinion, whatever disappearing trail of its legalistic argle-bargle one chooses to follow, is that DOMA is motivated by "bare . . . desire to harm" couples in same-sex marriages. How easy it is, indeed how inevitable, to reach the same conclusion with regard to state laws denying same-sex couples marital status. Consider how easy (inevitable) it is to make the following substitutions in a passage from today's opinion:

> *This state law's* principal effect is to identify a subset of *constitutionally protected sexual relationships*, see *Lawrence,* and make them unequal. The principal purpose is to impose inequality, not for other reasons like governmental efficiency. Responsibilities, as well as rights, enhance the dignity and integrity of the person. And *this state law* contrives to deprive some couples *enjoying constitutionally protected sexual relationships,* but not other couples, of both rights and responsibilities.

Or try this passage:

> *This state law* tells those couples, and all the world, that their otherwise valid *relationships* are unworthy of *state* recognition. This places same-sex couples in an unstable position of being in a second-tier *relationship*. The differentiation demeans the couple, whose moral and sexual choices the Constitution protects, see *Lawrence*. . . .

Or this, which does not even require alteration, except as to the invented number:

> And it humiliates thousands of children now being raised by same-sex couples. The law in question makes it even more difficult for the children to understand the integrity and closeness of their own family and its concord with other families in their community and in their daily lives.

Similarly transposable passages — deliberately transposable, I think — abound. In sum, that Court which finds it so horrific that Congress irrationally and hatefully robbed same-sex couples of the "personhood and dignity" which state legislatures conferred upon them, will of a certitude be similarly appalled by state legislatures' irrational and hateful failure to acknowledge that "personhood and dignity" in the first place. As far as this Court is concerned, no one should be fooled; it is just a matter of listening and waiting for the other shoe.

By formally declaring anyone opposed to same-sex marriage an enemy of human decency, the majority arms well every challenger to a state law restricting marriage to its traditional definition. Henceforth those challengers will lead with this Court's declaration that there is "no legitimate purpose" served by such a law, and will claim that the traditional definition has "the purpose and effect to disparage and to injure" the "personhood and dignity" of same-sex couples. The majority's limiting assurance will be meaningless in the face of language like that, as the majority well knows. That is why the language is there. The result will be a judicial distortion of our society's debate over marriage—a debate that can seem in need of our clumsy "help" only to a member of this institution.

As to that debate: Few public controversies touch an institution so central to the lives of so many, and few inspire such attendant passion by good people on all sides. Few public controversies will ever demonstrate so vividly the beauty of what our Framers gave us, a gift the Court pawns today to buy its stolen moment in the spotlight: a system of government that permits us to rule *ourselves*. Since DOMA's passage, citizens on all sides of the question have seen victories and they have seen defeats. There have been plebiscites, legislation, persuasion, and loud voices—in other words, democracy. Victories in one place for some, see North Carolina Const., Amdt. 1 (providing that "[m]arriage between one man and one woman is the only domestic legal union that shall be valid or recognized in this State") (approved by a popular vote, 61% to 39% on May 8, 2012), are offset by victories in other places for others, see Maryland Question 6 (establishing "that Maryland's civil marriage laws allow gay and lesbian couples to obtain a civil marriage license") (approved by a popular vote, 52% to 48%, on November 6, 2012). Even in a *single State,* the question has come out differently on different occasions. Compare Maine Question 1 (permitting "the State of Maine to issue marriage licenses to same-sex couples") (approved by a popular vote, 53% to 47%, on November 6, 2012) with Maine Question 1 (rejecting "the new law that lets same-sex couples marry") (approved by a popular vote, 53% to 47%, on November 3, 2009).

In the majority's telling, this story is black-and-white: Hate your neighbor or come along with us. The truth is more complicated. It is hard to admit that one's political opponents are not monsters, especially in a struggle like this one, and the challenge in the end proves more than today's Court can handle. Too bad. A reminder that disagreement over something so fundamental as marriage can still be politically legitimate would have been a fit task for what in earlier times was called the judicial temperament. We might have covered ourselves with honor today, by promising all sides of this debate that it was theirs to settle and that we would respect their resolution. We might have let the People decide.

But that the majority will not do. Some will rejoice in today's decision, and some will despair at it; that is the nature of a controversy that matters so much to so many. But the Court has cheated both sides, robbing the winners of an honest victory, and the losers of the peace that comes from a fair defeat. We owed both of them better. I dissent.

JUSTICE ALITO, with whom JUSTICE THOMAS joins as to Parts II and III, dissenting.

Our Nation is engaged in a heated debate about same-sex marriage. That debate is, at bottom, about the nature of the institution of marriage. Respondent Edith Windsor, supported by the United States, asks this Court to intervene in that debate, and although she couches her argument in different terms, what she seeks is a holding that enshrines in the Constitution a particular understanding of marriage under which the sex of the partners makes no difference. The Constitution, however, does not dictate that choice. It leaves the choice to the people, acting through their elected representatives at both the federal and state levels. I would therefore hold that Congress did not violate Windsor's constitutional rights by enacting §3 of the Defense of Marriage Act (DOMA), which defines the meaning of marriage under federal statutes that either confer upon married persons certain federal benefits or impose upon them certain federal obligations. . . .

II

. . . Same-sex marriage presents a highly emotional and important question of public policy — but not a difficult question of constitutional law. The Constitution does not guarantee the right to enter into a same-sex marriage. Indeed, no provision of the Constitution speaks to the issue.

The Court has sometimes found the Due Process Clauses to have a substantive component that guarantees liberties beyond the absence of physical restraint. And the Court's holding that "DOMA is unconstitutional as a deprivation of the liberty of the person protected by the Fifth Amendment of the Constitution," suggests that substantive due process may partially underlie the Court's decision today. But it is well established that any "substantive" component to the Due Process Clause protects only "those fundamental rights and liberties which are, objectively, 'deeply rooted in this Nation's history and tradition,' " *Washington v. Glucksberg* (1997), as well as " 'implicit in the concept of ordered liberty,' such that 'neither liberty nor justice would exist if they were sacrificed.' " *Glucksberg* (quoting *Palko v. Connecticut* (1937)).

It is beyond dispute that the right to same-sex marriage is not deeply rooted in this Nation's history and tradition. In this country, no State permitted same-sex marriage until the Massachusetts Supreme Judicial Court held in 2003 that limiting marriage to opposite-sex couples violated the State Constitution. Nor is the right to same-sex marriage deeply rooted in the traditions of other nations. No country allowed same-sex couples to marry until the Netherlands did so in 2000.

What Windsor and the United States seek, therefore, is not the protection of a deeply rooted right but the recognition of a very new right, and they seek this innovation not from a legislative body elected by the people, but from unelected judges. Faced with such a request, judges have cause for both caution and humility.

The family is an ancient and universal human institution. Family structure reflects the characteristics of a civilization, and changes in family structure and in the popular understanding of marriage and the family can have profound effects. Past changes in the understanding of marriage — for example, the gradual ascendance of the idea that romantic love is a prerequisite to marriage — have had far-reaching consequences. But the process by which such consequences come about is complex, involving the interaction of numerous factors, and tends to occur over an extended period of time.

We can expect something similar to take place if same-sex marriage becomes widely accepted. The long-term consequences of this change are not now known and are unlikely to be ascertainable for some time to come. There are those who think that allowing same-sex marriage will seriously undermine the institution of marriage. Others think that recognition of same-sex marriage will fortify a now-shaky institution.

At present, no one—including social scientists, philosophers, and historians—can predict with any certainty what the long-term ramifications of widespread acceptance of same-sex marriage will be. And judges are certainly not equipped to make such an assessment. The Members of this Court have the authority and the responsibility to interpret and apply the Constitution. Thus, if the Constitution contained a provision guaranteeing the right to marry a person of the same sex, it would be our duty to enforce that right. But the Constitution simply does not speak to the issue of same-sex marriage. In our system of government, ultimate sovereignty rests with the people, and the people have the right to control their own destiny. Any change on a question so fundamental should be made by the people through their elected officials.

III

Perhaps because they cannot show that same-sex marriage is a fundamental right under our Constitution, Windsor and the United States couch their arguments in equal protection terms. They argue that §3 of DOMA discriminates on the basis of sexual orientation, that classifications based on sexual orientation should trigger a form of "heightened" scrutiny, and that §3 cannot survive such scrutiny. They further maintain that the governmental interests that §3 purports to serve are not sufficiently important and that it has not been adequately shown that §3 serves those interests very well. The Court's holding, too, seems to rest on "the equal protection guarantee of the Fourteenth Amendment," although the Court is careful not to adopt most of Windsor's and the United States' argument. In my view, the approach that Windsor and the United States advocate is misguided. Our equal protection framework, upon which Windsor and the United States rely, is a judicial construct that provides a useful mechanism for analyzing a certain universe of equal protection cases. But that framework is ill suited for use in evaluating the constitutionality of laws based on the traditional understanding of marriage, which fundamentally turn on what marriage is.

Underlying our equal protection jurisprudence is the central notion that "[a] classification 'must be reasonable, not arbitrary, and must rest upon some ground of difference having a fair and substantial relation to the object of the legislation, so that all persons similarly circumstanced shall be treated alike.'" *Reed v. Reed* (1971). The modern tiers of scrutiny—on which Windsor and the United States rely so heavily—are a heuristic to help judges determine when classifications have that "fair and substantial relation to the object of the legislation." *Reed*.

So, for example, those classifications subject to strict scrutiny—*i.e.*, classifications that must be "narrowly tailored" to achieve a "compelling" government interest, *Parents Involved in Community Schools v. Seattle School Dist. No. 1* (2007)—are those that are "so seldom relevant to the achievement of any legitimate state interest that laws grounded in such considerations are deemed to reflect prejudice and antipathy." *Cleburne v. Cleburne Living Center, Inc.* (1985).

In contrast, those characteristics subject to so-called intermediate scrutiny—*i.e.,* those classifications that must be "'substantially related'" to the achievement of "important governmental objective[s]," *United States v. Virginia* (1996)—are those that are *sometimes* relevant considerations to be taken into account by legislators, but "generally provid[e] no sensible ground for different treatment," *Cleburne*. For example, the Court has held that statutory rape laws that criminalize sexual intercourse with a woman under the age of 18 years, but place no similar liability on partners of underage men, are grounded in the very real distinction that "young men and young women are not similarly situated with respect to the problems and the risks of sexual intercourse." *Michael M. v. Superior Court, Sonoma Cty.* (1981) (plurality opinion). The plurality reasoned that "[o]nly women may become pregnant, and they suffer disproportionately the profound physical, emotional, and psychological consequences of sexual activity." In other contexts, however, the Court has found that classifications based on gender are "arbitrary," and based on "outmoded notions of the relative capabilities of men and women," *Cleburne,* as when a State provides that a man must always be preferred to an equally qualified woman when both seek to administer the estate of a deceased party.

Finally, so-called rational-basis review applies to classifications based on "distinguishing characteristics relevant to interests the State has the authority to implement." *Cleburne*. We have long recognized that "the equal protection of the laws must coexist with the practical necessity that most legislation classifies for one purpose or another, with resulting disadvantages to various groups or persons." *Romer v. Evans* (1996). As a result, in rational-basis cases, where the court does not view the classification at issue as "inherently suspect," *Adarand Constructors, Inc. v. Peña* (1995), "the courts have been very reluctant, as they should be in our federal system and with our respect for the separation of powers, to closely scrutinize legislative choices as to whether, how, and to what extent those interests should be pursued." *Cleburne*.

In asking the Court to determine that §3 of DOMA is subject to and violates heightened scrutiny, Windsor and the United States thus ask us to rule that the presence of two members of the opposite sex is as rationally related to marriage as white skin is to voting or a Y-chromosome is to the ability to administer an estate. That is a striking request and one that unelected judges should pause before granting. Acceptance of the argument would cast all those who cling to traditional beliefs about the nature of marriage in the role of bigots or superstitious fools.

By asking the Court to strike down DOMA as not satisfying some form of heightened scrutiny, Windsor and the United States are really seeking to have the Court resolve a debate between two competing views of marriage.

The first and older view, which I will call the "traditional" or "conjugal" view, sees marriage as an intrinsically opposite-sex institution. BLAG notes that virtually every culture, including many not influenced by the Abrahamic religions, has limited marriage to people of the opposite sex. And BLAG attempts to explain this phenomenon by arguing that the institution of marriage was created for the purpose of channeling heterosexual intercourse into a structure that supports child rearing. Others explain the basis for the institution in more philosophical terms. They argue that marriage is essentially the solemnizing of a comprehensive, exclusive, permanent union that is intrinsically ordered to producing new life, even if it does not always do so. While modern cultural changes have weakened the link between marriage and procreation in the popular mind, there is no doubt that, throughout human history and across many cultures, marriage has been viewed as an exclusively opposite-sex institution and as one inextricably linked to procreation and biological kinship. The other, newer view is what I will call the "consent-based" vision of marriage, a vision that primarily defines marriage as the solemnization of mutual commitment—marked by strong emotional attachment and sexual attraction—between two persons. At least as it applies to heterosexual couples, this view of marriage now plays a very prominent role in the popular understanding of the institution. Indeed, our popular culture is infused with this understanding of marriage. Proponents of same-sex marriage argue that because gender differentiation is not relevant to this vision, the exclusion of same-sex couples from the institution of marriage is rank discrimination. The Constitution does not codify either of these views of marriage (although I suspect it would have been hard at the time of the adoption of the Constitution or the Fifth Amendment to find Americans who did not take the traditional view for granted). The silence of the Constitution on this question should be enough to end the matter as far as the judiciary is concerned. Yet, Windsor and the United States implicitly ask us to endorse the consent-based view of marriage and to reject the traditional view, thereby arrogating to ourselves the power to decide a question that philosophers, historians, social scientists, and theologians are better qualified to explore. Because our constitutional order assigns the resolution of questions of this nature to the people, I would not presume to enshrine either vision of marriage in our constitutional jurisprudence.

Legislatures, however, have little choice but to decide between the two views. We have long made clear that neither the political branches of the Federal Government nor state governments are required to be neutral between competing visions of the good, provided that the vision of the good that they adopt is not countermanded by the Constitution. Accordingly, both Congress and the States are entitled to enact laws recognizing either of the two understandings of marriage. And given the size of government and the degree to which it now regulates daily life, it seems unlikely that either Congress or the States could maintain complete neutrality even if they tried assiduously to do so.

Rather than fully embracing the arguments made by Windsor and the United States, the Court strikes down §3 of DOMA as a classification not properly supported by its objectives. The Court reaches this conclusion in part because it believes that §3 encroaches upon the States' sovereign prerogative to define marriage. Indeed, the Court's ultimate conclusion is that DOMA falls afoul of the

Fifth Amendment because it "singles out a class of persons deemed *by a State* entitled to recognition and protection to enhance their own liberty" and "imposes a disability on the class by refusing to acknowledge a status *the State finds* to be dignified and proper." (emphasis added).

To the extent that the Court takes the position that the question of same-sex marriage should be resolved primarily at the state level, I wholeheartedly agree. I hope that the Court will ultimately permit the people of each State to decide this question for themselves. Unless the Court is willing to allow this to occur, the whiffs of federalism in the today's opinion of the Court will soon be scattered to the wind.

In any event, §3 of DOMA, in my view, does not encroach on the prerogatives of the States, assuming of course that the many federal statutes affected by DOMA have not already done so. Section 3 does not prevent any State from recognizing same-sex marriage or from extending to same-sex couples any right, privilege, benefit, or obligation stemming from state law. All that §3 does is to define a class of persons to whom federal law extends certain special benefits and upon whom federal law imposes certain special burdens. In these provisions, Congress used marital status as a way of defining this class—in part, I assume, because it viewed marriage as a valuable institution to be fostered and in part because it viewed married couples as comprising a unique type of economic unit that merits special regulatory treatment. Assuming that Congress has the power under the Constitution to enact the laws affected by §3, Congress has the power to define the category of persons to whom those laws apply.

* * *

For these reasons, I would hold that §3 of DOMA does not violate the Fifth Amendment. I respectfully dissent.

Chapter 7

The Freedom of Speech and Press

ASSIGNMENT S-9

What Constitutes Speech?

When Is Conduct Speech?

Regulating Time, Place, and Manner

STUDY GUIDE:

- The next case concerns whether the regulation of "conduct" constitutes a restriction on "speech." The doctrines governing "time, place, and manner" regulations of speech are complex and are not covered in the casebook.
- The next case provides a brief introduction to those doctrines in the context of a recent controversy.

McCULLEN v. COAKLEY

No. 12-1168

Argued Jan. 15, 2014 | Decided June 26, 2014

CHIEF JUSTICE ROBERTS delivered the opinion of the Court.

A Massachusetts statute makes it a crime to knowingly stand on a "public way or sidewalk" within 35 feet of an entrance or driveway to any place, other than a hospital, where abortions are performed. Petitioners are individuals who approach and talk to women outside such facilities, attempting to dissuade them from having abortions. The statute prevents petitioners from doing so near the facilities' entrances. The question presented is whether the statute violates the First Amendment.

I

A

In 2000, the Massachusetts Legislature enacted the Massachusetts Reproductive Health Care Facilities Act. The law was designed to address clashes between abortion opponents and advocates of abortion rights that were occurring outside clinics where abortions were performed. The Act established a defined area with an 18-foot radius around the entrances and driveways of such facilities. Anyone could enter that area, but once within it, no one (other than certain exempt individuals) could knowingly approach within six feet of another person—unless that person consented—"for the purpose of passing a leaflet or handbill to, displaying a sign to, or engaging in oral protest, education, or counseling with such other person." A separate provision subjected to criminal punishment anyone who "knowingly obstructs, detains, hinders, impedes or blocks another person's entry to or exit from a reproductive health care facility."

The statute was modeled on a similar Colorado law that this Court had upheld in *Hill v. Colorado* (2000). Relying on *Hill,* the United States Court of Appeals for the First Circuit sustained the Massachusetts statute against a First Amendment challenge.

By 2007, some Massachusetts legislators and law enforcement officials had come to regard the 2000 statute as inadequate. At legislative hearings, multiple witnesses recounted apparent violations of the law. Massachusetts Attorney General Martha Coakley, for example, testified that protestors violated the statute "on a routine basis." . . .

To address these concerns, the Massachusetts Legislature amended the statute in 2007, replacing the six-foot no-approach zones (within the 18-foot area) with a 35-foot fixed buffer zone from which individuals are categorically excluded. The statute now provides:

> No person shall knowingly enter or remain on a public way or sidewalk adjacent to a reproductive health care facility within a radius of 35 feet of any portion of an entrance, exit or driveway of a reproductive health care facility or within the area within a rectangle created by extending the outside boundaries of any entrance, exit or driveway of a reproductive health care facility in straight lines to the point where such lines intersect the sideline of the street in front of such entrance, exit or driveway. Mass. Gen. Laws, ch. 266, §120E½(b).

A "reproductive health care facility," in turn, is defined as "a place, other than within or upon the grounds of a hospital, where abortions are offered or performed."

The 35-foot buffer zone applies only "during a facility's business hours," and the area must be "clearly marked and posted." In practice, facilities typically mark the zones with painted arcs and posted signs on adjacent sidewalks and streets. A first violation of the statute is punishable by a fine of up to $500, up to three months in prison, or both, while a subsequent offense is punishable by a fine of between $500 and $5,000, up to two and a half years in prison, or both.

The Act exempts four classes of individuals: (1) "persons entering or leaving such facility"; (2) "employees or agents of such facility acting within the scope of their employment"; (3) "law enforcement, ambulance, firefighting, construction, utilities, public works and other municipal agents acting within the scope of their employment"; and (4) "persons using the public sidewalk or street right-of-way adjacent to such facility solely for the purpose of reaching a destination other than such facility." The legislature also retained the separate provision from the 2000 version that proscribes the knowing obstruction of access to a facility.

B

Some of the individuals who stand outside Massachusetts abortion clinics are fairly described as protestors, who express their moral or religious opposition to abortion through signs and chants or, in some cases, more aggressive methods such as face-to-face confrontation. Petitioners take a different tack. They attempt to engage women approaching the clinics in what they call "sidewalk counseling," which involves offering information about alternatives to abortion and help pursuing those options. . . .

The buffer zones have displaced petitioners from their previous positions outside the clinics. . . . Before the Act was amended to create the buffer zones, petitioners stood near the entryway to the foyer. Now a buffer zone—marked by a painted arc and a sign—surrounds the entrance. This zone extends 23 feet down the sidewalk in one direction, 26 feet in the other, and outward just one foot short of the curb. The clinic's entrance adds another seven feet to the width of the zone. The upshot is that petitioners are effectively excluded from a 56-foot-wide expanse of the public sidewalk in front of the clinic.

Petitioners at all three clinics claim that the buffer zones have considerably hampered their counseling efforts. Although they have managed to conduct some counseling and to distribute some literature outside the buffer zones—particularly at the Boston clinic—they say they have had many fewer conversations and distributed many fewer leaflets since the zones went into effect.

The second statutory exemption allows clinic employees and agents acting within the scope of their employment to enter the buffer zones. Relying on this exemption, the Boston clinic uses "escorts" to greet women as they approach the clinic, accompanying them through the zones to the clinic entrance. Petitioners claim that the escorts sometimes thwart petitioners' attempts to communicate with patients by blocking petitioners from handing literature to patients, telling patients not to "pay any attention" or "listen to" petitioners, and disparaging petitioners as "crazy." . . .

I

By its very terms, the Massachusetts Act regulates access to "public way[s]" and "sidewalk[s]." Such areas occupy a "special position in terms of First Amendment protection" because of their historic role as sites for discussion and debate. *United States v. Grace* (1983). These places—which we have labeled "traditional public fora"—"have immemorially been held in trust for the use of the public and, time out of mind, have been used for purposes of assembly, communicating thoughts between citizens, and discussing public questions." *Pleasant Grove City v. Summum* (2009).

It is no accident that public streets and sidewalks have developed as venues for the exchange of ideas. Even today, they remain one of the few places where a speaker can be confident that he is not simply preaching to the choir. With respect to other means of communication, an individual confronted with an uncomfortable message can always turn the page, change the channel, or leave the Web site. Not so on public streets and sidewalks. There, a listener often encounters speech he might otherwise tune out. In light of the First Amendment's purpose "to preserve an uninhibited marketplace of ideas in which truth will ultimately prevail," *FCC v. League of Women Voters of Cal.* (1984), this aspect of traditional public fora is a virtue, not a vice.

In short, traditional public fora are areas that have historically been open to the public for speech activities. Thus, even though the Act says nothing about speech on its face, there is no doubt—and respondents do not dispute—that it restricts access to traditional public fora and is therefore subject to First Amendment scrutiny.

Consistent with the traditionally open character of public streets and sidewalks, we have held that the government's ability to restrict speech in such locations is "very limited." *Grace.* In particular, the guiding First Amendment principle that the "government has no power to restrict expression because of its message, its ideas, its subject matter, or its content" applies with full force in a traditional public forum. *Police Dept. of Chicago v. Mosley* (1972). As a general rule, in such a forum the government may not "selectively . . . shield the public from some kinds of speech on the ground that they are more offensive than others." *Erznoznik v. Jacksonville* (1975).

We have, however, afforded the government somewhat wider leeway to regulate features of speech unrelated to its content. "[E]ven in a public forum the government may impose reasonable restrictions on the time, place, or manner of protected speech, provided the restrictions 'are justified without reference to the content of the regulated speech, that they are narrowly tailored to serve a significant governmental interest, and that they leave open ample alternative channels for communication of the information.'" [*Ward v. Rock Against Racism* (1989).]

While the parties agree that this test supplies the proper framework for assessing the constitutionality of the Massachusetts Act, they disagree about whether the Act satisfies the test's three requirements.

III

Petitioners contend that the Act is not content neutral for two independent reasons: First, they argue that it discriminates against abortion-related speech because it establishes buffer zones only at clinics that perform abortions. Second, petitioners contend that the Act, by exempting clinic employees and agents, favors one viewpoint about abortion over the other. If either of these arguments is correct, then the Act must satisfy strict scrutiny—that is, it must be the least restrictive means of achieving a compelling state interest. Respondents do not argue that the Act can survive this exacting standard. . . .

A

The Act applies only at a "reproductive health care facility," defined as "a place, other than within or upon the grounds of a hospital, where abortions are offered or performed." Given this definition, petitioners argue, "virtually all speech affected by the Act is speech concerning abortion," thus rendering the Act content based.

We disagree. To begin, the Act does not draw content-based distinctions on its face. The Act would be content based if it required "enforcement authorities" to "examine the content of the message that is conveyed to determine whether" a violation has occurred. But it does not. Whether petitioners violate the Act "depends" not "on what they say," [*Holder v. Humanitarian Law Project* (2010)], but simply on where they say it. Indeed, petitioners can violate the Act merely by standing in a buffer zone, without displaying a sign or uttering a word.

It is true, of course, that by limiting the buffer zones to abortion clinics, the Act has the "inevitable effect" of restricting abortion-related speech more than speech on other subjects. Brief for Petitioners (quoting *United States v. O'Brien* (1968)). But a facially neutral law does not become content based simply because it may disproportionately affect speech on certain topics. On the contrary, "[a] regulation that serves purposes unrelated to the content of expression is deemed neutral, even if it has an incidental effect on some speakers or messages but not others." *Ward*. The question in such a case is whether the law is "'justified without reference to the content of the regulated speech.'" *Renton v. Playtime Theatres, Inc.* (1986) (quoting *Virginia Pharmacy Board v. Virginia Citizens Consumer Council, Inc.* (1976)).

The Massachusetts Act is. Its stated purpose is to "increase forthwith public safety at reproductive health care facilities." . . .

We have previously deemed the foregoing concerns to be content neutral. Obstructed access and congested sidewalks are problems no matter what caused them. A group of individuals can obstruct clinic access and clog sidewalks just as much when they loiter as when they protest abortion or counsel patients.

To be clear, the Act would not be content neutral if it were concerned with undesirable effects that arise from "the direct impact of speech on its audience" or "[l]isteners' reactions to speech." If, for example, the speech outside Massachusetts abortion clinics caused offense or made listeners uncomfortable, such offense or discomfort would not give the Commonwealth a content-neutral justification to restrict the speech. All of the problems identified by the Commonwealth here, however, arise irrespective of any listener's reactions. Whether or not a single person reacts to abortion protestors' chants or petitioners' counseling, large crowds outside abortion clinics can still compromise public safety, impede access, and obstruct sidewalks.

Petitioners do not really dispute that the Commonwealth's interests in ensuring safety and preventing obstruction are, as a general matter, content neutral. But petitioners note that these interests "apply outside every building in the State that hosts any activity that might occasion protest or comment," not just abortion clinics. By choosing to pursue these interests only at abortion clinics, petitioners argue, the Massachusetts Legislature evinced a purpose to "single[ ] out for regulation speech about one particular topic: abortion."

We cannot infer such a purpose from the Act's limited scope. The broad reach of a statute can help confirm that it was not enacted to burden a narrower category of disfavored speech. See Kagan, Private Speech, Public Purpose: The Role of Governmental Motive in First Amendment Doctrine, 63 U. Chi. L. Rev. 413, 451-452 (1996). At the same time, however, "States adopt laws to address the problems that confront them. The First Amendment does not require States to regulate for problems that do not exist." *Burson v. Freeman* (1992) (plurality opinion). The Massachusetts Legislature amended the Act in 2007 in response to a problem that was, in its experience, limited to abortion clinics. There was a record of crowding, obstruction, and even violence outside such clinics. There were apparently no similar recurring problems associated with other kinds of healthcare facilities, let alone with "every building in the State that hosts any activity that might occasion protest or comment." In light of the limited nature of the problem, it was reasonable for the Massachusetts Legislature to enact a limited solution. When selecting among various options for combating a particular problem, legislatures should be encouraged to choose the one that restricts less speech, not more.

B

Petitioners also argue that the Act is content based because it exempts four classes of individuals, one of which comprises "employees or agents of [a reproductive healthcare] facility acting within the scope of their employment." This exemption, petitioners say, favors one side in the abortion debate and thus constitutes viewpoint discrimination—an "egregious form of content discrimination," *Rosenberger v. Rector and Visitors of Univ. of Va.* (1995). In particular, petitioners argue that the exemption allows clinic employees and agents—including the volunteers who "escort" patients arriving at the Boston clinic—to speak inside the buffer zones.

It is of course true that "an exemption from an otherwise permissible regulation of speech may represent a governmental 'attempt to give one side of a debatable public question an advantage in expressing its views to the people.'" *City of Ladue v. Gilleo* (1994). At least on the record before us, however, the statutory exemption for clinic employees and agents acting within the scope of their employment does not appear to be such an attempt.

There is nothing inherently suspect about providing some kind of exemption to allow individuals who work at the clinics to enter or remain within the buffer zones. In particular, the exemption cannot be regarded as simply a carve-out for the clinic escorts; it also covers employees such as the maintenance worker shoveling a snowy sidewalk or the security guard patrolling a clinic entrance.

Given the need for an exemption for clinic employees, the "scope of their employment" qualification simply ensures that the exemption is limited to its purpose of allowing the employees to do their jobs. It performs the same function as the identical "scope of their employment" restriction on the exemption for "law enforcement, ambulance, fire-fighting, construction, utilities, public works and other municipal agents." . . . The limitation . . . makes clear—with respect to both clinic employees and municipal agents—that exempted individuals are allowed inside the zones only to perform those acts authorized by their employers. There is no suggestion in the record that any of the clinics authorize their employees to speak about abortion in the buffer zones. The "scope of their employment" limitation thus seems designed to protect against exactly the sort of conduct that petitioners and Justice Scalia fear.

Petitioners did testify in this litigation about instances in which escorts at the Boston clinic had expressed views about abortion to the women they were accompanying, thwarted petitioners' attempts to speak and hand literature to the women, and disparaged petitioners in various ways. It is unclear from petitioners' testimony whether these alleged incidents occurred within the buffer zones. There is no viewpoint discrimination problem if the incidents occurred outside the zones because petitioners are equally free to say whatever they would like in that area.

Even assuming the incidents occurred inside the zones, the record does not suggest that they involved speech within the scope of the escorts' employment. If the speech was beyond the scope of their employment, then each of the alleged incidents would violate the Act's express terms. Petitioners' complaint would then be that the police were failing to *enforce* the Act equally against clinic escorts. . . .

It would be a very different question if it turned out that a clinic authorized escorts to speak about abortion inside the buffer zones. In that case, the escorts would not seem to be violating the Act because the speech would be within the scope of their employment. The Act's exemption for clinic employees would then facilitate speech on only one side of the abortion debate—a clear form of viewpoint discrimination that would support an as-applied challenge to the buffer zone at that clinic. But the record before us contains insufficient evidence to show that the exemption operates in this way at any of the clinics, perhaps because the clinics do not want to doom the Act by allowing their employees to speak about abortion within the buffer zones.[1]

We thus conclude that the Act is neither content nor viewpoint based and therefore need not be analyzed under strict scrutiny.

1. Of course we do not hold that "[s]peech restrictions favoring one viewpoint over another are not content based unless it can be shown that the favored viewpoint has actually been expressed." *Post.* We instead apply an uncontroversial principle of constitutional adjudication: that a plaintiff generally cannot prevail on an *as-applied* challenge without showing that the law has in fact been (or is sufficiently likely to be) unconstitutionally *applied* to him. Specifically, when someone challenges a law as viewpoint discriminatory but it is not clear from the face of the law which speakers will be allowed to speak, he must show that he was prevented from speaking while someone espousing another viewpoint was permitted to do so. Justice Scalia can decry this analysis as "astonishing" only by quoting a sentence that is explicitly limited to as-applied challenges and treating it as relevant to facial challenges. *Ibid.*

IV

Even though the Act is content neutral, it still must be "narrowly tailored to serve a significant governmental interest." *Ward*. . . . For a content-neutral time, place, or manner regulation to be narrowly tailored, it must not "burden substantially more speech than is necessary to further the government's legitimate interests." *Ward*. Such a regulation, unlike a content-based restriction of speech, "need not be the least restrictive or least intrusive means of" serving the government's interests. But the government still "may not regulate expression in such a manner that a substantial portion of the burden on speech does not serve to advance its goals."

A

As noted, respondents claim that the Act promotes "public safety, patient access to healthcare, and the unobstructed use of public sidewalks and roadways." . . . The buffer zones clearly serve these interests.

At the same time, the buffer zones impose serious burdens on petitioners' speech. At each of the three Planned Parenthood clinics where petitioners attempt to counsel patients, the zones carve out a significant portion of the adjacent public sidewalks, pushing petitioners well back from the clinics' entrances and driveways. The zones thereby compromise petitioners' ability to initiate the close, personal conversations that they view as essential to "sidewalk counseling." . . .

The buffer zones have also made it substantially more difficult for petitioners to distribute literature to arriving patients. As explained, because petitioners in Boston cannot readily identify patients before they enter the zone, they often cannot approach them in time to place literature near their hands—the most effective means of getting the patients to accept it. In Worcester and Springfield, the zones have pushed petitioners so far back from the clinics' driveways that they can no longer even attempt to offer literature as drivers turn into the parking lots. In short, the Act operates to deprive petitioners of their two primary methods of communicating with patients. . . .

In the context of petition campaigns, we have observed that "one-on-one communication" is "the most effective, fundamental, and perhaps economical avenue of political discourse." *Meyer v. Grant* (1988). And "handing out leaflets in the advocacy of a politically controversial viewpoint . . . is the essence of First Amendment expression"; "[n]o form of speech is entitled to greater constitutional protection." *McIntyre v. Ohio Elections Comm'n* (1995). When the government makes it more difficult to engage in these modes of communication, it imposes an especially significant First Amendment burden.

Respondents also emphasize that the Act does not prevent petitioners from engaging in various forms of "protest"—such as chanting slogans and displaying signs—outside the buffer zones. That misses the point. Petitioners are not protestors. They seek not merely to express their opposition to abortion, but to inform women of various alternatives and to provide help in pursuing them.

Petitioners believe that they can accomplish this objective only through personal, caring, consensual conversations. And for good reason: It is easier to ignore a strained voice or a waving hand than a direct greeting or an outstretched arm. While the record indicates that petitioners have been able to have a number of quiet conversations outside the buffer zones, respondents have not refuted petitioners' testimony that the conversations have been far less frequent and far less successful since the buffer zones were instituted. It is thus no answer to say that petitioners can still be "seen and heard" by women within the buffer zones. If all that the women can see and hear are vociferous opponents of abortion, then the buffer zones have effectively stifled petitioners' message.

Finally, respondents suggest that, at the Worcester and Springfield clinics, petitioners are prevented from communicating with patients not by the buffer zones but by the fact that most patients arrive by car and park in the clinics' private lots. It is true that the layout of the two clinics would prevent petitioners from approaching the clinics' *doorways,* even without the buffer zones. But petitioners do not claim a right to trespass on the clinics' property. They instead claim a right to stand on the public sidewalks by the driveway as cars turn into the parking lot. Before the buffer zones, they could do so. Now they must stand a substantial distance away. The Act alone is responsible for that restriction on their ability to convey their message.

B

1

The buffer zones burden substantially more speech than necessary to achieve the Commonwealth's asserted interests. At the outset, we note that the Act is truly exceptional: Respondents and their *amici* identify no other State with a law that creates fixed buffer zones around abortion clinics. That of course does not mean that the law is invalid. It does, however, raise concern that the Commonwealth has too readily forgone options that could serve its interests just as well, without substantially burdening the kind of speech in which petitioners wish to engage.

That is the case here. The Commonwealth's interests include ensuring public safety outside abortion clinics, preventing harassment and intimidation of patients and clinic staff, and combating deliberate obstruction of clinic entrances. The Act itself contains a separate provision, subsection (e)—unchallenged by petitioners—that prohibits much of this conduct. . . .

The Commonwealth points to a substantial public safety risk created when protestors obstruct driveways leading to the clinics. That is, however, an example of its failure to look to less intrusive means of addressing its concerns. Any such obstruction can readily be addressed through existing local ordinances.

All of the foregoing measures are, of course, in addition to available generic criminal statutes forbidding assault, breach of the peace, trespass, vandalism, and the like. . . .

The Commonwealth also asserts an interest in preventing congestion in front of abortion clinics. According to respondents, even when individuals do not deliberately obstruct access to clinics, they can inadvertently do so simply by gathering in large numbers. But the Commonwealth could address that problem through more targeted means. Some localities, for example, have ordinances that require crowds blocking a clinic entrance to disperse when ordered to do so by the police, and that forbid the individuals to reassemble within a certain distance of the clinic for a certain period. . . .

And to the extent the Commonwealth argues that even these types of laws are ineffective, it has another problem. The portions of the record that respondents cite to support the anticongestion interest pertain mainly to one place at one time: the Boston Planned Parenthood clinic on Saturday mornings. Respondents point us to no evidence that individuals regularly gather at other clinics, or at other times in Boston, in sufficiently large groups to obstruct access. For a problem shown to arise only once a week in one city at one clinic, creating 35-foot buffer zones at every clinic across the Commonwealth is hardly a narrowly tailored solution. . . .

2

Respondents have but one reply: "We have tried other approaches, but they do not work." Respondents emphasize the history in Massachusetts of obstruction at abortion clinics, and the Commonwealth's allegedly failed attempts to combat such obstruction with injunctions and individual prosecutions. They also point to the Commonwealth's experience under the 2000 version of the Act, during which the police found it difficult to enforce the six-foot no-approach zones given the "frenetic" activity in front of clinic entrances. According to respondents, this history shows that Massachusetts has tried less restrictive alternatives to the buffer zones, to no avail.

We cannot accept that contention. Although respondents claim that Massachusetts "tried other laws already on the books," they identify not a single prosecution brought under those laws within at least the last 17 years. And while they also claim that the Commonwealth "tried injunctions," the last injunctions they cite date to the 1990s. In short, the Commonwealth has not shown that it seriously undertook to address the problem with less intrusive tools readily available to it. Nor has it shown that it considered different methods that other jurisdictions have found effective. . . .

To meet the requirement of narrow tailoring, the government must demonstrate that alternative measures that burden substantially less speech would fail to achieve the government's interests, not simply that the chosen route is easier. A painted line on the sidewalk is easy to enforce, but the prime objective of the First Amendment is not efficiency. In any case, we do not think that showing intentional obstruction is nearly so difficult in this context as respondents suggest. To determine whether a protestor intends to block access to a clinic, a police officer need only order him to move. If he refuses, then there is no question that his continued conduct is knowing or intentional. . . .

Given the vital First Amendment interests at stake, it is not enough for Massachusetts simply to say that other approaches have not worked.[2]

* * *

Petitioners wish to converse with their fellow citizens about an important subject on the public streets and sidewalks—sites that have hosted discussions about the issues of the day throughout history. Respondents assert undeniably significant interests in maintaining public safety on those same streets and sidewalks, as well as in preserving access to adjacent healthcare facilities. But here the Commonwealth has pursued those interests by the extreme step of closing a substantial portion of a traditional public forum to all speakers. It has done so without seriously addressing the problem through alternatives that leave the forum open for its time-honored purposes. The Commonwealth may not do that consistent with the First Amendment.

The judgment of the Court of Appeals for the First Circuit is reversed, and the case is remanded for further proceedings consistent with this opinion.

It is so ordered.

JUSTICE SCALIA, with whom JUSTICE KENNEDY and JUSTICE THOMAS join, concurring in the judgment.

Today's opinion carries forward this Court's practice of giving abortion-rights advocates a pass when it comes to suppressing the free-speech rights of their opponents. There is an entirely separate, abridged edition of the First Amendment applicable to speech against abortion.

The second half of the Court's analysis today, invalidating the law at issue because of inadequate "tailoring," is certainly attractive to those of us who oppose an abortion-speech edition of the First Amendment. But think again. This is an opinion that has Something for Everyone, and the more significant portion continues the onward march of abortion-speech-only jurisprudence. That is the first half of the Court's analysis, which concludes that a statute of this sort is not content based and hence not subject to so-called strict scrutiny. The Court reaches out to decide that question unnecessarily—or at least unnecessarily insofar as legal analysis is concerned

I disagree with the Court's dicta (Part III) and hence see no reason to opine on its holding (Part IV).

I. THE COURT'S CONTENT-NEUTRALITY DISCUSSION IS UNNECESSARY

The gratuitous portion of today's opinion is Part III, which concludes—in seven pages of the purest dicta—that subsection (b) of the Massachusetts Reproductive Health Care Facilities Act is not specifically directed at speech

2. Because we find that the Act is not narrowly tailored, we need not consider whether the Act leaves open ample alternative channels of communication. Nor need we consider petitioners' overbreadth challenge.

opposing (or even concerning) abortion and hence need not meet the strict-scrutiny standard applicable to content-based speech regulations. . . .

II. The Statute Is Content Based and Fails Strict Scrutiny

Having eagerly volunteered to take on the level-of-scrutiny question, the Court provides the wrong answer. Petitioners argue for two reasons that subsection (b) articulates a content-based speech restriction — and that we must therefore evaluate it through the lens of strict scrutiny.

A. Application to Abortion Clinics Only

First, petitioners maintain that the Act targets abortion-related — for practical purposes, abortion-opposing — speech because it applies outside abortion clinics only (rather than outside other buildings as well). . . . Every objective indication shows that the provision's primary purpose is to restrict speech that opposes abortion.

I begin, as suggested above, with the fact that the Act burdens only the public spaces outside abortion clinics. . . . [A]lthough the statute applies to all abortion clinics in Massachusetts, only one is known to have been beset by the problems that the statute supposedly addresses. The Court uses this striking fact (a smoking gun, so to speak) as a basis for concluding that the law is insufficiently "tailored" to safety and access concerns (Part IV) rather than as a basis for concluding that it is not *directed* to those concerns at all, but to the suppression of antiabortion speech. That is rather like invoking the eight missed human targets of a shooter who has killed one victim to prove, not that he is guilty of attempted mass murder, but that *he has bad aim.*

Whether the statute "restrict[s] more speech than necessary" in light of the problems that it allegedly addresses is, to be sure, relevant to the tailoring component of the First Amendment analysis (the shooter doubtless did have bad aim), but it is also relevant — powerfully relevant — to whether the law is really directed to safety and access concerns or rather to the suppression of a particular type of speech. Showing that a law that suppresses speech on a specific subject is so far-reaching that it applies even when the asserted non-speech-related problems are not present is persuasive evidence that the law is content based. In its zeal to treat abortion-related speech as a special category, the majority distorts not only the First Amendment but also the ordinary logic of probative inferences.

The structure of the Act also indicates that it rests on content-based concerns. The goals of "public safety, patient access to healthcare, and the unobstructed use of public sidewalks and roadways," are already achieved by an earlier-enacted subsection of the statute, which provides criminal penalties for "[a]ny person who knowingly obstructs, detains, hinders, impedes or blocks another person's entry to or exit from a reproductive health care facility." As the majority recognizes, that provision is easy to enforce. Thus, the speech-free zones carved out by subsection (b) add nothing to safety and access; what they achieve, and what they were obviously designed to achieve, is the suppression of speech opposing abortion.

Further contradicting the Court's fanciful defense of the Act is the fact that subsection (b) was enacted as a more easily enforceable substitute for a prior provision. That provision did not exclude people entirely from the restricted areas around abortion clinics; rather, it forbade people in those areas to approach within six feet of another person *without that person's consent* "for the purpose of passing a leaflet or handbill to, displaying a sign to, or engaging in oral protest, education or counseling with such other person." As the majority acknowledges, that provision was "modeled on a . . . Colorado law that this Court had upheld in *Hill*." And in that case, the Court recognized that the statute in question was directed at the suppression of unwelcome speech, vindicating what *Hill* called "[t]he unwilling listener's interest in avoiding unwanted communication." The Court held that interest to be content neutral.

The provision at issue here was indisputably meant to serve the same interest in protecting citizens' supposed right to avoid speech that they would rather not hear. For that reason, we granted a second question for review in this case (though one would not know that from the Court's opinion, which fails to mention it): whether *Hill* should be cut back or cast aside. The majority avoids that question by declaring the Act content neutral on other (entirely unpersuasive) grounds. In concluding that the statute is content based and therefore subject to strict scrutiny, I necessarily conclude that *Hill* should be overruled. Reasons for doing so are set forth in the dissents in that case, and in the abundance of scathing academic commentary describing how *Hill* stands in contradiction to our First Amendment jurisprudence.[3] Protecting people from speech they do not want to hear is not a function that the First Amendment allows the government to undertake in the public streets and sidewalks. . . .

B. EXEMPTION FOR ABORTION-CLINIC EMPLOYEES OR AGENTS

Petitioners contend that the Act targets speech opposing abortion (and thus constitutes a presumptively invalid viewpoint-discriminatory restriction) for another reason as well: It exempts "employees or agents" of an abortion clinic "acting within the scope of their employment."

It goes without saying that "[g]ranting waivers to favored speakers (or . . . denying them to disfavored speakers) would of course be unconstitutional." *Thomas v. Chicago Park Dist.* (2002). The majority opinion . . . jumps right over the prong that asks whether the provision "draw[s] . . . distinctions on its face," and instead proceeds directly to the purpose-related prong asking whether the

3. *Hill* . . . is inexplicable on standard free-speech grounds[,] and . . . it is shameful the Supreme Court would have upheld this piece of legislation on the reasoning that it gave." Constitutional Law Symposium, Professor Michael W. McConnell's Response, 28 Pepperdine L. Rev. 747 (2001). "I don't think [*Hill*] was a difficult case. I think it was slam-dunk simple and slam-dunk wrong." *Id.*, at 750 (remarks of Laurence Tribe). The list could go on.

exemption "represent[s] a governmental attempt to give one side of a debatable public question an advantage in expressing its views to the people," (internal quotation marks omitted). I disagree with the majority's negative answer to that question, but that is beside the point if the text of the statute—whatever its purposes might have been—"license[s] one side of a debate to fight freestyle, while requiring the other to follow Marquis of Queensberry rules." *R.A.V. v. St. Paul* (1992).

Is there any serious doubt that *abortion-clinic employees or agents* "acting within the scope of their employment" near clinic entrances may—indeed, often will—speak in favor of abortion ("You are doing the right thing")? Or speak in opposition to the message of abortion opponents—saying, for example, that "this is a safe facility" to rebut the statement that it is not? See Tr. of Oral Arg. The Court's contrary assumption is simply incredible. And the majority makes no attempt to establish the further necessary proposition that abortion-clinic employees and agents do not engage in nonspeech activities directed to the suppression of antiabortion speech by hampering the efforts of counselors to speak to prospective clients. Are we to believe that a clinic employee sent out to "escort" prospective clients into the building would not seek to prevent a counselor like Eleanor McCullen from communicating with them? He could pull a woman away from an approaching counselor, cover her ears, or make loud noises to drown out the counselor's pleas. . . .

The Court takes the peculiar view that, so long as the clinics have not specifically authorized their employees to speak in favor of abortion (or, presumably, to impede antiabortion speech), there is no viewpoint discrimination. But it is axiomatic that "where words are employed in a statute which had at the time a well-known meaning at common law or in the law of this country[,] they are presumed to have been used in that sense unless the context compels to the contrary." *Standard Oil Co. of N.J. v. United States* (1911). The phrase "scope of employment" is a well-known common-law concept that includes "[t]he range of reasonable and foreseeable activities that an employee engages in while carrying out the employer's business." Black's Law Dictionary (9th ed. 2009). The employer need not specifically direct or sanction each aspect of an employee's conduct for it to qualify. Indeed, employee conduct can qualify even if the employer specifically forbids it. In any case, it is implausible that clinics would bar escorts from engaging in the sort of activity mentioned above. Moreover, a statute that forbids one side but not the other to convey its message does not become viewpoint neutral simply because the favored side chooses voluntarily to abstain from activity that the statute permits.

There is not a shadow of a doubt that the assigned or foreseeable conduct of a clinic employee or agent can include both speaking in favor of abortion rights and countering the speech of people like petitioners. Indeed, as the majority acknowledges, the trial record includes testimony that escorts at the Boston clinic "expressed views about abortion to the women they were accompanying, thwarted petitioners' attempts to speak and hand literature to the women, and disparaged petitioners in various ways," including by calling them " 'crazy.' " What a surprise! The Web site for the Planned Parenthood League of Massachusetts (which operates the three abortion facilities where petitioners attempt to counsel women), urges readers to "Become a Clinic Escort Volunteer" in order to "provide a safe space for patients by escorting them through protestors to the health center." The dangers that the Web site attributes to "protestors" are related entirely to speech, not to safety or access. "Protestors," it reports, "hold signs, try to speak to patients entering the building, and distribute literature that can be misleading." The "safe space" provided by escorts is protection from that speech.

Going from bad to worse, the majority's opinion contends that "the record before us contains insufficient evidence to show" that abortion-facility escorts have actually spoken in favor of abortion (or, presumably, hindered antiabortion speech) while acting within the scope of their employment. Here is a brave new First Amendment test: Speech restrictions favoring one viewpoint over another are not content based unless it can be shown that the favored viewpoint has actually been expressed. A city ordinance closing a park adjoining the Republican National Convention to all speakers except those whose remarks have been approved by the Republican National Committee is thus not subject to strict scrutiny unless it can be shown that someone has given committee-endorsed remarks. For this Court to suggest such a test is astonishing.[4]

C. CONCLUSION

In sum, the Act should be reviewed under the strict-scrutiny standard applicable to content-based legislation. That standard requires that a regulation represent "the least restrictive means" of furthering "a compelling Government interest." *United States v. Playboy Entertainment Group, Inc.* (2000) (internal quotation marks omitted). Respondents do not even attempt to argue that subsection (b) survives this test. "Suffice it to say that if protecting people from unwelcome communications"—the actual purpose of the provision—"is a compelling state interest, the First Amendment is a dead letter." *Hill* (Scalia, J., dissenting).

---

4. The Court states that I can make this assertion "only by quoting a sentence that is explicitly limited to as-applied challenges and treating it as relevant to facial challenges." That is not so. The sentence in question appears in a paragraph immediately following rejection of the facial challenge, which begins: "It would be a very different question if it turned out that a clinic authorized escorts to speak about abortion inside the buffer zones." And the prior discussion regarding the facial challenge points to the fact that "[t]here is no suggestion in the record that any of the clinics authorize their employees to speak about abortion in the buffer zones." To be sure, the paragraph in question then goes on to concede only that the statute's constitutionality *as applied* would depend upon explicit clinic authorization. Even that seems to me wrong. Saying that voluntary action by a third party can cause an otherwise valid statute to violate the First Amendment as applied seems to me little better than saying it can cause such a statute to violate the First Amendment facially. A statute that punishes me for speaking unless *x* chooses to speak is unconstitutional facially and as applied, without reference to *x*'s action.

III. NARROW TAILORING

. . . The obvious purpose of the challenged portion of the Massachusetts Reproductive Health Care Facilities Act is to "protect" prospective clients of abortion clinics from having to hear abortion-opposing speech on public streets and sidewalks. The provision is thus unconstitutional root and branch and cannot be saved, as the majority suggests, by limiting its application to the single facility that has experienced the safety and access problems to which it is quite obviously not addressed. I concur only in the judgment that the statute is unconstitutional under the First Amendment.

JUSTICE ALITO, concurring in the judgment.

I agree that the Massachusetts statute at issue in this case violates the First Amendment. As the Court recognizes, if the Massachusetts law discriminates on the basis of viewpoint, it is unconstitutional, and I believe the law clearly discriminates on this ground. . . .

It is clear on the face of the Massachusetts law that it discriminates based on viewpoint. Speech in favor of the clinic and its work by employees and agents is permitted; speech criticizing the clinic and its work is a crime. This is blatant viewpoint discrimination. . . .

In this case, I do not think that it is possible to reach a judgment about the intent of the Massachusetts Legislature without taking into account the fact that the law that the legislature enacted blatantly discriminates based on viewpoint. In light of this feature, as well as the overbreadth that the Court identifies, it cannot be said, based on the present record, that the law would be content neutral even if the exemption for clinic employees and agents were excised. However, if the law were truly content neutral, I would agree with the Court that the law would still be unconstitutional on the ground that it burdens more speech than is necessary to serve the Commonwealth's asserted interests.

ASSIGNMENT S-10

What Constitutes "Speech"?

Does Money Equal Speech?

STUDY GUIDE:

- The next case continues the line of cases we have been studying in which the Roberts Court is using the First Amendment to increasingly constrain the power of Congress to regulate the financing of campaigns.
- As we have already seen, its technique is to limit the purpose for which such restrictions can be imposed to the prevention of quid pro quo corruption (and its appearance).
- In contrast, the dissent takes a broader view of the appropriate use of Congress's power (or perhaps a narrower view of what the First Amendment prohibits).

McCUTCHEON v. FEDERAL ELECTION COMMISSION

No. 12-536

Argued Oct. 8, 2013 | Decided Apr. 2, 2014

Chief Justice Roberts announced the judgment of the Court and delivered an opinion, in which Justice Scalia, Justice Kennedy, and Justice Alito join.

There is no right more basic in our democracy than the right to participate in electing our political leaders. Citizens can exercise that right in a variety of ways: They can run for office themselves, vote, urge others to vote for a particular candidate, volunteer to work on a campaign, and contribute to a candidate's campaign. This case is about the last of those options.

The right to participate in democracy through political contributions is protected by the First Amendment, but that right is not absolute. Our cases have held that Congress may regulate campaign contributions to protect against corruption or the appearance of corruption. See, *e.g., Buckley v. Valeo* (1976). At the same time, we have made clear that Congress may not regulate contributions simply to reduce the amount of money in politics, or to restrict the political participation of some in order to enhance the relative influence of others. See, *e.g., Arizona Free Enterprise Club's Freedom Club PAC v. Bennett (2011).*

Many people might find those latter objectives attractive: They would be delighted to see fewer television commercials touting a candidate's accomplishments or disparaging an opponent's character. Money in politics may at times seem repugnant to some, but so too does much of what the First Amendment vigorously protects. If the First Amendment protects flag burning, funeral protests, and Nazi parades—despite the profound offense such spectacles cause—it surely protects political campaign speech despite popular opposition. See *Texas v. Johnson* (1989); *Snyder v. Phelps* (2011); *National Socialist Party of America v. Skokie* (1977). Indeed, as we have emphasized, the First Amendment "has its fullest and most urgent application precisely to the conduct of campaigns for political office." *Monitor Patriot Co. v. Roy* (1971).

In a series of cases over the past 40 years, we have spelled out how to draw the constitutional line between the permissible goal of avoiding corruption in the political process and the impermissible desire simply to limit political speech. We have said that government regulation may not target the general gratitude a candidate may feel toward those who support him or his allies, or the political access such support may afford. "Ingratiation and access . . . are not corruption." *Citizens United v. Federal Election Comm'n* (2010). They embody a central feature of democracy—that constituents support candidates who share their beliefs and interests, and candidates who are elected can be expected to be responsive to those concerns.

Any regulation must instead target what we have called "*quid pro quo*" corruption or its appearance. That Latin phrase captures the notion of a direct exchange of an official act for money. "The hallmark of corruption is the financial *quid pro quo*: dollars for political favors." *Federal Election Comm'n v. National Conservative Political Action Comm.* (1985). Campaign finance restrictions that pursue other objectives, we have explained, impermissibly inject the Government "into the debate over who should govern." *Bennett*. And those who govern should be the *last* people to help decide who *should* govern.

The statute at issue in this case imposes two types of limits on campaign contributions. The first, called base limits, restricts how much money a donor may contribute to a particular candidate or committee. The second, called aggregate limits, restricts how much money a donor may contribute in total to all candidates or committees.

This case does not involve any challenge to the base limits, which we have previously upheld as serving the permissible objective of combatting corruption. The Government contends that the aggregate limits also serve that objective, by preventing circumvention of the base limits. We conclude, however, that the aggregate limits do little, if anything, to address that concern, while seriously restricting participation in the democratic process. The aggregate limits are therefore invalid under the First Amendment. . . .

II

A

Buckley v. Valeo presented this Court with its first opportunity to evaluate the constitutionality of the original contribution and expenditure limits set forth in FECA. . . . [I]n one paragraph of its 139-page opinion, the Court turned to the $25,000 aggregate limit under FECA. As a preliminary matter, it noted that the constitutionality of the aggregate limit "ha[d] not been separately addressed at length by the parties." Then, in three sentences, the Court disposed of any constitutional objections to the aggregate limit that the challengers might have had:

> The overall $25,000 ceiling does impose an ultimate restriction upon the number of candidates and committees with which an individual may associate himself by means of financial support. But this quite modest restraint upon protected political activity serves to prevent evasion of the $1,000 contribution limitation by a person who might otherwise contribute massive amounts of money to a particular candidate through the use of unearmarked contributions to political committees likely to contribute to that candidate, or huge contributions to the candidate's political party. The limited, additional restriction on associational freedom imposed by the overall ceiling is thus no more than a corollary of the basic individual contribution limitation that we have found to be constitutionally valid.

B

. . .

2

Buckley treated the constitutionality of the $25,000 aggregate limit as contingent upon that limit's ability to prevent circumvention of the $1,000 base limit, describing the aggregate limit as "no more than a corollary" of the base limit. The Court determined that circumvention could occur when an individual legally contributes "massive amounts of money to a particular candidate through the use of unearmarked contributions" to entities that are themselves likely to contribute to the candidate. For that reason, the Court upheld the $25,000 aggregate limit.

Although *Buckley* provides some guidance, we think that its ultimate conclusion about the constitutionality of the aggregate limit in place under FECA does not control here. *Buckley* spent a total of three sentences analyzing that limit; in fact, the opinion pointed out that the constitutionality of the aggregate limit "ha[d] not been separately addressed at length by the parties." We are now asked to address appellants' direct challenge to the aggregate limits in place under BCRA. BCRA is a different statutory regime, and the aggregate limits it imposes operate against a distinct legal backdrop.

Most notably, statutory safeguards against circumvention have been considerably strengthened since *Buckley* was decided, through both statutory additions and the introduction of a comprehensive regulatory scheme. With more targeted anticircumvention measures in place today, the indiscriminate aggregate limits under BCRA appear particularly heavy-handed. . . .

We are confronted with a different statute and different legal arguments, at a different point in the development of campaign finance regulation. Appellants' substantial First Amendment challenge to the system of aggregate limits currently in place thus merits our plenary consideration.

III

The First Amendment "is designed and intended to remove governmental restraints from the arena of public discussion, putting the decision as to what views shall be voiced largely into the hands of each of us, . . . in the belief that no other approach would comport with the premise of individual dignity and choice upon which our political system rests." *Cohen v. California* (1971). As relevant here, the First Amendment safeguards an individual's right to participate in the public debate through political expression and political association. When an individual contributes money to a candidate, he exercises both of those rights: The contribution "serves as a general expression of support for the candidate and his views" and "serves to affiliate a person with a candidate." . . .

Buckley acknowledged that aggregate limits at least diminish an individual's right of political association. As the Court explained, the "overall $25,000 ceiling does impose an ultimate restriction upon the number of candidates and committees with which an individual may associate himself by means of financial support." But the Court characterized that restriction as a "quite modest restraint upon protected political activity." We cannot agree with that characterization. An aggregate limit on *how many* candidates and committees an individual may support through contributions is not a "modest restraint" at all. The Government may no more restrict how many candidates or causes a donor may support than it may tell a newspaper how many candidates it may endorse.

To put it in the simplest terms, the aggregate limits prohibit an individual from fully contributing to the primary and general election campaigns of ten or more candidates, even if all contributions fall within the base limits Congress views as adequate to protect against corruption. The individual may give up to $5,200 each to nine candidates, but the aggregate limits constitute an outright ban on further contributions to any other candidate (beyond the additional $1,800 that may be spent before reaching the $48,600 aggregate limit). At that point, the limits deny the individual all ability to exercise his expressive and associational rights by contributing to someone who will advocate for his policy preferences. A donor must limit the number of candidates he supports, and may have to choose which of several policy concerns he will advance—clear First Amendment harms that the dissent never acknowledges.

It is no answer to say that the individual can simply contribute less money to more people. To require one person to contribute at lower levels than others because he wants to support more candidates or causes is to impose a special burden on broader participation in the democratic process. And as we have recently admonished, the Government may not penalize an individual for "robustly exercis[ing]" his First Amendment rights. *Davis.*

The First Amendment burden is especially great for individuals who do not have ready access to alternative avenues for supporting their preferred politicians and policies. In the context of base contribution limits, *Buckley* observed that a supporter could vindicate his associational interests by personally volunteering his time and energy on behalf of a candidate. Such personal volunteering is not a realistic alternative for those who wish to support a wide variety of candidates or causes. Other effective methods of supporting preferred candidates or causes without contributing money are reserved for a select few, such as entertainers capable of raising hundreds of thousands of dollars in a single evening.

The dissent faults this focus on "the individual's right to engage in political speech," saying that it fails to take into account "the public's interest" in "collective speech." This "collective" interest is said to promote "a government where laws reflect the very thoughts, views, ideas, and sentiments, the expression of which the First Amendment protects."

But there are compelling reasons not to define the boundaries of the First Amendment by reference to such a generalized conception of the public good. First, the dissent's "collective speech" reflected in laws is of course the will of the majority, and plainly can include laws that restrict free speech. The whole point of the First Amendment is to afford individuals protection against such infringements. The First Amendment does not protect the government, even when the government purports to act through legislation reflecting "collective speech."

Second, the degree to which speech is protected cannot turn on a legislative or judicial determination that particular speech is useful to the democratic process. The First Amendment does not contemplate such "ad hoc balancing of relative social costs and benefits." *Stevens.*

Third, our established First Amendment analysis already takes account of any "collective" interest that may justify restrictions on individual speech. Under that accepted analysis, such restrictions are measured against the asserted public interest (usually framed as an important or compelling governmental interest). As explained below, we do not doubt the compelling nature of the "collective" interest in preventing corruption in the electoral process. But we permit Congress to pursue that interest only so long as it does not unnecessarily infringe an individual's right to freedom of speech; we do not truncate this tailoring test at the outset.

IV

A

With the significant First Amendment costs for individual citizens in mind, we turn to the governmental interests asserted in this case. This Court has identified only one legitimate governmental interest for restricting campaign finances: preventing corruption or the appearance of corruption. We have consistently rejected attempts to suppress campaign speech based on other legislative objectives. No matter how desirable it may seem, it is not an acceptable governmental objective to "level the playing field," or to "level electoral opportunities," or to "equaliz[e] the financial resources of candidates." *Bennett.* The First Amendment prohibits such legislative attempts to "fine-tun[e]" the electoral process, no matter how well intentioned. *Bennett.*

As we framed the relevant principle in *Buckley,* "the concept that government may restrict the speech of some elements of our society in order to enhance the relative voice of others is wholly foreign to the First Amendment." The dissent's suggestion that *Buckley* supports the opposite proposition simply ignores what *Buckley* actually said on the matter.

Moreover, while preventing corruption or its appearance is a legitimate objective, Congress may target only a specific type of corruption — "*quid pro quo*" corruption. As *Buckley* explained, Congress may permissibly seek to rein in "large contributions [that] are given to secure a political *quid pro quo* from current and potential office holders." In addition to "actual *quid pro quo* arrangements," Congress may permissibly limit "the appearance of corruption stemming from public awareness of the opportunities for abuse inherent in a regime of large individual financial contributions" to particular candidates.

Spending large sums of money in connection with elections, but not in connection with an effort to control the exercise of an officeholder's official duties, does not give rise to such *quid pro quo* corruption. Nor does the possibility that an individual who spends large sums may garner "influence over or access to" elected officials or political parties. And because the Government's interest in preventing the appearance of corruption is equally confined to the appearance of *quid pro quo* corruption, the Government may not seek to limit the appearance of mere influence or access. . . .

The dissent advocates a broader conception of corruption, and would apply the label to any individual contributions above limits deemed necessary to protect "collective speech." Thus, under the dissent's view, it is perfectly fine to contribute $5,200 to nine candidates but somehow corrupt to give the same amount to a tenth. . . . The definition of corruption that we apply today, however, has firm roots in *Buckley* itself. . . .

The line between *quid pro quo* corruption and general influence may seem vague at times, but the distinction must be respected in order to safeguard basic First Amendment rights. In addition, "[i]n drawing that line, the First Amendment requires us to err on the side of protecting political speech rather than suppressing it." *Federal Election Comm'n v. Wisconsin Right to Life* (2007) (opinion of Roberts, C.J.).

The dissent laments that our opinion leaves only remnants of FECA and BCRA that are inadequate to combat corruption. Such rhetoric ignores the fact that we leave the base limits undisturbed. Those base limits remain the primary means of regulating campaign contributions—the obvious explanation for why the aggregate limits received a scant few sentences of attention in *Buckley*.

B

"When the Government restricts speech, the Government bears the burden of proving the constitutionality of its actions." *United States v. Playboy Entertainment Group, Inc.* (2000). Here, the Government seeks to carry that burden by arguing that the aggregate limits further the permissible objective of preventing *quid pro quo* corruption.

The difficulty is that once the aggregate limits kick in, they ban all contributions of *any* amount. But Congress's selection of a $5,200 base limit indicates its belief that contributions of that amount or less do not create a cognizable risk of corruption. If there is no corruption concern in giving nine candidates up to $5,200 each, it is difficult to understand how a tenth candidate can be regarded as corruptible if given $1,801, and all others corruptible if given a dime. And if there is no risk that additional candidates will be corrupted by donations of up to $5,200, then the Government must defend the aggregate limits by demonstrating that they prevent circumvention of the base limits. . . .

As an initial matter, there is not the same risk of *quid pro quo* corruption or its appearance when money flows through independent actors to a candidate, as when a donor contributes to a candidate directly. When an individual contributes to a candidate, a party committee, or a PAC, the individual must by law cede control over the funds. The Government admits that if the funds are subsequently re-routed to a particular candidate, such action occurs at the initial recipient's discretion—not the donor's. As a consequence, the chain of attribution grows longer, and any credit must be shared among the various actors along the way. For those reasons, the risk of *quid pro quo* corruption is generally applicable only to "the narrow category of money gifts that are directed, in some manner, to a candidate or officeholder." *McConnell* (opinion of Kennedy, J.).

Buckley nonetheless focused on the possibility that "unearmarked contributions" could eventually find their way to a candidate's coffers. Even accepting the validity of *Buckley*'s circumvention theory, it is hard to see how a candidate today could receive a "massive amount[ ] of money" that could be traced back to a particular contributor uninhibited by the aggregate limits. The Government offers a series of scenarios in support of that possibility. But each is sufficiently implausible that the Government has not carried its burden of demonstrating that the aggregate limits further its anticircumvention interest. . . .

The primary example of circumvention, in one form or another, envisions an individual donor who contributes the maximum amount under the base limits to a particular candidate, say, Representative Smith. Then the donor also channels "massive amounts of money" to Smith through a series of contributions to PACs that have stated their intention to support Smith.

Various earmarking and antiproliferation rules disarm this example. Importantly, the donor may not contribute to the most obvious PACs: those that support only Smith. Nor may the donor contribute to the slightly less obvious PACs that he knows will route "a substantial portion" of his contribution to Smith.

The donor must instead turn to other PACs that are likely to give to Smith. When he does so, however, he discovers that his contribution will be significantly diluted by all the contributions from others to the same PACs. After all, the donor cannot give more than $5,000 to a PAC and so cannot dominate the PAC's total receipts, as he could when *Buckley* was decided. He cannot retain control over his contribution, direct his money "in any way" to Smith, or even *imply* that he would like his money to be recontributed to Smith. His salience as a Smith supporter has been diminished, and with it the potential for corruption.

It is not clear how many candidates a PAC must support before our dedicated donor can avoid being tagged with the impermissible knowledge that "a substantial portion" of his contribution will go to Smith. But imagine that the donor is one of ten equal donors to a PAC that gives the highest possible contribution to Smith. The PAC may give no more than $2,600 per election to Smith. Of that sum, just $260 will be attributable to the donor intent on circumventing the base limits. Thus far he has hardly succeeded in funneling "massive amounts of money" to Smith. *Buckley*.

But what if this donor does the same thing via, say, 100 different PACs? His $260 contribution will balloon to $26,000, ten times what he may contribute directly to Smith in any given election. . . . [I]t is hard to believe that a rational actor would engage in such machinations. In the example described, a dedicated donor spent $500,000—donating the full $5,000 to 100 different PACs—to add just $26,000 to Smith's campaign coffers. That same donor, meanwhile, could have spent unlimited funds on independent expenditures on behalf of Smith. Indeed, he could have spent his entire $500,000 advocating for Smith, without the risk that his selected PACs would choose not to give to Smith, or that he would have to share credit with other contributors to the PACs.

We have said in the context of independent expenditures that " '[t]he absence of prearrangement and coordination of an expenditure with the candidate or his agent . . . undermines the value of the expenditure to the candidate.' " *Citizens United*. But probably not by 95 percent. And at least from the *donor's* point of view, it strikes us as far more likely that he will want to see his full $500,000 spent on behalf of his favored candidate—even if it must be spent independently—rather than see it diluted to a small fraction so that it can be contributed directly by someone else. . . .

These scenarios, along with others that have been suggested, are either illegal under current campaign finance laws or divorced from reality. The three examples posed by the dissent are no exception. The dissent does not explain how the large sums it postulates can be legally rerouted to a particular candidate, why most state committees would participate in a plan to redirect their donations to a candidate in another State, or how a donor or group of donors can avoid regulations prohibiting contributions to a committee "with the knowledge that a substantial portion" of the contribution will support a candidate to whom the donor has already contributed. . . .

Buckley upheld aggregate limits only on the ground that they prevented channeling money to candidates beyond the base limits. The absence of such a prospect today belies the Government's asserted objective of preventing corruption or its appearance. The improbability of circumvention indicates that the aggregate limits instead further the impermissible objective of simply limiting the amount of money in political campaigns.

C

Quite apart from the foregoing, the aggregate limits violate the First Amendment because they are not "closely drawn to avoid unnecessary abridgment of associational freedoms." *Buckley*. In the First Amendment context, fit matters. Even when the Court is not applying strict scrutiny, we still require "a fit that is not necessarily perfect, but reasonable; that represents not necessarily the single best disposition but one whose scope is 'in proportion to the interest served,' . . . that employs not necessarily the least restrictive means but . . . a means narrowly tailored to achieve the desired objective." *Board of Trustees of State Univ. of N.Y. v. Fox* (1989). Here, because the statute is poorly tailored to the Government's interest in preventing circumvention of the base limits, it impermissibly restricts participation in the political process.

1

The Government argues that the aggregate limits are justified because they prevent an individual from giving to too many initial recipients who might subsequently recontribute a donation. After all, only recontributed funds can conceivably give rise to circumvention of the base limits. Yet all indications are that many types of recipients have scant interest in regifting donations they receive. . . .

Based on what we can discern from experience, the indiscriminate ban on all contributions above the aggregate limits is disproportionate to the Government's interest in preventing circumvention. The Government has not given us any reason to believe that parties or candidates would dramatically shift their priorities if the aggregate limits were lifted. Absent such a showing, we cannot conclude that the sweeping aggregate limits are appropriately tailored to guard against any contributions that might implicate the Government's anticircumvention interest.

A final point: It is worth keeping in mind that the *base limits* themselves are a prophylactic measure. As we have explained, "restrictions on direct contributions are preventative, because few if any contributions to candidates will involve *quid pro quo* arrangements." *Citizens United.* The aggregate limits are then layered on top, ostensibly to prevent circumvention of the base limits. This "prophylaxis-upon-prophylaxis approach" requires that we be particularly diligent in scrutinizing the law's fit. *Wisconsin Right to Life* (opinion of Roberts, C.J.).

2

Importantly, there are multiple alternatives available to Congress that would serve the Government's anticircumvention interest, while avoiding "unnecessary abridgment" of First Amendment rights. *Buckley.* The most obvious might involve targeted restrictions on transfers among candidates and political committees. . . .

One possible option for restricting transfers would be to require contributions above the current aggregate limits to be deposited into segregated, nontransferable accounts and spent only by their recipients. Such a solution would address the same circumvention possibilities as the current aggregate limits, while not completely barring contributions beyond the aggregate levels. In addition (or as an alternative), if Congress believes that circumvention is especially likely to occur through creation of a joint fundraising committee, it could require that funds received through those committees be spent by their recipients (or perhaps it could simply limit the size of joint fundraising committees). Such alternatives to the aggregate limits properly refocus the inquiry on the delinquent actor: the recipient of a contribution within the base limits, who then routes the money in a manner that undermines those limits. . . .

We do not mean to opine on the validity of any particular proposal. The point is that there are numerous alternative approaches available to Congress to prevent circumvention of the base limits. . . .

* * *

For the past 40 years, our campaign finance jurisprudence has focused on the need to preserve authority for the Government to combat corruption, without at the same time compromising the political responsiveness at the heart of the democratic process, or allowing the Government to favor some participants in that process over others. As Edmund Burke explained in his famous speech to the electors of Bristol, a representative owes constituents the exercise of his "mature judgment," but judgment informed by "the strictest union, the closest correspondence, and the most unreserved communication with his constituents."

The Speeches of the Right Hon. Edmund Burke 129-130 (J. Burke ed. 1867). Constituents have the right to support candidates who share their views and concerns. Representatives are not to follow constituent orders, but can be expected to be cognizant of and responsive to those concerns. Such responsiveness is key to the very concept of self-governance through elected officials.

The Government has a strong interest, no less critical to our democratic system, in combatting corruption and its appearance. We have, however, held that this interest must be limited to a specific kind of corruption—*quid pro quo* corruption—in order to ensure that the Government's efforts do not have the effect of restricting the First Amendment right of citizens to choose who shall govern them. For the reasons set forth, we conclude that the aggregate limits on contributions do not further the only governmental interest this Court accepted as legitimate in *Buckley*. They instead intrude without justification on a citizen's ability to exercise "the most fundamental First Amendment activities." *Buckley*.

The judgment of the District Court is reversed, and the case is remanded for further proceedings.

It is so ordered.

JUSTICE THOMAS, concurring in the judgment.

I adhere to the view that this Court's decision in *Buckley v. Valeo* (1976) (*per curiam*), denigrates core First Amendment speech and should be overruled. . . . I am wholly in agreement with the plurality's conclusion on this point: "[T]he Government may not penalize an individual for 'robustly exercis[ing]' his First Amendment rights." I regret only that the plurality does not acknowledge that today's decision, although purporting not to overrule *Buckley,* continues to chip away at its footings.

In sum, what remains of *Buckley* is a rule without a rationale. Contributions and expenditures are simply "two sides of the same First Amendment coin," and our efforts to distinguish the two have produced mere "word games" rather than any cognizable principle of constitutional law. *Buckley* (Burger, C.J., concurring in part and dissenting in part). For that reason, I would overrule *Buckley* and subject the aggregate limits in BCRA to strict scrutiny, which they would surely fail.

This case represents yet another missed opportunity to right the course of our campaign finance jurisprudence by restoring a standard that is faithful to the First Amendment. Until we undertake that reexamination, we remain in a "halfway house" of our own design. For these reasons, I concur only in the judgment.

JUSTICE BREYER, with whom JUSTICE GINSBURG, JUSTICE SOTOMAYOR, and JUSTICE KAGAN join, dissenting.

Nearly 40 years ago in *Buckley* v. *Valeo*, this Court considered the constitutionality of laws that imposed limits upon the overall amount a single person can contribute to all federal candidates, political parties, and committees taken together. The Court held that those limits did not violate the Constitution. The *Buckley* Court focused upon the same problem that concerns the Court today, and it wrote:

> The overall $25,000 ceiling does impose an ultimate restriction upon the number of candidates and committees with which an individual may associate himself by means of financial support. But this quite modest restraint upon protected political activity serves to prevent evasion of the $1,000 contribution limitation by a person who might otherwise contribute massive amounts of money to a particular candidate through the use of unearmarked contributions to political committees likely to contribute to that candidate, or huge contributions to the candidate's political party. The limited, additional restriction on associational freedom imposed by the overall ceiling is thus no more than a corollary of the basic individual contribution limitation that we have found to be constitutionally valid.

Today a majority of the Court overrules this holding. It is wrong to do so. Its conclusion rests upon its own, not a record-based, view of the facts. Its legal analysis is faulty: It misconstrues the nature of the competing constitutional interests at stake. It understates the importance of protecting the political integrity of our governmental institutions. It creates a loophole that will allow a single individual to contribute millions of dollars to a political party or to a candidate's campaign. Taken together with *Citizens United v. Federal Election Comm'n* (2010), today's decision eviscerates our Nation's campaign finance laws, leaving a remnant incapable of dealing with the grave problems of democratic legitimacy that those laws were intended to resolve.

I

The plurality concludes that the aggregate contribution limits " 'unnecessar[ily] abridg[e]' " First Amendment rights. Aggregate contribution ceilings limit an individual's ability to engage in such "broader participation in the democratic process," while insufficiently advancing any legitimate governmental objective. Hence, the plurality finds, they violate the Constitution. . . .

II

The plurality's first claim—that large aggregate contributions do not "give rise" to "corruption"—is plausible only because the plurality defines "corruption" too narrowly. The plurality describes the constitutionally permissible objective of campaign finance regulation as follows: "Congress may target only a specific type of corruption—'*quid pro quo*' corruption." It then defines *quid pro quo* corruption to mean no more than "a direct exchange of an official act for money"—an act akin to bribery. It adds specifically that corruption does *not* include efforts to "garner 'influence over or access to' elected officials or political parties." Moreover, the Government's efforts to prevent the "appearance of corruption" are "equally confined to the appearance of *quid pro quo* corruption," as narrowly defined. In the plurality's view, a federal statute could not prevent an individual from writing a million dollar check to a political party (by donating to its various committees), because the rationale for any limit would "dangerously broade[n] the circumscribed definition of *quid pro quo* corruption articulated in our prior cases."

This critically important definition of "corruption" is inconsistent with the Court's prior case law (with the possible exception of *Citizens United,* as I will explain below). It is virtually impossible to reconcile with this Court's decision in *McConnell,* upholding the Bipartisan Campaign Reform Act of 2002 (BCRA). And it misunderstands the constitutional importance of the interests at stake. In fact, constitutional interests—indeed, First Amendment interests—lie on both sides of the legal equation.

A

. . . Speech does not exist in a vacuum. Rather, political communication seeks to secure government action. A politically oriented "marketplace of ideas" seeks to form a public opinion that can and will influence elected representatives. . . . Accordingly, the First Amendment advances not only the individual's right to engage in political speech, but also the public's interest in preserving a democratic order in which collective speech *matters*. . . .

Corruption breaks the constitutionally necessary "chain of communication" between the people and their representatives. It derails the essential speech-to-government-action tie. Where enough money calls the tune, the general public will not be heard. Insofar as corruption cuts the link between political thought and political action, a free marketplace of political ideas loses its point. That is one reason why the Court has stressed the constitutional importance of Congress' concern that a few large donations not drown out the voices of the many. . . .

The "appearance of corruption" can make matters worse. It can lead the public to believe that its efforts to communicate with its representatives or to help sway public opinion have little purpose. And a cynical public can lose interest in political participation altogether. Democracy, the Court has often said, cannot work unless "the people have faith in those who govern." *United States v. Mississippi Valley Generating Co.* (1961).

The upshot is that the interests the Court has long described as preventing "corruption" or the "appearance of corruption" are more than ordinary factors to be weighed against the constitutional right to political speech. Rather, they are interests rooted in the First Amendment itself. They are rooted in the constitutional effort to create a democracy responsive to the people—a government where laws reflect the very thoughts, views, ideas, and sentiments, the expression of which the First Amendment protects. Given that end, we can and should understand campaign finance laws as resting upon a broader and more significant constitutional rationale than the plurality's limited definition of "corruption" suggests. We should see these laws as seeking in significant part to strengthen, rather than weaken, the First Amendment. To say this is not to deny the potential for conflict between (1) the need to permit contributions that pay for the diffusion of ideas, and (2) the need to limit payments in order to help maintain the integrity of the electoral process. But that conflict takes place within, not outside, the First Amendment's boundaries.

B

Since the kinds of corruption that can destroy the link between public opinion and governmental action extend well beyond those the plurality describes, the plurality's notion of corruption is flatly inconsistent with the basic constitutional rationale I have just described. Thus, it should surprise no one that this Court's case law (*Citizens United* excepted) insists upon a considerably broader definition. . . .

C

Most important, in *McConnell,* this Court considered the constitutionality of the Bipartisan Campaign Reform Act of 2002, an Act that set new limits on "soft money" contributions to political parties. . . . The Court in *McConnell* upheld these new contribution restrictions under the First Amendment for the very reason the plurality today discounts or ignores. Namely, the Court found they thwarted a significant risk of corruption—understood not as *quid pro quo* bribery, but as privileged access to and pernicious influence upon elected representatives. . . .

We specifically rejected efforts to define "corruption" in ways similar to those the plurality today accepts. We added: "Just as troubling to a functioning democracy as classic *quid pro quo* corruption is the danger that officeholders will decide issues not on the merits or the desires of their constituencies, but according to the wishes of those who have made large financial contributions valued by the officeholder."

Insofar as today's decision sets forth a significantly narrower definition of "corruption," and hence of the public's interest in political integrity, it is flatly inconsistent with *McConnell.*

D

One case, however, contains language that offers the plurality support. That case is *Citizens United.* There, as the plurality points out, the Court said that "[w]hen *Buckley* identified a sufficiently important governmental interest in preventing corruption or the appearance of corruption, that interest was limited to *quid pro quo* corruption." Further, the Court said that *quid pro quo* corruption does not include "influence over or access to elected officials," because " 'generic favoritism or influence theory . . . is at odds with standard First Amendment analyses.' "

How should we treat these statements from *Citizens United* now? They are not essential to the Court's holding in the case—at least insofar as it can be read to require federal law to treat corporations and trade unions like individuals when they independently pay for, *e.g.,* television advertising during the last 60 days of a federal election. Taken literally, the statements cited simply refer to and characterize still-earlier Court cases. They do not require the more absolute reading that the plurality here gives them.

More than that. Read as the plurality reads them today, the statements from *Citizens United* about the proper contours of the corruption rationale conflict not just with language in the *McConnell* opinion, but with *McConnell*'s very holding. . . . So: Does the Court intend today to overrule *McConnell*? Or does it intend to leave *McConnell* and BCRA in place? The plurality says the latter. But how does the plurality explain its rejection of the broader definition of corruption, upon which *McConnell*'s holding depends?

III

. . . Here, as in *Buckley*, in the absence of limits on aggregate political contributions, donors can and likely will find ways to channel millions of dollars to parties and to individual candidates, producing precisely the kind of "corruption" or "appearance of corruption" that previously led the Court to hold aggregate limits constitutional. Those opportunities for circumvention will also produce the type of corruption that concerns the plurality today. The methods for using today's opinion to evade the law's individual contribution limits are complex, but they are well known, or will become well known, to party fundraisers. I shall describe three.

A

Example One: Gifts for the Benefit of the Party. Campaign finance law permits each individual to give $64,800 over two years to a national party committee. The two major political parties each have three national committees. Federal law also entitles an individual to give $20,000 to a state party committee over two years. Each major political party has 50 such committees. Those individual limits mean that, in the absence of any aggregate limit, an individual could legally give to the Republican Party or to the Democratic Party about $1.2 million over two years. To make it easier for contributors to give gifts of this size, each party could create a "Joint Party Committee," comprising all of its national and state party committees. . . . A contributor could then write a single check to the Joint Party Committee—and its staff would divide the funds so that each constituent unit receives no more than it could obtain from the contributor directly ($64,800 for a national committee over two years, $20,000 for a state committee over the same). Before today's decision, the total size of Rich Donor's check to the Joint Party Committee was capped at $74,600—the aggregate limit for donations to political parties over a 2-year election cycle. After today's decision, Rich Donor can write a single check to the Joint Party Committee in an amount of about $1.2 million. . . . Will elected officials be particularly grateful to the large donor, feeling obliged to provide him special access and influence, and perhaps even a *quid pro quo* legislative favor? That is what we have previously believed. See *McConnell* ("Large soft-money donations at a candidate's or officeholder's behest give rise to all of the same corruption concerns posed by contributions made directly to the candidate or officeholder"). And . . . we have believed this with good reason.

Example Two: Donations to Individual Candidates (The $3.6 Million Check). The first example significantly *understates* the problem. That is because federal election law also allows a single contributor to give $5,200 to each party candidate over a 2-year election cycle (assuming the candidate is running in both a primary and a general election). There are 435 party candidates for House seats and 33 party candidates for Senate seats in any given election year. That makes an additional $2.4 million in allowable contributions. Thus, without an aggregate limit, the law will permit a wealthy individual to write a check, over a 2-year election cycle, for $3.6 million—all to benefit his political party and its candidates. . . . The law will also permit a party and its candidates to shift most of Rich Donor's contributions to a *single* candidate, say Smith. Here is how:

The law permits each candidate and each party committee in the Smith Victory Committee to write Candidate Smith a check directly. For his primary and general elections combined, they can write checks of up to $4,000 (from each candidate's authorized campaign committee) and $10,000 (from each state and national committee). This yields a potential $1,872,000 (from candidates) plus $530,000 (from party committees). Thus, the law permits the candidates and party entities to redirect $2.37 million of Rich Donor's $3.6 million check to Candidate Smith. It also permits state and national committees to contribute to Smith's general election campaign through making coordinated expenditures—in amounts that range from $46,600 to $2.68 million for a general election (depending upon the size of Smith's State and whether he is running for a House or Senate seat).

The upshot is that Candidate Smith can receive at least $2.37 million and possibly the full $3.6 million contributed by Rich Donor to the Smith Victory Committee, even though the funds must first be divided up among the constituent units before they can be rerouted to Smith. . . .

Example Three: Proliferating Political Action Committees (PACs). Campaign finance law . . . does not prohibit an individual from contributing (within the current $123,200 biannual aggregate limit) $5,000 to each of an unlimited total number of PACs. And there, so to speak, lies the rub.

Here is how, without any aggregate limits, a party will be able to channel $2 million from each of ten Rich Donors to each of ten Embattled Candidates. Groups of party supporters—individuals, corporations, or trade unions—create 200 PACs. Each PAC claims it will use the funds it raises to support several candidates from the party, though it will favor those who are most endangered. . . . Over a 2-year election cycle, Rich Donor One gives $10,000 to each PAC ($5,000 per year)—yielding $2 million total. Rich Donor 2 does the same. So, too, do the other eight Rich Donors. This brings their total donations to $20 million, disbursed among the 200 PACs. Each PAC will have collected $100,000, and each can use its money to write ten checks of $10,000—to each of the ten most Embattled Candidates in the party (over two years). Every Embattled Candidate, receiving a $10,000 check from 200 PACs, will have collected $2 million.

The upshot is that ten Rich Donors will have contributed $2 million each, and ten Embattled Candidates will have collected $2 million each. In this example, unlike *Example Two,* the recipient candidates may not know which of the ten Rich Donors is personally responsible for the $2 million he or she receives. But the recipient candidate is highly likely to know who the ten Rich Donors are, and to feel appropriately grateful. . . .

B

. . . The plurality believes that the three scenarios I have just depicted either pose no threat, or cannot or will not take place. It does not believe the scenario depicted in *Example One* is any cause for concern, because it involves only "general, broad-based support of a political party." Not so. A candidate who solicits a multimillion dollar check for his party will be deeply grateful to the checkwriter, and surely could reward him with a *quid pro quo* favor. The plurality discounts the scenarios depicted in *Example Two* and *Example Three* because it finds such circumvention tactics "illegal under current campaign finance laws," "implausible," or "divorced from reality." But they are not.

The plurality's view depends in large part upon its claim that since this Court decided *Buckley* in 1976, changes in either statutory law or in applicable regulations have come to make it difficult, if not impossible, for these circumvention scenarios to arise. Hence, it concludes, there is no longer a need for aggregate contribution limits. But a closer examination of the five legal changes to which the plurality points makes clear that those changes cannot effectively stop the abuses that I have depicted. . . .

[For example,] . . . the plurality points to [an] FEC regulation . . . , which says that "an individual who has contributed to a candidate" may not "also contribute to a political committee that has supported or anticipates supporting the same candidate if the individual knows that 'a substantial portion [of his contribution] will be contributed to, or expended on behalf of,' that candidate." This regulation is important, for in principle, the FEC might use it to prevent the circumstances that *Examples Two* and *Three* set forth from arising. And it is not surprising that the plurality relies upon the existence of this rule when it describes those circumstances as "implausible," "illegal," or "divorced from reality."

In fact, however, this regulation is not the strong anti-circumvention weapon that the plurality imagines. Despite the plurality's assurances, it does not "disarm" the possibilities for circumvention. That is because the regulation requires a showing that donors have "*knowledge* that a substantial portion" of their contributions will be used by a PAC to support a candidate to whom they have already contributed. §110.1(h)(2) (emphasis added). And "knowledge" is hard to prove. . . .

IV

The plurality concludes that even if circumvention were a threat, the aggregate limits are "poorly tailored" to address it. The First Amendment requires " 'a fit that is . . . reasonable,' " and there is no such "fit" here because there are several alternative ways Congress could prevent evasion of the base limits. . . . The plurality, however, does not show, or try to show, that these hypothetical alternatives could effectively replace aggregate contribution limits. Indeed, it does not even "opine on the validity of any particular proposal,"—presumably because these proposals themselves could be subject to constitutional challenges. For the most part, the alternatives the plurality mentions were similarly available at the time of *Buckley.* Their hypothetical presence did not prevent the Court from upholding aggregate limits in 1976. How can their continued hypothetical presence lead the plurality now to conclude that aggregate limits are "poorly tailored"? How can their continued hypothetical presence lead the Court to overrule *Buckley* now?

In sum, the explanation of why aggregate limits are needed is complicated, as is the explanation of why other methods will not work. But the conclusion is simple: There is no "substantial mismatch" between Congress' legitimate objective and the "means selected to achieve it." The Court, as in *Buckley*, should hold that aggregate contribution limits are constitutional.

V

. . . The justification for aggregate contribution restrictions is strongly rooted in the need to assure political integrity and ultimately in the First Amendment itself. The threat to that integrity posed by the risk of special access and influence remains real. Even taking the plurality on its own terms and considering solely the threat of *quid pro quo* corruption (*i.e.,* money-for-votes exchanges), the aggregate limits are a necessary tool to stop circumvention. And there is no basis for finding a lack of "fit" between the threat and the means used to combat it, namely the aggregate limits.

The plurality reaches the opposite conclusion. The result, as I said at the outset, is a decision that substitutes judges' understandings of how the political process works for the understanding of Congress; that fails to recognize the difference between influence resting upon public opinion and influence bought by money alone; that overturns key precedent; that creates huge loopholes in the law; and that undermines, perhaps devastates, what remains of campaign finance reform.

With respect, I dissent.

Chapter 8

The Free Exercise of Religion

ASSIGNMENT S-11

Applying the Religious Freedom Restoration Act

STUDY GUIDE:

- As we saw in *O Centro*, the *Smith* doctrine was rejected by Congress when it enacted the Religious Freedom Restoration Act (RFRA). Although the Supreme Court in *City of Boerne v. Flores* held that Congress had exceeded its powers under the Fourteenth Amendment when it applied the heightened standard of RFRA to the states, Congress was free to impose on *itself* by statute an approach that was more accommodating to religious free exercise.
- The next case is a much discussed application of RFRA to federal regulations adopted by the Obama administration pursuant to the Affordable Care Act. These regulations required employers that provided health insurance to their employees to include insurance coverage for certain specified forms of contraceptives.
- So, when reading the opinions, it is important to remember that this is not a First Amendment case, but one of statutory interpretation. On the other hand, there is some dispute between the majority and the dissent about whether RFRA imported the entirety of the Supreme Court doctrine (like *Sherbert*) that preceded *Smith*, or whether the Supreme Court is free to apply the statute more broadly or narrowly than the pre-*Smith* doctrine applied the First Amendment.

BURWELL, SECRETARY OF HEALTH AND HUMAN SERVICES, et al. v. HOBBY LOBBY STORES, INC.

Nos. 13-354 and 13-356

Argued Mar. 25, 2014 | Decided June 30, 2014

JUSTICE ALITO delivered the opinion of the Court.

We must decide in these cases whether the Religious Freedom Restoration Act of 1993 (RFRA) permits the United States Department of Health and Human

Services (HHS) to demand that three closely held corporations provide health-insurance coverage for methods of contraception that violate the sincerely held religious beliefs of the companies' owners. We hold that the regulations that impose this obligation violate RFRA, which prohibits the Federal Government from taking any action that substantially burdens the exercise of religion unless that action constitutes the least restrictive means of serving a compelling government interest.

In holding that the HHS mandate is unlawful, we reject HHS's argument that the owners of the companies forfeited all RFRA protection when they decided to organize their businesses as corporations rather than sole proprietorships or general partnerships. The plain terms of RFRA make it perfectly clear that Congress did not discriminate in this way against men and women who wish to run their businesses as for-profit corporations in the manner required by their religious beliefs.

Since RFRA applies in these cases, we must decide whether the challenged HHS regulations substantially burden the exercise of religion, and we hold that they do. The owners of the businesses have religious objections to abortion, and according to their religious beliefs the four contraceptive methods at issue are abortifacients. If the owners comply with the HHS mandate, they believe they will be facilitating abortions, and if they do not comply, they will pay a very heavy price—as much as $1.3 million per day, or about $475 million per year, in the case of one of the companies. If these consequences do not amount to a substantial burden, it is hard to see what would.

Under RFRA, a Government action that imposes a substantial burden on religious exercise must serve a compelling government interest, and we assume that the HHS regulations satisfy this requirement. But in order for the HHS mandate to be sustained, it must also constitute the least restrictive means of serving that interest, and the mandate plainly fails that test.[1] There are other ways in which Congress or HHS could equally ensure that every woman has cost-free access to the particular contraceptives at issue here and, indeed, to all FDA-approved contraceptives.

In fact, HHS has already devised and implemented a system that seeks to respect the religious liberty of religious nonprofit corporations while ensuring that the employees of these entities have precisely the same access to all FDA-approved contraceptives as employees of companies whose owners have no religious objections to providing such coverage. The employees of these religious nonprofit corporations still have access to insurance coverage without cost sharing for all FDA-approved contraceptives; and according to HHS, this system imposes no net economic burden on the insurance companies that are required to provide or secure the coverage.

---

1. In *City of Boerne v. Flores* (1997), we wrote that RFRA's "least restrictive means requirement was not used in the pre-*Smith* jurisprudence RFRA purported to codify." On this understanding of our pre-*Smith* cases, RFRA did more than merely restore the balancing test used in the *Sherbert* line of cases; it provided even broader protection for religious liberty than was available under those decisions. [This footnote appears in a portion of the opinion omitted from this excerpt.—Ed.]

Although HHS has made this system available to religious nonprofits that have religious objections to the contraceptive mandate, HHS has provided no reason why the same system cannot be made available when the owners of for-profit corporations have similar religious objections. We therefore conclude that this system constitutes an alternative that achieves all of the Government's aims while providing greater respect for religious liberty. And under RFRA, that conclusion means that enforcement of the HHS contraceptive mandate against the objecting parties in these cases is unlawful.

As this description of our reasoning shows, our holding is very specific. We do not hold, as the principal dissent alleges, that for-profit corporations and other commercial enterprises can "opt out of any law (saving only tax laws) they judge incompatible with their sincerely held religious beliefs." Nor do we hold, as the dissent implies, that such corporations have free rein to take steps that impose "disadvantages . . . on others" or that require "the general public [to] pick up the tab." And we certainly do not hold or suggest that "RFRA demands accommodation of a for-profit corporation's religious beliefs no matter the impact that accommodation may have on . . . thousands of women employed by Hobby Lobby." The effect of the HHS-created accommodation on the women employed by Hobby Lobby and the other companies involved in these cases would be precisely zero. Under that accommodation, these women would still be entitled to all FDA-approved contraceptives without cost sharing. . . .

I

. . .

B

At issue in these cases are HHS regulations promulgated under the Patient Protection and Affordable Care Act of 2010 (ACA). ACA generally requires employers with 50 or more full-time employees to offer "a group health plan or group health insurance coverage" that provides "minimum essential coverage." Any covered employer that does not provide such coverage must pay a substantial price. Specifically, if a covered employer provides group health insurance but its plan fails to comply with ACA's group-health-plan requirements, the employer may be required to pay $100 per day for each affected "individual." And if the employer decides to stop providing health insurance altogether and at least one full-time employee enrolls in a health plan and qualifies for a subsidy on one of the government-run ACA exchanges, the employer must pay $2,000 per year for each of its full-time employees.

Unless an exception applies, ACA requires an employer's group health plan or group-health-insurance coverage to furnish "preventive care and screenings" for women without "any cost sharing requirements." Congress itself, however, did not specify what types of preventive care must be covered. Instead, Congress authorized the Health Resources and Services Administration (HRSA), a component of HHS, to make that important and sensitive decision. The HRSA in turn consulted the Institute of Medicine, a nonprofit group of volunteer advisers, in determining which preventive services to require.

In August 2011, based on the Institute's recommendations, the HRSA promulgated the Women's Preventive Services Guidelines. The Guidelines provide that nonexempt employers are generally required to provide "coverage, without cost sharing" for "[a]ll Food and Drug Administration [(FDA)] approved contraceptive methods, sterilization procedures, and patient education and counseling." Although many of the required, FDA-approved methods of contraception work by preventing the fertilization of an egg, four of those methods (those specifically at issue in these cases) may have the effect of preventing an already fertilized egg from developing any further by inhibiting its attachment to the uterus.

HHS also authorized the HRSA to establish exemptions from the contraceptive mandate for "religious employers." That category encompasses "churches, their integrated auxiliaries, and conventions or associations of churches," as well as "the exclusively religious activities of any religious order." In its Guidelines, HRSA exempted these organizations from the requirement to cover contraceptive services.

In addition, HHS has effectively exempted certain religious nonprofit organizations, described under HHS regulations as "eligible organizations," from the contraceptive mandate. An "eligible organization" means a nonprofit organization that "holds itself out as a religious organization" and "opposes providing coverage for some or all of any contraceptive services required to be covered . . . on account of religious objections." To qualify for this accommodation, an employer must certify that it is such an organization. When a group-health-insurance issuer receives notice that one of its clients has invoked this provision, the issuer must then exclude contraceptive coverage from the employer's plan and provide separate payments for contraceptive services for plan participants without imposing any cost-sharing requirements on the eligible organization, its insurance plan, or its employee beneficiaries. Although this procedure requires the issuer to bear the cost of these services, HHS has determined that this obligation will not impose any net expense on issuers because its cost will be less than or equal to the cost savings resulting from the services.

In addition to these exemptions for religious organizations, ACA exempts a great many employers from most of its coverage requirements. Employers providing "grandfathered health plans"—those that existed prior to March 23, 2010, and that have not made specified changes after that date—need not comply with many of the Act's requirements, including the contraceptive mandate. And employers with fewer than 50 employees are not required to provide health insurance at all.

All told, the contraceptive mandate "presently does not apply to tens of millions of people." This is attributable, in large part, to grandfathered health plans: Over one-third of the 149 million nonelderly people in America with employer-sponsored health plans were enrolled in grandfathered plans in 2013. The count for employees working for firms that do not have to provide insurance at all because they employ fewer than 50 employees is 34 million workers.

II

A

Norman and Elizabeth Hahn and their three sons are devout members of the Mennonite Church, a Christian denomination. The Mennonite Church opposes abortion and believes that "[t]he fetus in its earliest stages . . . shares humanity with those who conceived it."

Fifty years ago, Norman Hahn started a wood-working business in his garage, and since then, this company, Conestoga Wood Specialties, has grown and now has 950 employees. Conestoga is organized under Pennsylvania law as a for-profit corporation. The Hahns exercise sole ownership of the closely held business; they control its board of directors and hold all of its voting shares. One of the Hahn sons serves as the president and CEO. . . .

The Hahns and Conestoga sued HHS and other federal officials and agencies under RFRA and the Free Exercise Clause of the First Amendment, seeking to enjoin application of ACA's contraceptive mandate insofar as it requires them to provide health-insurance coverage for four FDA-approved contraceptives that may operate after the fertilization of an egg. These include two forms of emergency contraception commonly called "morning after" pills and two types of intrauterine devices.

In opposing the requirement to provide coverage for the contraceptives to which they object, the Hahns argued that "it is immoral and sinful for [them] to intentionally participate in, pay for, facilitate, or otherwise support these drugs." The District Court denied a preliminary injunction, and the Third Circuit affirmed in a divided opinion, holding that "for-profit, secular corporations cannot engage in religious exercise" within the meaning of RFRA or the First Amendment. The Third Circuit also rejected the claims brought by the Hahns themselves because it concluded that the HHS "[m]andate does not impose any requirements on the Hahns" in their personal capacity.

B

David and Barbara Green and their three children are Christians who own and operate two family businesses. Forty-five years ago, David Green started an arts-and-crafts store that has grown into a nationwide chain called Hobby Lobby. There are now 500 Hobby Lobby stores, and the company has more than 13,000 employees. Hobby Lobby is organized as a for-profit corporation under Oklahoma law.

One of David's sons started an affiliated business, Mardel, which operates 35 Christian bookstores and employs close to 400 people. Mardel is also organized as a for-profit corporation under Oklahoma law.

Though these two businesses have expanded over the years, they remain closely held, and David, Barbara, and their children retain exclusive control of both companies. David serves as the CEO of Hobby Lobby, and his three children serve as the president, vice president, and vice CEO. . . .

Like the Hahns, the Greens believe that life begins at conception and that it would violate their religion to facilitate access to contraceptive drugs or devices that operate after that point. They specifically object to the same four contraceptive methods as the Hahns and, like the Hahns, they have no objection to the other 16 FDA-approved methods of birth control. Although their group-health-insurance plan predates the enactment of ACA, it is not a grandfathered plan because Hobby Lobby elected not to retain grandfathered status before the contraceptive mandate was proposed.

The Greens, Hobby Lobby, and Mardel sued HHS and other federal agencies and officials to challenge the contraceptive mandate under RFRA and the Free Exercise Clause. The District Court denied a preliminary injunction, and the plaintiffs appealed, moving for initial en banc consideration. The Tenth Circuit granted that motion and reversed in a divided opinion. Contrary to the conclusion of the Third Circuit, the Tenth Circuit held that the Greens' two for-profit businesses are "persons" within the meaning of RFRA and therefore may bring suit under that law.

The court then held that the corporations had established a likelihood of success on their RFRA claim. The court concluded that the contraceptive mandate substantially burdened the exercise of religion by requiring the companies to choose between "compromis[ing] their religious beliefs" and paying a heavy fee—either "close to $475 million more in taxes every year" if they simply refused to provide coverage for the contraceptives at issue, or "roughly $26 million" annually if they "drop[ped] health-insurance benefits for all employees."

The court next held that HHS had failed to demonstrate a compelling interest in enforcing the mandate against the Greens' businesses and, in the alternative, that HHS had failed to prove that enforcement of the mandate was the "least restrictive means" of furthering the Government's asserted interests. After concluding that the companies had "demonstrated irreparable harm," the court reversed and remanded for the District Court to consider the remaining factors of the preliminary-injunction test.

We granted certiorari.

III

A

RFRA prohibits the "Government [from] substantially burden[ing] *a person's* exercise of religion even if the burden results from a rule of general applicability" unless the Government "demonstrates that application of the burden to *the person*—(1) is in furtherance of a compelling governmental interest; and (2) is the least restrictive means of furthering that compelling governmental interest." The first question that we must address is whether this provision applies to regulations that govern the activities of for-profit corporations like Hobby Lobby, Conestoga, and Mardel.

HHS contends that neither these companies nor their owners can even be heard under RFRA. According to HHS, the companies cannot sue because they seek to make a profit for their owners, and the owners cannot be heard because the regulations, at least as a formal matter, apply only to the companies and not to the owners as individuals. HHS's argument would have dramatic consequences.

Consider this Court's decision in *Braunfeld v. Brown* (1961) (plurality opinion). In that case, five Orthodox Jewish merchants who ran small retail businesses in Philadelphia challenged a Pennsylvania Sunday closing law as a violation of the Free Exercise Clause. Because of their faith, these merchants closed their shops on Saturday, and they argued that requiring them to remain shut on Sunday threatened them with financial ruin. The Court entertained their claim (although it ruled against them on the merits), and if a similar claim were raised today under RFRA against a jurisdiction still subject to the Act, the merchants would be entitled to be heard. According to HHS, however, if these merchants chose to incorporate their businesses — without in any way changing the size or nature of their businesses — they would forfeit all RFRA (and free-exercise) rights. HHS would put these merchants to a difficult choice: either give up the right to seek judicial protection of their religious liberty or forgo the benefits, available to their competitors, of operating as corporations.

As we have seen, RFRA was designed to provide very broad protection for religious liberty. By enacting RFRA, Congress went far beyond what this Court has held is constitutionally required. Is there any reason to think that the Congress that enacted such sweeping protection put small-business owners to the choice that HHS suggests? An examination of RFRA's text, to which we turn in the next part of this opinion, reveals that Congress did no such thing. . . .

B

1

As we noted above, RFRA applies to "a person's" exercise of religion, and RFRA itself does not define the term "person." We therefore look to the Dictionary Act, which we must consult "[i]n determining the meaning of any Act of Congress, unless the context indicates otherwise."

Under the Dictionary Act, "the wor[d] 'person' . . . include[s] corporations, companies, associations, firms, partnerships, societies, and joint stock companies, as well as individuals." Thus, unless there is something about the RFRA context that "indicates otherwise," the Dictionary Act provides a quick, clear, and affirmative answer to the question whether the companies involved in these cases may be heard.

We see nothing in RFRA that suggests a congressional intent to depart from the Dictionary Act definition, and HHS makes little effort to argue otherwise. We have entertained RFRA and free-exercise claims brought by nonprofit corporations, see *Gonzales v. O Centro Esprita Beneficiente Unio do Vegetal* (RFRA); *Hosanna-Tabor Evangelical Lutheran Church and School v. EEOC* (2012) (Free Exercise); *Church of the Lukumi Babalu Aye, Inc. v. Hialeah* (1993) (Free Exercise), and HHS concedes that a nonprofit corporation can be a "person" within the meaning of RFRA.

This concession effectively dispatches any argument that the term "person" as used in RFRA does not reach the closely held corporations involved in these cases. No known understanding of the term "person" includes *some* but not all corporations. The term "person" sometimes encompasses artificial persons (as the Dictionary Act instructs), and it sometimes is limited to natural persons. But no conceivable definition of the term includes natural persons and nonprofit corporations, but not for-profit corporations.

2

The principal argument advanced by HHS and the principal dissent regarding RFRA protection for Hobby Lobby, Conestoga, and Mardel focuses not on the statutory term "person," but on the phrase "exercise of religion." According to HHS and the dissent, these corporations are not protected by RFRA because they cannot exercise religion. Neither HHS nor the dissent, however, provides any persuasive explanation for this conclusion.

Is it because of the corporate form? The corporate form alone cannot provide the explanation because, as we have pointed out, HHS concedes that nonprofit corporations can be protected by RFRA. . . .

If the corporate form is not enough, what about the profit-making objective? In *Braunfeld*, we entertained the free-exercise claims of individuals who were attempting to make a profit as retail merchants, and the Court never even hinted that this objective precluded their claims. . . . If, as *Braunfeld* recognized, a sole proprietorship that seeks to make a profit may assert a free-exercise claim,[2] why can't Hobby Lobby, Conestoga, and Mardel do the same? . . .

4

Finally, HHS contends that Congress could not have wanted RFRA to apply to for-profit corporations because it is difficult as a practical matter to ascertain the sincere "beliefs" of a corporation. HHS goes so far as to raise the specter of "divisive, polarizing proxy battles over the religious identity of large, publicly traded corporations such as IBM or General Electric."

These cases, however, do not involve publicly traded corporations, and it seems unlikely that the sort of corporate giants to which HHS refers will often assert RFRA claims. HHS has not pointed to any example of a publicly traded corporation asserting RFRA rights, and numerous practical restraints would likely prevent that from occurring. For example, the idea that unrelated shareholders—including institutional investors with their own set of stakeholders—would agree to run a corporation under the same religious beliefs seems improbable. In any event, we have no occasion in these cases to consider RFRA's applicability

---

2. It is revealing that the principal dissent cannot even bring itself to acknowledge that *Braunfeld* was correct in entertaining the merchants' claims. See *Post* (dismissing the relevance of *Braunfeld* in part because "[t]he free exercise claim asserted there was promptly rejected on the merits").

to such companies. The companies in the cases before us are closely held corporations, each owned and controlled by members of a single family, and no one has disputed the sincerity of their religious beliefs. . . .

For all these reasons, we hold that a federal regulation's restriction on the activities of a for-profit closely held corporation must comply with RFRA.

IV

Because RFRA applies in these cases, we must next ask whether the HHS contraceptive mandate "substantially burden[s]" the exercise of religion. We have little trouble concluding that it does.

A

As we have noted, the Hahns and Greens have a sincere religious belief that life begins at conception. They therefore object on religious grounds to providing health insurance that covers methods of birth control that, as HHS acknowledges, may result in the destruction of an embryo. By requiring the Hahns and Greens and their companies to arrange for such coverage, the HHS mandate demands that they engage in conduct that seriously violates their religious beliefs.

If the Hahns and Greens and their companies do not yield to this demand, the economic consequences will be severe. If the companies continue to offer group health plans that do not cover the contraceptives at issue, they will be taxed $100 per day for each affected individual. For Hobby Lobby, the bill could amount to $1.3 million per day or about $475 million per year; for Conestoga, the assessment could be $90,000 per day or $33 million per year; and for Mardel, it could be $40,000 per day or about $15 million per year. These sums are surely substantial.

It is true that the plaintiffs could avoid these assessments by dropping insurance coverage altogether and thus forcing their employees to obtain health insurance on one of the exchanges established under ACA. But if at least one of their full-time employees were to qualify for a subsidy on one of the government-run exchanges, this course would also entail substantial economic consequences. The companies could face penalties of $2,000 per employee each year. These penalties would amount to roughly $26 million for Hobby Lobby, $1.8 million for Conestoga, and $800,000 for Mardel. . . .

C

In taking the position that the HHS mandate does not impose a substantial burden on the exercise of religion, HHS's main argument (echoed by the principal dissent) is basically that the connection between what the objecting parties must do (provide health-insurance coverage for four methods of contraception that may operate after the fertilization of an egg) and the end that they find to be morally wrong (destruction of an embryo) is simply too attenuated. HHS and the dissent note that providing the coverage would not itself result in the destruction of an embryo; that would occur only if an employee chose to take advantage of the coverage and to use one of the four methods at issue.[3]

This argument dodges the question that RFRA presents (whether the HHS mandate imposes a substantial burden on the ability of the objecting parties to conduct business in accordance with *their religious beliefs*) and instead addresses a very different question that the federal courts have no business addressing (whether the religious belief asserted in a RFRA case is reasonable). The Hahns and Greens believe that providing the coverage demanded by the HHS regulations is connected to the destruction of an embryo in a way that is sufficient to make it immoral for them to provide the coverage. This belief implicates a difficult and important question of religion and moral philosophy, namely, the circumstances under which it is wrong for a person to perform an act that is innocent in itself but that has the effect of enabling or facilitating the commission of an immoral act by another. Arrogating the authority to provide a binding national answer to this religious and philosophical question, HHS and the principal dissent in effect tell the plaintiffs that their beliefs are flawed. For good reason, we have repeatedly refused to take such a step.

Moreover, in *Thomas v. Review Bd. of Indiana Employment Security Div.* (1981), we considered and rejected an argument that is nearly identical to the one now urged by HHS and the dissent. In *Thomas*, a Jehovah's Witness was initially employed making sheet steel for a variety of industrial uses, but he was later transferred to a job making turrets for tanks. Because he objected on religious grounds to participating in the manufacture of weapons, he lost his job and sought unemployment compensation. Ruling against the employee, the state court had difficulty with the line that the employee drew between work that he found to be consistent with his religious beliefs (helping to manufacture steel that was used in making weapons) and work that he found morally objectionable (helping to make the weapons themselves). This Court, however, held that "it is not for us to say that the line he drew was an unreasonable one."

Similarly, in these cases, the Hahns and Greens and their companies sincerely believe that providing the insurance coverage demanded by the HHS regulations lies on the forbidden side of the line, and it is not for us to say that their religious beliefs are mistaken or insubstantial. Instead, our "narrow function . . . in this

---

3. This argument is not easy to square with the position taken by HHS in providing exemptions from the contraceptive mandate for religious employers, such as churches, that have the very same religious objections as the Hahns and Greens and their companies. The connection between what these religious employers would be required to do if not exempted (provide insurance coverage for particular contraceptives) and the ultimate event that they find morally wrong (destruction of an embryo) is exactly the same. Nevertheless, as discussed, HHS and the Labor and Treasury Departments authorized the exemption from the contraceptive mandate of group health plans of certain religious employers, and later expanded the exemption to include certain nonprofit organizations with religious objections to contraceptive coverage. 78 Fed. Reg. 39871. When this was done, the Government made clear that its objective was to "protec[t]" these religious objectors "from having to contract, arrange, pay, or refer for such coverage." *Ibid.* Those exemptions would be hard to understand if the plaintiffs' objections here were not substantial.

context is to determine" whether the line drawn reflects "an honest conviction," and there is no dispute that it does. . . .

V

Since the HHS contraceptive mandate imposes a substantial burden on the exercise of religion, we must move on and decide whether HHS has shown that the mandate both "(1) is in furtherance of a compelling governmental interest; and (2) is the least restrictive means of furthering that compelling governmental interest."

A

HHS asserts that the contraceptive mandate serves a variety of important interests, but many of these are couched in very broad terms, such as promoting "public health" and "gender equality." RFRA, however, contemplates a "more focused" inquiry: It "requires the Government to demonstrate that the compelling interest test is satisfied through application of the challenged law 'to the person'—the particular claimant whose sincere exercise of religion is being substantially burdened." This requires us to "loo[k] beyond broadly formulated interests" and to "scrutiniz[e] the asserted harm of granting specific exemptions to particular religious claimants"—in other words, to look to the marginal interest in enforcing the contraceptive mandate in these cases. . . .

We find it unnecessary to adjudicate this issue. We will assume that the interest in guaranteeing cost-free access to the four challenged contraceptive methods is compelling within the meaning of RFRA, and we will proceed to consider the final prong of the RFRA test, *i.e.*, whether HHS has shown that the contraceptive mandate is "the least restrictive means of furthering that compelling governmental interest."

B

The least-restrictive-means standard is exceptionally demanding, and it is not satisfied here. HHS has not shown that it lacks other means of achieving its desired goal without imposing a substantial burden on the exercise of religion by the objecting parties in these cases.

The most straightforward way of doing this would be for the Government to assume the cost of providing the four contraceptives at issue to any women who are unable to obtain them under their health-insurance policies due to their employers' religious objections. This would certainly be less restrictive of the plaintiffs' religious liberty, and HHS has not shown that this is not a viable alternative. . . . If, as HHS tells us, providing all women with cost-free access to all FDA-approved methods of contraception is a Government interest of the highest order, it is hard to understand HHS's argument that it cannot be required under RFRA to pay *anything* in order to achieve this important goal.

HHS contends that RFRA does not permit us to take this option into account because "RFRA cannot be used to require creation of entirely new programs." But we see nothing in RFRA that supports this argument, and drawing the line between the "creation of an entirely new program" and the modification of an existing program (which RFRA surely allows) would be fraught with problems. We do not doubt that cost may be an important factor in the least-restrictive-means analysis, but . . . RFRA . . . may in some circumstances require the Government to expend additional funds to accommodate citizens' religious beliefs. HHS's view that RFRA can never require the Government to spend even a small amount reflects a judgment about the importance of religious liberty that was not shared by the Congress that enacted that law.

In the end, however, we need not rely on the option of a new, government-funded program in order to conclude that the HHS regulations fail the least-restrictive-means test. HHS itself has demonstrated that it has at its disposal an approach that is less restrictive than requiring employers to fund contraceptive methods that violate their religious beliefs. As we explained above, HHS has already established an accommodation for nonprofit organizations with religious objections. Under that accommodation, the organization can self-certify that it opposes providing coverage for particular contraceptive services.

We do not decide today whether an approach of this type complies with RFRA for purposes of all religious claims. At a minimum, however, it does not impinge on the plaintiffs' religious belief that providing insurance coverage for the contraceptives at issue here violates their religion, and it serves HHS's stated interests equally well.[4] . . .

C

HHS and the principal dissent argue that a ruling in favor of the objecting parties in these cases will lead to a flood of religious objections regarding a wide variety of medical procedures and drugs, such as vaccinations and blood transfusions, but HHS has made no effort to substantiate this prediction. . . .

In any event, our decision in these cases is concerned solely with the contraceptive mandate. Our decision should not be understood to hold that an insurance-coverage mandate must necessarily fall if it conflicts with an employer's religious beliefs. Other coverage requirements, such as immunizations, may be supported by different interests (for example, the need to combat the spread of infectious diseases) and may involve different arguments about the least restrictive means of providing them. . . .

4. The principal dissent faults us for being "noncommital" in refusing to decide a case that is not before us here. The less restrictive approach we describe accommodates the religious beliefs asserted in these cases, and that is the only question we are permitted to address.

HHS also raises for the first time in this Court the argument that applying the contraceptive mandate to for-profit employers with sincere religious objections is essential to the comprehensive health-insurance scheme that ACA establishes. HHS analogizes the contraceptive mandate to the requirement to pay Social Security taxes, which we upheld in [*United States v. Lee* (1982)] despite the religious objection of an employer, but these cases are quite different. Our holding in *Lee* turned primarily on the special problems associated with a national system of taxation. We noted that "[t]he obligation to pay the social security tax initially is not fundamentally different from the obligation to pay income taxes." . . . We observed that "[t]he tax system could not function if denominations were allowed to challenge the tax system because tax payments were spent in a manner that violates their religious belief."

Lee was a free-exercise, not a RFRA, case, but if the issue in *Lee* were analyzed under the RFRA framework, the fundamental point would be that there simply is no less restrictive alternative to the categorical requirement to pay taxes. . . .

* * *

The contraceptive mandate, as applied to closely held corporations, violates RFRA. Our decision on that statutory question makes it unnecessary to reach the First Amendment claim raised by Conestoga and the Hahns.

The judgment of the Tenth Circuit is affirmed; the judgment of the Third Circuit is reversed, and that case is remanded for further proceedings consistent with this opinion.

It is so ordered.

JUSTICE GINSBURG, with whom JUSTICE SOTOMAYOR joins, and with whom JUSTICE BREYER and JUSTICE KAGAN join as to all but Part III-C-1, dissenting.

In a decision of startling breadth, the Court holds that commercial enterprises, including corporations, along with partnerships and sole proprietorships, can opt out of any law (saving only tax laws) they judge incompatible with their sincerely held religious beliefs. Compelling governmental interests in uniform compliance with the law, and disadvantages that religion-based opt-outs impose on others, hold no sway, the Court decides, at least when there is a "less restrictive alternative." And such an alternative, the Court suggests, there always will be whenever, in lieu of tolling an enterprise claiming a religion-based exemption, the government, *i.e.,* the general public, can pick up the tab.

The Court does not pretend that the First Amendment's Free Exercise Clause demands religion-based accommodations so extreme, for our decisions leave no doubt on that score. . . . In the Court's view, RFRA demands accommodation of a for-profit corporation's religious beliefs no matter the impact that accommodation may have on third parties who do not share the corporation owners' religious faith — in these cases, thousands of women employed by Hobby Lobby and Conestoga or dependents of persons those corporations employ. Persuaded that Congress enacted RFRA to serve a far less radical purpose, and mindful of the havoc the Court's judgment can introduce, I dissent. . . .

II

Any First Amendment Free Exercise Clause claim Hobby Lobby or Conestoga might assert is foreclosed by this Court's decision in *Employment Div., Dept. of Human Resources of Ore. v. Smith*, 494 U.S. 872 (1990). . . . The First Amendment is not offended, *Smith* held, when "prohibiting the exercise of religion . . . is not the object of [governmental regulation] but merely the incidental effect of a generally applicable and otherwise valid provision." *Id.*, at 878. The ACA's contraceptive coverage requirement applies generally, it is "otherwise valid," it trains on women's well being, not on the exercise of religion, and any effect it has on such exercise is incidental.

Even if *Smith* did not control, the Free Exercise Clause would not require the exemption Hobby Lobby and Conestoga seek. Accommodations to religious beliefs or observances, the Court has clarified, must not significantly impinge on the interests of third parties.

The exemption sought by Hobby Lobby and Conestoga would override significant interests of the corporations' employees and covered dependents. It would deny legions of women who do not hold their employers' beliefs access to contraceptive coverage that the ACA would otherwise secure. In sum, with respect to free exercise claims no less than free speech claims, " '[y]our right to swing your arms ends just where the other man's nose begins.' " Chafee, Freedom of Speech in War Time, 32 Harv. L. Rev. 932, 957 (1919).

III

A

. . . RFRA's purpose is specific and written into the statute itself. The Act was crafted to "restore the compelling interest test as set forth in *Sherbert v. Verner* (1963) and *Wisconsin v. Yoder* (1972) and to guarantee its application in all cases where free exercise of religion is substantially burdened." . . . In line with this restorative purpose, Congress expected courts considering RFRA claims to "look to free exercise cases decided prior to *Smith* for guidance." In short, the Act reinstates the law as it was prior to *Smith*, without "creat[ing] . . . new rights for any religious practice or for any potential litigant." Given the Act's moderate purpose, it is hardly surprising that RFRA's enactment in 1993 provoked little controversy. . . .

C

With RFRA's restorative purpose in mind, I turn to the Act's application to the instant lawsuits. That task, in view of the positions taken by the Court, requires consideration of several questions, each potentially dispositive of Hobby Lobby's and Conestoga's claims: Do for-profit corporations rank among "person[s]" who "exercise . . . religion"? Assuming that they do, does the contraceptive coverage requirement "substantially burden" their religious exercise? If so, is the requirement "in furtherance of a compelling government interest"? And last, does the requirement represent the least restrictive means for furthering that interest? . . . [T]he Court falters at each step of its analysis.

1

RFRA's compelling interest test . . . applies to government actions that "substantially burden *a person's exercise of religion*." This reference, the Court submits, incorporates the definition of "person" found in the Dictionary Act, which extends to "corporations, companies, associations, firms, partnerships, societies, and joint stock companies, as well as individuals." The Dictionary Act's definition, however, controls only where "context" does not "indicat[e] otherwise." Here, context does so indicate. RFRA speaks of "a person's *exercise of religion*." Whether a corporation qualifies as a "person" capable of exercising religion is an inquiry one cannot answer without reference to the "full body" of pre-*Smith* "free-exercise caselaw." There is in that case law no support for the notion that free exercise rights pertain to for-profit corporations. . . .

Reading RFRA, as the Court does, to require extension of religion-based exemptions to for-profit corporations surely is not grounded in the pre-*Smith* precedent Congress sought to preserve. Had Congress intended RFRA to initiate a change so huge, a clarion statement to that effect likely would have been made in the legislation. The text of RFRA makes no such statement and the legislative history does not so much as mention for-profit corporations.

The Court notes that for-profit corporations may support charitable causes and use their funds for religious ends, and therefore questions the distinction between such corporations and religious nonprofit organizations. Again, the Court forgets that religious organizations exist to serve a community of believers. For-profit corporations do not fit that bill. Moreover, history is not on the Court's side. Recognition of the discrete characters of "ecclesiastical and lay" corporations dates back to Blackstone, see 1 W. Blackstone, Commentaries on the Laws of England 458 (1765), and was reiterated by this Court centuries before the enactment of the Internal Revenue Code. To reiterate, "for-profit corporations are different from religious non-profits in that they use labor to make a profit, rather than to perpetuate [the] religious value[s] [shared by a community of believers]." [*Gilardi v. United States Dept. of Health and Human Servs.* (CADC 2013) (Edwards, J., concurring in part and dissenting in part) (emphasis deleted).]

Citing *Braunfeld v. Brown*, 366 U.S. 599 (1961), the Court questions why, if "a sole proprietorship that seeks to make a profit may assert a free-exercise claim, [Hobby Lobby and Conestoga] can't . . . do the same?" But even accepting, *arguendo*, the premise that unincorporated business enterprises may gain religious accommodations under the Free Exercise Clause, the Court's conclusion is unsound. In a sole proprietorship, the business and its owner are one and the same. By incorporating a business, however, an individual separates herself from the entity and escapes personal responsibility for the entity's obligations. . . .

2

Even if Hobby Lobby and Conestoga were deemed RFRA "person[s]," to gain an exemption, they must demonstrate that the contraceptive coverage requirement "substantially burden[s] [their] exercise of religion." Congress no doubt meant the modifier "substantially" to carry weight. In the original draft of RFRA, the word "burden" appeared unmodified. The word "substantially" was inserted pursuant to a clarifying amendment offered by Senators Kennedy and Hatch. In proposing the amendment, Senator Kennedy stated that RFRA, in accord with the Court's pre-*Smith* case law, "does not require the Government to justify every action that has some effect on religious exercise." . . .

I agree with the Court that the Green and Hahn families' religious convictions regarding contraception are sincerely held. But those beliefs, however deeply held, do not suffice to sustain a RFRA claim. RFRA, properly understood, distinguishes between "factual allegations that [plaintiffs'] beliefs are sincere and of a religious nature," which a court must accept as true, and the "legal conclusion . . . that [plaintiffs'] religious exercise is substantially burdened," an inquiry the court must undertake. . . .

Undertaking the inquiry that the Court forgoes, I would conclude that the connection between the families' religious objections and the contraceptive coverage requirement is too attenuated to rank as substantial. The requirement carries no command that Hobby Lobby or Conestoga purchase or provide the contraceptives they find objectionable. Instead, it calls on the companies covered by the requirement to direct money into undifferentiated funds that finance a wide variety of benefits under comprehensive health plans. Those plans, in order to comply with the ACA, must offer contraceptive coverage without cost sharing, just as they must cover an array of other preventive services.

Importantly, the decisions whether to claim benefits under the plans are made not by Hobby Lobby or Conestoga, but by the covered employees and dependents, in consultation with their health care providers. Should an employee of Hobby Lobby or Conestoga share the religious beliefs of the Greens and Hahns, she is of course under no compulsion to use the contraceptives in question. But "[n]o individual decision by an employee and her physician—be it to use contraception, treat an infection, or have a hip replaced—is in any meaningful sense [her employer's] decision or action." *Grote v. Sebelius*, 708 F.3d 850, 865 (CA7 2013) (Rovner, J., dissenting). It is doubtful that Congress, when it specified that burdens must be "substantia[l]," had in mind a linkage thus interrupted by independent decisionmakers (the woman and her health counselor) standing between the challenged government action and the religious exercise claimed to be infringed. Any decision to use contraceptives made by a woman covered under Hobby Lobby's or Conestoga's plan will not be propelled by the Government, it will be the woman's autonomous choice, informed by the physician she consults.

3

Even if one were to conclude that Hobby Lobby and Conestoga meet the substantial burden requirement, the Government has shown that the contraceptive coverage for which the ACA provides furthers compelling interests in public health and women's well being. Those interests are concrete, specific, and demonstrated by a wealth of empirical evidence. . . . Perhaps the gravity of the interests at stake has led the Court to assume, for purposes of its RFRA analysis, that the compelling interest criterion is met in these cases. . . . The Court ultimately acknowledges a critical point: RFRA's application "*must* take adequate account of the burdens a requested accommodation may impose on nonbeneficiaries." No tradition, and no prior decision under RFRA, allows a religion-based exemption when the accommodation would be harmful to others—here, the very persons the contraceptive coverage requirement was designed to protect.

4

After assuming the existence of compelling government interests, the Court holds that the contraceptive coverage requirement fails to satisfy RFRA's least restrictive means test. But the Government has shown that there is no less restrictive, equally effective means that would both (1) satisfy the challengers' religious objections to providing insurance coverage for certain contraceptives (which they believe cause abortions); and (2) carry out the objective of the ACA's contraceptive coverage requirement, to ensure that women employees receive, at no cost to them, the preventive care needed to safeguard their health and well being. A "least restrictive means" cannot require employees to relinquish benefits accorded them by federal law in order to ensure that their commercial employers can adhere unreservedly to their religious tenets.

Then let the government pay (rather than the employees who do not share their employer's faith), the Court suggests. . . . The ACA, however, requires coverage of preventive services through the existing employer-based system of health insurance "so that [employees] face minimal logistical and administrative obstacles." Impeding women's receipt of benefits "by requiring them to take steps to learn about, and to sign up for, a new [government funded and administered] health benefit" was scarcely what Congress contemplated. . . .

Ultimately, the Court hedges on its proposal to align for-profit enterprises with nonprofit religion-based organizations. "We do not decide today whether [the] approach [the opinion advances] complies with RFRA for purposes of all religious claims." Counsel for Hobby Lobby was similarly noncommittal. Asked at oral argument whether the Court-proposed alternative was acceptable, counsel responded: "We haven't been offered that accommodation, so we haven't had to decide what kind of objection, if any, we would make to that."

Conestoga suggests that, if its employees had to acquire and pay for the contraceptives (to which the corporation objects) on their own, a tax credit would qualify as a less restrictive alternative. A tax credit, of course, is one variety of "let the government pay." In addition to departing from the existing employer-based system of health insurance, Conestoga's alternative would require a woman to reach into her own pocket in the first instance, and it would do nothing for the woman too poor to be aided by a tax credit.

In sum, in view of what Congress sought to accomplish, *i.e.,* comprehensive preventive care for women furnished through employer-based health plans, none of the proffered alternatives would satisfactorily serve the compelling interests to which Congress responded.

IV

Among the pathmarking pre-*Smith* decisions RFRA preserved is *United States v. Lee*, 455 U.S. 252 (1982). . . . The Government urges that *Lee* should control the challenges brought by Hobby Lobby and Conestoga. In contrast, today's Court dismisses *Lee* as a tax case. Indeed, it was a tax case and the Court in *Lee* homed in on "[t]he difficulty in attempting to accommodate religious beliefs in the area of taxation." . . .

There is an overriding interest, I believe, in keeping the courts "out of the business of evaluating the relative merits of differing religious claims," *Lee*, 455 U.S., at 263, n. 2 (Stevens, J., concurring in judgment), or the sincerity with which an asserted religious belief is held. Indeed, approving some religious claims while deeming others unworthy of accommodation could be "perceived as favoring one religion over another," the very "risk the Establishment Clause was designed to preclude." *Ibid.* The Court, I fear, has ventured into a minefield by its immoderate reading of RFRA. I would confine religious exemptions under that Act to organizations formed "for a religious purpose," "engage[d] primarily in carrying out that religious purpose," and not "engaged . . . substantially in the exchange of goods or services for money beyond nominal amounts."

* * *

For the reasons stated, I would reverse the judgment of the Court of Appeals for the Tenth Circuit and affirm the judgment of the Court of Appeals for the Third Circuit.

JUSTICE BREYER and JUSTICE KAGAN, dissenting.

We agree with Justice Ginsburg that the plaintiffs' challenge to the contraceptive coverage requirement fails on the merits. We need not and do not decide whether either for-profit corporations or their owners may bring claims under the Religious Freedom Restoration Act of 1993. Accordingly, we join all but Part III-C-1 of Justice Ginsburg's dissenting opinion.

Chapter 9

No Establishment of Religion

ASSIGNMENT S-12

Government Endorsement of Religion

STUDY GUIDE:

- The next case applies the principles identified in *Marsh* and *Lee* to meetings of a municipal city council. How does Justice Kennedy distinguish this use of prayer from the one he found to be unconstitutional in *Lee*?
- Notice the ways in which the plurality's analysis (and Justice Alito's concurrence) differs from the dissent in characterizing the nature of the practices and proceedings in the previous cases and the practices being challenged here.
- This excerpt also includes a brief summary of Justice Thomas's long-standing stance that, because the Establishment Clause was a "federalism" provision and not one protecting an individual right, it should not have been incorporated against the states via the Fourteenth Amendment. Hence, on his reading of the First and Fourteenth Amendments, there is no constitutional bar on what the city was doing.

GREECE v. GALLOWAY

No. 12-696

Argued Nov. 6, 2013 | Decided May 5, 2014

JUSTICE KENNEDY delivered the opinion of the Court, except as to Part II-B.[1]

The Court must decide whether the town of Greece, New York, imposes an impermissible establishment of religion by opening its monthly board meetings with a prayer. It must be concluded, consistent with the Court's opinion in *Marsh v. Chambers* (1983), that no violation of the Constitution has been shown.

1. The Chief Justice and Justice Alito join this opinion in full. Justice Scalia and Justice Thomas join this opinion except as to Part II-B.

I

Greece, a town with a population of 94,000, is in upstate New York. For some years, it began its monthly town board meetings with a moment of silence. In 1999, the newly elected town supervisor, John Auberger, decided to replicate the prayer practice he had found meaningful while serving in the county legislature. Following the roll call and recitation of the Pledge of Allegiance, Auberger would invite a local clergyman to the front of the room to deliver an invocation. After the prayer, Auberger would thank the minister for serving as the board's "chaplain for the month" and present him with a commemorative plaque. The prayer was intended to place town board members in a solemn and deliberative frame of mind, invoke divine guidance in town affairs, and follow a tradition practiced by Congress and dozens of state legislatures.

The town followed an informal method for selecting prayer givers, all of whom were unpaid volunteers. A town employee would call the congregations listed in a local directory until she found a minister available for that month's meeting. The town eventually compiled a list of willing "board chaplains" who had accepted invitations and agreed to return in the future. The town at no point excluded or denied an opportunity to a would-be prayer giver. Its leaders maintained that a minister or layperson of any persuasion, including an atheist, could give the invocation. But nearly all of the congregations in town were Christian; and from 1999 to 2007, all of the participating ministers were too.

Greece neither reviewed the prayers in advance of the meetings nor provided guidance as to their tone or content, in the belief that exercising any degree of control over the prayers would infringe both the free exercise and speech rights of the ministers. The town instead left the guest clergy free to compose their own devotions. . . .

Respondents Susan Galloway and Linda Stephens attended town board meetings to speak about issues of local concern, and they objected that the prayers violated their religious or philosophical views. At one meeting, Galloway admonished board members that she found the prayers "offensive," "intolerable," and an affront to a "diverse community." After respondents complained that Christian themes pervaded the prayers, to the exclusion of citizens who did not share those beliefs, the town invited a Jewish layman and the chairman of the local Baha'i temple to deliver prayers. A Wiccan priestess who had read press reports about the prayer controversy requested, and was granted, an opportunity to give the invocation.

Galloway and Stephens brought suit in the United States District Court for the Western District of New York. They alleged that the town violated the First Amendment's Establishment Clause by preferring Christians over other prayer givers and by sponsoring sectarian prayers, such as those given "in Jesus' name." They did not seek an end to the prayer practice, but rather requested an injunction that would limit the town to "inclusive and ecumenical" prayers that referred only to a "generic God" and would not associate the government with any one faith or belief. The Court of Appeals for the Second Circuit . . . held that some aspects of the prayer program, viewed in their totality by a reasonable observer, conveyed the message that Greece was endorsing Christianity. . . .

Having granted certiorari to decide whether the town's prayer practice violates the Establishment Clause, the Court now reverses the judgment of the Court of Appeals.

II

In *Marsh*, the Court found no First Amendment violation in the Nebraska Legislature's practice of opening its sessions with a prayer delivered by a chaplain paid from state funds. The decision concluded that legislative prayer, while religious in nature, has long been understood as compatible with the Establishment Clause. As practiced by Congress since the framing of the Constitution, legislative prayer lends gravity to public business, reminds lawmakers to transcend petty differences in pursuit of a higher purpose, and expresses a common aspiration to a just and peaceful society. The Court has considered this symbolic expression to be a "tolerable acknowledgement of beliefs widely held," *Marsh* rather than a first, treacherous step towards establishment of a state church.

Marsh is sometimes described as "carving out an exception" to the Court's Establishment Clause jurisprudence, because it sustained legislative prayer without subjecting the practice to "any of the formal 'tests' that have traditionally structured" this inquiry. *Id.* (Brennan, J., dissenting). The Court in *Marsh* found those tests unnecessary because history supported the conclusion that legislative invocations are compatible with the Establishment Clause. The First Congress made it an early item of business to appoint and pay official chaplains, and both the House and Senate have maintained the office virtually uninterrupted since that time. When *Marsh* was decided, in 1983, legislative prayer had persisted in the Nebraska Legislature for more than a century, and the majority of the other States also had the same, consistent practice. Although no information has been cited by the parties to indicate how many local legislative bodies open their meetings with prayer, this practice too has historical precedent. "In light of the unambiguous and unbroken history of more than 200 years, there can be no doubt that the practice of opening legislative sessions with a prayer has become part of the fabric of our society." *Marsh*.

Yet *Marsh* must not be understood as permitting a practice that would amount to a constitutional violation if not for its historical foundation. The case teaches instead that the Establishment Clause must be interpreted "by reference to historical practices and understandings." [*County of Allegheny v. American Civil Liberties Union, Greater Pittsburg Chapter* (1989)] (Kennedy, J., concurring in judgment in part and dissenting in part). That the First Congress provided for the appointment of chaplains only days after approving language for the First Amendment demonstrates that the Framers considered legislative prayer a benign acknowledgment of religion's role in society. In the 1850's, the judiciary committees in both the House and Senate reevaluated the practice of official chaplaincies after receiving petitions to abolish the office. The committees concluded that the office posed no threat of an establishment because lawmakers were not compelled to attend the daily prayer; no faith was excluded by law, nor any favored; and the cost of the chaplain's salary imposed a vanishingly small burden on taxpayers. *Marsh* stands for the proposition that it is not necessary to define the precise boundary of the Establishment Clause where history shows that the specific practice is permitted. Any test the Court adopts must acknowledge a practice that was accepted by the Framers and has withstood the critical scrutiny of time and political change. A test that would sweep away what has so long been settled would create new controversy and begin anew the very divisions along religious lines that the Establishment Clause seeks to prevent. See *Van Orden v. Perry* (2005) (Breyer, J., concurring in judgment).

The Court's inquiry, then, must be to determine whether the prayer practice in the town of Greece fits within the tradition long followed in Congress and the state legislatures. Respondents assert that the town's prayer exercise falls outside that tradition and transgresses the Establishment Clause for two independent but mutually reinforcing reasons. First, they argue that *Marsh* did not approve prayers containing sectarian language or themes, such as the prayers offered in Greece that referred to the "death, resurrection, and ascension of the Savior Jesus Christ," and the "saving sacrifice of Jesus Christ on the cross." Second, they argue that the setting and conduct of the town board meetings create social pressures that force nonadherents to remain in the room or even feign participation in order to avoid offending the representatives who sponsor the prayer and will vote on matters citizens bring before the board. The sectarian content of the prayers compounds the subtle coercive pressures, they argue, because the nonbeliever who might tolerate ecumenical prayer is forced to do the same for prayer that might be inimical to his or her beliefs.

A

Respondents maintain that prayer must be nonsectarian, or not identifiable with any one religion; and they fault the town for permitting guest chaplains to deliver prayers that "use overtly Christian terms" or "invoke specifics of Christian theology." A prayer is fitting for the public sphere, in their view, only if it contains the "most general, nonsectarian reference to God," and eschews mention of doctrines associated with any one faith. They argue that prayer which contemplates "the workings of the Holy Spirit, the events of Pentecost, and the belief that God 'has raised up the Lord Jesus' and 'will raise us, in our turn, and put us by His side' " would be impermissible, as would any prayer that reflects dogma particular to a single faith tradition.

An insistence on nonsectarian or ecumenical prayer as a single, fixed standard is not consistent with the tradition of legislative prayer outlined in the Court's cases. The Court found the prayers in *Marsh* consistent with the First Amendment not because they espoused only a generic theism but because our history and tradition have shown that prayer in this limited context could "coexis[t] with the principles of disestablishment and religious freedom." The Congress that drafted the First Amendment would have been accustomed to invocations containing explicitly religious themes of the sort respondents find objectionable. One of the Senate's first chaplains, the Rev. William White, gave prayers in a series that included the Lord's Prayer, the Collect for Ash Wednesday, prayers for peace and grace, a general thanksgiving, St. Chrysostom's Prayer, and a prayer seeking "the grace of our Lord Jesus Christ, &c." Letter from W. White to H. Jones (Dec. 29, 1830). The decidedly Christian nature of these prayers must not be dismissed as the relic of a time when our Nation was less pluralistic than it is today. Congress continues to permit its appointed and visiting chaplains to express themselves in a religious idiom. It acknowledges our growing diversity not by proscribing sectarian content but by welcoming ministers of many creeds.

The contention that legislative prayer must be generic or nonsectarian . . . is irreconcilable with the facts of *Marsh* and with its holding and reasoning. *Marsh* nowhere suggested that the constitutionality of legislative prayer turns on the neutrality of its content. The opinion noted that Nebraska's chaplain, the Rev. Robert E. Palmer, modulated the "explicitly Christian" nature of his prayer and "removed all references to Christ" after a Jewish lawmaker complained. With this footnote, the Court did no more than observe the practical demands placed on a minister who holds a permanent, appointed position in a legislature and chooses to write his or her prayers to appeal to more members, or at least to give less offense to those who object. *Marsh* did not suggest that Nebraska's prayer practice would have failed had the chaplain not acceded to the legislator's request. Nor did the Court imply the rule that prayer violates the Establishment Clause any time it is given in the name of a figure deified by only one faith or creed. To the contrary, the Court instructed that the "content of the prayer is not of concern to judges," provided "there is no indication that the prayer opportunity has been exploited to proselytize or advance any one, or to disparage any other, faith or belief."

To hold that invocations must be nonsectarian would force the legislatures that sponsor prayers and the courts that are asked to decide these cases to act as supervisors and censors of religious speech, a rule that would involve government in religious matters to a far greater degree than is the case under the town's current practice of neither editing or approving prayers in advance nor criticizing their content after the fact. . . .

The First Amendment is not a majority rule, and government may not seek to define permissible categories of religious speech. Once it invites prayer into the public sphere, government must permit a prayer giver to address his or her own God or gods as conscience dictates, unfettered by what an administrator or judge considers to be nonsectarian.

In rejecting the suggestion that legislative prayer must be nonsectarian, the Court does not imply that no constraints remain on its content. The relevant constraint derives from its place at the opening of legislative sessions, where it is meant to lend gravity to the occasion and reflect values long part of the Nation's heritage. Prayer that is solemn and respectful in tone, that invites lawmakers to reflect upon shared ideals and common ends before they embark on the fractious business of governing, serves that legitimate function. If the course and practice over time shows that the invocations denigrate nonbelievers or religious minorities, threaten damnation, or preach conversion, many present may consider the prayer to fall short of the desire to elevate the purpose of the occasion and to unite lawmakers in their common effort. That circumstance would present a different case than the one presently before the Court.

The tradition reflected in *Marsh* permits chaplains to ask their own God for blessings of peace, justice, and freedom that find appreciation among people of all faiths. That a prayer is given in the name of Jesus, Allah, or Jehovah, or that it makes passing reference to religious doctrines, does not remove it from that tradition. These religious themes provide particular means to universal ends. Prayer that reflects beliefs specific to only some creeds can still serve to solemnize the occasion, so long as the practice over time is not "exploited to proselytize or advance any one, or to disparage any other, faith or belief." *Marsh*. . . .

From the earliest days of the Nation, these invocations have been addressed to assemblies comprising many different creeds. These ceremonial prayers strive for the idea that people of many faiths may be united in a community of tolerance and devotion. Even those who disagree as to religious doctrine may find common ground in the desire to show respect for the divine in all aspects of their lives and being. Our tradition assumes that adult citizens, firm in their own beliefs, can tolerate and perhaps appreciate a ceremonial prayer delivered by a person of a different faith.

The prayers delivered in the town of Greece do not fall outside the tradition this Court has recognized. A number of the prayers did invoke the name of Jesus, the Heavenly Father, or the Holy Spirit, but they also invoked universal themes, as by celebrating the changing of the seasons or calling for a "spirit of cooperation" among town leaders. . . .

Respondents point to other invocations that disparaged those who did not accept the town's prayer practice. One guest minister characterized objectors as a "minority" who are "ignorant of the history of our country," while another lamented that other towns did not have "God-fearing" leaders. Although these two remarks strayed from the rationale set out in *Marsh*, they do not despoil a practice that on the whole reflects and embraces our tradition. Absent a pattern of prayers that over time denigrate, proselytize, or betray an impermissible government purpose, a challenge based solely on the content of a prayer will not likely establish a constitutional violation. *Marsh,* indeed, requires an inquiry into the prayer opportunity as a whole, rather than into the contents of a single prayer.

Finally, the Court disagrees with the view taken by the Court of Appeals that the town of Greece contravened the Establishment Clause by inviting a predominantly Christian set of ministers to lead the prayer. The town made reasonable efforts to identify all of the congregations located within its borders and represented that it would welcome a prayer by any minister or layman who wished to give one. That nearly all of the congregations in town turned out to be Christian does not reflect an aversion or bias on the part of town leaders against minority faiths. So long as the town maintains a policy of nondiscrimination, the Constitution does not require it to search beyond its borders for non-Christian prayer givers in an effort to achieve religious balancing. The quest to promote "a 'diversity' of religious views" would require the town "to make wholly inappropriate judgments about the number of religions [it] should sponsor and the relative frequency with which it should sponsor each," [*Lee v. Weisman* (1992)] (Souter, J., concurring), a form of government entanglement with religion that is far more troublesome than the current approach.

B

Respondents further seek to distinguish the town's prayer practice from the tradition upheld in *Marsh* on the ground that it coerces participation by nonadherents. . . .

It is an elemental First Amendment principle that government may not coerce its citizens "to support or participate in any religion or its exercise." *County of Allegheny* (Kennedy, J., concurring in judgment in part and dissenting in part). On the record in this case the Court is not persuaded that the town of Greece, through the act of offering a brief, solemn, and respectful prayer to open its monthly meetings, compelled its citizens to engage in a religious observance. The inquiry remains a fact-sensitive one that considers both the setting in which the prayer arises and the audience to whom it is directed.

The prayer opportunity in this case must be evaluated against the backdrop of historical practice. As a practice that has long endured, legislative prayer has become part of our heritage and tradition, part of our expressive idiom, similar to the Pledge of Allegiance, inaugural prayer, or the recitation of "God save the United States and this honorable Court" at the opening of this Court's sessions. It is presumed that the reasonable observer is acquainted with this tradition and understands that its purposes are to lend gravity to public proceedings and to acknowledge the place religion holds in the lives of many private citizens, not to afford government an opportunity to proselytize or force truant constituents into the pews. That many appreciate these acknowledgments of the divine in our public institutions does not suggest that those who disagree are compelled to join the expression or approve its content.

The principal audience for these invocations is not, indeed, the public but lawmakers themselves, who may find that a moment of prayer or quiet reflection sets the mind to a higher purpose and thereby eases the task of governing. The District Court in *Marsh* described the prayer exercise as "an internal act" directed at the Nebraska Legislature's "own members," rather than an effort to promote religious observance among the public. To be sure, many members of the public find these prayers meaningful and wish to join them. But their purpose is largely to accommodate the spiritual needs of lawmakers and connect them to a tradition dating to the time of the Framers. For members of town boards and commissions, who often serve part-time and as volunteers, ceremonial prayer may also reflect the values they hold as private citizens. The prayer is an opportunity for them to show who and what they are without denying the right to dissent by those who disagree.

The analysis would be different if town board members directed the public to participate in the prayers, singled out dissidents for opprobrium, or indicated that their decisions might be influenced by a person's acquiescence in the prayer opportunity. No such thing occurred in the town of Greece. . . .

In their declarations in the trial court, respondents stated that the prayers gave them offense and made them feel excluded and disrespected. Offense, however, does not equate to coercion. Adults often encounter speech they find disagreeable; and an Establishment Clause violation is not made out any time a person experiences a sense of affront from the expression of contrary religious views in a legislative forum, especially where, as here, any member of the public is welcome in turn to offer an invocation reflecting his or her own convictions. . . .

This case can be distinguished from the conclusions and holding of *Lee v. Weisman*. There the Court found that, in the context of a graduation where school authorities maintained close supervision over the conduct of the students and the substance of the ceremony, a religious invocation was coercive as to an objecting student. Four Justices dissented in *Lee,* but the circumstances the Court confronted there are not present in this case and do not control its outcome. Nothing in the record suggests that members of the public are dissuaded from leaving the meeting room during the prayer, arriving late, or even, as happened here, making a later protest. In this case, as in *Marsh,* board members and constituents are "free to enter and leave with little comment and for any number of reasons." *Lee*. Should nonbelievers choose to exit the room during a prayer they find distasteful, their absence will not stand out as disrespectful or even noteworthy. And should they remain, their quiet acquiescence will not, in light of our traditions, be interpreted as an agreement with the words or ideas expressed. Neither choice represents an unconstitutional imposition as to mature adults, who "presumably" are "not readily susceptible to religious indoctrination or peer pressure." *Marsh* (internal quotation marks and citations omitted).

In the town of Greece, the prayer is delivered during the ceremonial portion of the town's meeting. Board members are not engaged in policymaking at this time, but in more general functions, such as swearing in new police officers, inducting high school athletes into the town hall of fame, and presenting proclamations to volunteers, civic groups, and senior citizens. It is a moment for town leaders to recognize the achievements of their constituents and the aspects of community life that are worth celebrating. By inviting ministers to serve as chaplain for the month, and welcoming them to the front of the room alongside civic leaders, the town is acknowledging the central place that religion, and religious institutions, hold in the lives of those present. Indeed, some congregations are not simply spiritual homes for town residents but also the provider of social services for citizens regardless of their beliefs. The inclusion of a brief, ceremonial prayer as part of a larger exercise in civic recognition suggests that its purpose and effect are to acknowledge religious leaders and the institutions they represent rather than to exclude or coerce nonbelievers.

Ceremonial prayer is but a recognition that, since this Nation was founded and until the present day, many Americans deem that their own existence must be understood by precepts far beyond the authority of government to alter or define and that willing participation in civic affairs can be consistent with a brief acknowledgment of their belief in a higher power, always with due respect for those who adhere to other beliefs. The prayer in this case has a permissible ceremonial purpose. It is not an unconstitutional establishment of religion.

* * *

The town of Greece does not violate the First Amendment by opening its meetings with prayer that comports with our tradition and does not coerce participation by nonadherents. The judgment of the U.S. Court of Appeals for the Second Circuit is reversed.

It is so ordered.

JUSTICE ALITO, with whom JUSTICE SCALIA joins, concurring.

I write separately to respond to the principal dissent. . . .

II

[T]he principal dissent's objection, in the end, is really quite niggling. According to the principal dissent, the town could have avoided any constitutional problem in either of two ways.

A

First, the principal dissent writes, "[i]f the Town Board had let its chaplains know that they should speak in nonsectarian terms, common to diverse religious groups, then no one would have valid grounds for complaint." "Priests and ministers, rabbis and imams," the principal dissent continues, "give such invocations all the time" without any great difficulty.

Both Houses of Congress now advise guest chaplains that they should keep in mind that they are addressing members from a variety of faith traditions, and as a matter of policy, this advice has much to recommend it. But any argument that nonsectarian prayer is constitutionally required runs headlong into a long history of contrary congressional practice. From the beginning, as the Court notes, many Christian prayers were offered in the House and Senate, and when rabbis and other non-Christian clergy have served as guest chaplains, their prayers have often been couched in terms particular to their faith traditions.[2]

---

2. For example, when a rabbi first delivered a prayer at a session of the House of Representatives in 1860, he appeared "in full rabbinic dress, 'piously bedecked in a white tallit and a large velvet skullcap,' " and his prayer "invoked several uniquely Jewish themes and repeated the Biblical priestly blessing in Hebrew." See Brief for Nathan Lewin as *Amicus Curiae*. Many other rabbis have given distinctively Jewish prayers, and distinctively Islamic, Buddhist, and Hindu prayers have also been delivered.

Not only is there no historical support for the proposition that only generic prayer is allowed, but as our country has become more diverse, composing a prayer that is acceptable to all members of the community who hold religious beliefs has become harder and harder. It was one thing to compose a prayer that is acceptable to both Christians and Jews; it is much harder to compose a prayer that is also acceptable to followers of Eastern religions that are now well represented in this country. Many local clergy may find the project daunting, if not impossible, and some may feel that they cannot in good faith deliver such a vague prayer.

In addition, if a town attempts to go beyond simply *recommending* that a guest chaplain deliver a prayer that is broadly acceptable to all members of a particular community (and the groups represented in different communities will vary), the town will inevitably encounter sensitive problems. . . .

B

If a town wants to avoid the problems associated with this first option, the principal dissent argues, it has another choice: It may "invit[e] clergy of many faiths." "When one month a clergy member refers to Jesus, and the next to Allah or Jehovah," the principal dissent explains, "the government does not identify itself with one religion or align itself with that faith's citizens, and the effect of even sectarian prayer is transformed."

If, as the principal dissent appears to concede, such a rotating system would obviate any constitutional problems, then despite all its high rhetoric, the principal dissent's quarrel with the town of Greece really boils down to this: The town's clerical employees did a bad job in compiling the list of potential guest chaplains. For that is really the only difference between what the town did and what the principal dissent is willing to accept. . . .

The effect of requiring such exactitude would be to pressure towns to forswear altogether the practice of having a prayer before meetings of the town council. Many local officials, puzzled by our often puzzling Establishment Clause jurisprudence and terrified of the legal fees that may result from a lawsuit claiming a constitutional violation, already think that the safest course is to ensure that local government is a religion-free zone. Indeed, the Court of Appeals' opinion in this case advised towns that constitutional difficulties "may well prompt municipalities to pause and think carefully before adopting legislative prayer." But if, as precedent and historic practice make clear (and the principal dissent concedes), prayer before a legislative session is not inherently inconsistent with the First Amendment, then a unit of local government should not be held to have violated the First Amendment simply because its procedure for lining up guest chaplains does not comply in all respects with what might be termed a "best practices" standard.

III

While the principal dissent, in the end, would demand no more than a small modification in the procedure that the town of Greece initially followed, much of the rhetoric in that opinion sweeps more broadly. Indeed, the logical thrust of many of its arguments is that prayer is *never* permissible prior to meetings of local government legislative bodies. At Greece Town Board meetings, the principal dissent pointedly notes, ordinary citizens (and even children!) are often present. The guest chaplains stand in front of the room facing the public. "[T]he setting is intimate," and ordinary citizens are permitted to speak and to ask the board to address problems that have a direct effect on their lives. The meetings are "occasions for ordinary citizens to engage with and petition their government, often on highly individualized matters." Before a session of this sort, the principal dissent argues, any prayer that is not acceptable to all in attendance is out of bounds.

The features of Greece meetings that the principal dissent highlights are by no means unusual. It is common for residents to attend such meetings, either to speak on matters on the agenda or to request that the town address other issues that are important to them. Nor is there anything unusual about the occasional attendance of students, and when a prayer is given at the beginning of such a meeting, I expect that the chaplain generally stands at the front of the room and faces the public. To do otherwise would probably be seen by many as rude. Finally, although the principal dissent, attaches importance to the fact that guest chaplains in the town of Greece often began with the words "Let us pray," that is also commonplace and for many clergy, I suspect, almost reflexive. In short, I see nothing out of the ordinary about any of the features that the principal dissent notes. Therefore, if prayer is not allowed at meetings with those characteristics, local government legislative bodies, unlike their national and state counterparts, cannot begin their meetings with a prayer. I see no sound basis for drawing such a distinction.

IV

The principal dissent claims to accept the Court's decision in *Marsh v. Chambers*, which upheld the constitutionality of the Nebraska Legislature's practice of prayer at the beginning of legislative sessions, but the principal dissent's acceptance of *Marsh* appears to be predicated on the view that the prayer at issue in that case was little more than a formality to which the legislators paid scant attention. The principal dissent describes this scene: A session of the state legislature begins with or without most members present; a strictly nonsectarian prayer is recited while some legislators remain seated; and few members of the public are exposed to the experience. This sort of perfunctory and hidden-away prayer, the principal dissent implies, is all that *Marsh* and the First Amendment can tolerate.

It is questionable whether the principal dissent accurately describes the Nebraska practice at issue in *Marsh*, but what is important is not so much what happened in Nebraska in the years prior to *Marsh*, but what happened before congressional sessions during the period leading up to the adoption of the First Amendment. By that time, prayer before legislative sessions already had an impressive pedigree, and it is important to recall that history and the events that led to the adoption of the practice.

The principal dissent paints a picture of "morning in Nebraska" circa 1983, but it is more instructive to consider "morning in Philadelphia," September 1774. The First Continental Congress convened in Philadelphia, and the need for the 13 colonies to unite was imperative. But "[m]any things set colony apart from colony," and prominent among these sources of division was religion. "Purely as a practical matter," however, the project of bringing the colonies together required that these divisions be overcome.

Samuel Adams sought to bridge these differences by prodding a fellow Massachusetts delegate to move to open the session with a prayer. As John Adams later recounted, this motion was opposed on the ground that the delegates were "so divided in religious sentiments, some Episcopalians, some Quakers, some Anabaptists, some Presbyterians, and some Congregationalists, that [they] could not join in the same act of worship." In response, Samuel Adams proclaimed that "he was no bigot, and could hear a prayer from a gentleman of piety and virtue, who was at the same time a friend to his country." Putting aside his personal prejudices, he moved to invite a local Anglican minister, Jacob Duché, to lead the first prayer.

The following morning, Duché appeared in full "pontificals" and delivered both the Anglican prayers for the day and an extemporaneous prayer. For many of the delegates — members of religious groups that had come to America to escape persecution in Britain — listening to a distinctively Anglican prayer by a minister of the Church of England represented an act of notable ecumenism. But Duché's prayer met with wide approval — John Adams wrote that it "filled the bosom of every man" in attendance — and the practice was continued. This first congressional prayer was emphatically Christian, and it was neither an empty formality nor strictly nondenominational. But one of its purposes, and presumably one of its effects, was not to divide, but to unite.

It is no wonder, then, that the practice of beginning congressional sessions with a prayer was continued after the Revolution ended and the new Constitution was adopted. One of the first actions taken by the new Congress when it convened in 1789 was to appoint chaplains for both Houses. The first Senate chaplain, an Episcopalian, was appointed on April 25, 1789, and the first House chaplain, a Presbyterian, was appointed on May 1. Three days later, Madison announced that he planned to introduce proposed constitutional amendments to protect individual rights; on June 8, 1789, those amendments were introduced; and on September 26, 1789, the amendments were approved to be sent to the States for ratification. In the years since the adoption of the First Amendment, the practice of prayer before sessions of the House and Senate has continued, and opening prayers from a great variety of faith traditions have been offered.

This Court has often noted that actions taken by the First Congress are presumptively consistent with the Bill of Rights, and this principle has special force when it comes to the interpretation of the Establishment Clause. This Court has always purported to base its Establishment Clause decisions on the original meaning of that provision. Thus, in *Marsh*, when the Court was called upon to decide whether prayer prior to sessions of a state legislature was consistent with the Establishment Clause, we relied heavily on the history of prayer before sessions of Congress and held that a state legislature may follow a similar practice.

There can be little doubt that the decision in *Marsh* reflected the original understanding of the First Amendment. It is virtually inconceivable that the First Congress, having appointed chaplains whose responsibilities prominently included the delivery of prayers at the beginning of each daily session, thought that this practice was inconsistent with the Establishment Clause. And since this practice was well established and undoubtedly well known, it seems equally clear that the state legislatures that ratified the First Amendment had the same understanding. In the case before us, the Court of Appeals appeared to base its decision on one of the Establishment Clause "tests" set out in the opinions of this Court, but if there is any inconsistency between any of those tests and the historic practice of legislative prayer, the inconsistency calls into question the validity of the test, not the historic practice.

V

. . . All that the Court does today is to allow a town to follow a practice that we have previously held is permissible for Congress and state legislatures. In seeming to suggest otherwise, the principal dissent goes far astray.

JUSTICE THOMAS, with whom JUSTICE SCALIA joins as to Part II, concurring in part and concurring in the judgment.

Except for Part II-B, I join the opinion of the Court, which faithfully applies *Marsh*. I write separately to reiterate my view that the Establishment Clause is "best understood as a federalism provision," *Elk Grove Unified School Dist. v. Newdow* (2004) (Thomas, J., concurring in judgment), and to state my understanding of the proper "coercion" analysis.

I

The Establishment Clause provides that "Congress shall make no law respecting an establishment of religion." U.S. Const., Amdt. 1. As I have explained before, the text and history of the Clause "resis[t] incorporation" against the States. If the Establishment Clause is not incorporated, then it has no application here, where only municipal action is at issue.

As an initial matter, the Clause probably prohibits Congress from establishing a national religion. The text of the Clause also suggests that Congress "could not interfere with state establishments, notwithstanding any argument that could be made based on Congress' power under the Necessary and Proper Clause." *Newdow* (opinion of Thomas, J.). The language of the First Amendment ("Congress shall make no law") "precisely tracked and inverted the exact wording" of the Necessary and Proper Clause ("Congress shall have power . . . to make all laws which shall be necessary and proper . . ."), which was the subject of fierce criticism by Anti-Federalists at the time of ratification. A. Amar, The Bill of Rights 39 (1998) (hereinafter Amar); see also Natelson, The Framing and Adoption of the Necessary and Proper Clause, in The Origins of the Necessary and Proper Clause 84, 94-96 (G. Lawson, G. Miller, R. Natelson, & G. Seidman eds. 2010) (summarizing Anti-Federalist claims that the Necessary and Proper Clause would aggrandize the powers of the Federal Government). That choice of language—"Congress shall make no law"—effectively denied Congress any power to regulate state establishments.

Construing the Establishment Clause as a federalism provision accords with the variety of church-state arrangements that existed at the Founding. At least six States had established churches in 1789. New England States like Massachusetts, Connecticut, and New Hampshire maintained local-rule establishments whereby the majority in each town could select the minister and religious denomination (usually Congregationalism, or "Puritanism"). In the South, Maryland, South Carolina, and Georgia eliminated their exclusive Anglican establishments following the American Revolution and adopted general establishments, which permitted taxation in support of all Christian churches (or, as in South Carolina, all Protestant churches). Virginia, by contrast, had recently abolished its official state establishment and ended direct government funding of clergy after a legislative battle led by James Madison. Other States—principally Rhode Island, Pennsylvania, and Delaware, which were founded by religious dissenters—had no history of formal establishments at all, although they still maintained religious tests for office.

The import of this history is that the relationship between church and state in the fledgling Republic was far from settled at the time of ratification. See Muõz, The Original Meaning of the Establishment Clause and the Impossibility of Its Incorporation, 8 U. Pa. J. Constitutional L. 585, 605 (2006). Although the remaining state establishments were ultimately dismantled—Massachusetts, the last State to disestablish, would do so in 1833—that outcome was far from assured when the Bill of Rights was ratified in 1791. That lack of consensus suggests that the First Amendment was simply agnostic on the subject of state establishments; the decision to establish or disestablish religion was reserved to the States.

The Federalist logic of the original Establishment Clause poses a special barrier to its mechanical incorporation against the States through the Fourteenth Amendment. Unlike the Free Exercise Clause, which "plainly protects individuals against congressional interference with the right to exercise their religion," the Establishment Clause "does not purport to protect individual rights." *Newdow* (opinion of Thomas, J.). Instead, the States are the particular beneficiaries of the Clause. Incorporation therefore gives rise to a paradoxical result: Applying the Clause against the States eliminates their right to establish a religion free from federal interference, thereby "prohibit[ing] exactly what the Establishment Clause protected."

Put differently, the structural reasons that counsel against incorporating the Tenth Amendment also apply to the Establishment Clause. To my knowledge, no court has ever suggested that the Tenth Amendment, which "reserve[s] to the States" powers not delegated to the Federal Government, could or should be applied against the States. To incorporate that limitation would be to divest the States of all powers not specifically delegated to them, thereby inverting the original import of the Amendment. Incorporating the Establishment Clause has precisely the same effect.

The most cogent argument in favor of incorporation may be that, by the time of Reconstruction, the framers of the Fourteenth Amendment had come to reinterpret the Establishment Clause (notwithstanding its Federalist origins) as expressing an individual right. On this question, historical evidence from the 1860's is mixed. Congressmen who catalogued the personal rights protected by the First Amendment commonly referred to speech, press, petition, and assembly, but not to a personal right of nonestablishment; instead, they spoke only of " 'free exercise' " or " 'freedom of conscience.' " Amar (collecting sources). There may be reason to think these lists were abbreviated, and silence on the issue is not dispositive. See Lash, The Second Adoption of the Establishment Clause: The Rise of the Nonestablishment Principle, 27 Ariz. St. L.J. 1085, 1141-1145 (1995). Given the textual and logical difficulties posed by incorporation, however, there is no warrant for transforming the meaning of the Establishment Clause without a firm historical foundation. The burden of persuasion therefore rests with those who claim that the Clause assumed a different meaning upon adoption of the Fourteenth Amendment.[3]

II

Even if the Establishment Clause were properly incorporated against the States, the municipal prayers at issue in this case bear no resemblance to the coercive state establishments that existed at the founding. "The coercion that was a hallmark of historical establishments of religion was coercion of religious orthodoxy and of financial support *by force of law and threat of penalty*." *Lee v. Weisman* (1992) (Scalia, J., dissenting). In a typical case, attendance at the established church was mandatory, and taxes were levied to generate church revenue. Dissenting ministers were barred from preaching, and political participation was limited to members of the established church.

3. This Court has never squarely addressed these barriers to the incorporation of the Establishment Clause. When the issue was first presented in *Everson v. Board of Ed. of Ewing* (1947), the Court casually asserted that "the Fourteenth Amendment [has been] interpreted to make the prohibitions of the First applicable to state action abridging religious freedom. There is every reason to give the same application and broad interpretation to the 'establishment of religion' clause." The cases the Court cited in support of that proposition involved the Free Exercise Clause—which had been incorporated seven years earlier. Thus, in the space of a single paragraph and a nonresponsive string citation, the *Everson* Court glibly effected a sea change in constitutional law. The Court's inattention to these doctrinal questions might be explained, although not excused, by the rise of popular conceptions about "separation of church and state" as an "American" constitutional right. See generally P. Hamburger, Separation of Church and State 454-463 (2002); see also *id.,* at 391-454 (discussing the role of nativist sentiment in the campaign for "separation" as an American ideal).

This is not to say that the state establishments in existence when the Bill of Rights was ratified were uniform. As previously noted, establishments in the South were typically governed through the state legislature or State Constitution, while establishments in New England were administered at the municipal level. Notwithstanding these variations, both state and local forms of establishment involved "actual legal coercion," *Newdow* (opinion of Thomas, J.): They exercised government power in order to exact financial support of the church, compel religious observance, or control religious doctrine.

None of these founding-era state establishments remained at the time of Reconstruction. But even assuming that the framers of the Fourteenth Amendment reconceived the nature of the Establishment Clause as a constraint on the States, nothing in the history of the intervening period suggests a fundamental transformation in their understanding of *what constituted an establishment*. At a minimum, there is no support for the proposition that the framers of the Fourteenth Amendment embraced wholly modern notions that the Establishment Clause is violated whenever the "reasonable observer" feels "subtle pressure," *ante,* or perceives governmental "endors[ement]," *ante*. For example, of the 37 States in existence when the Fourteenth Amendment was ratified, 27 State Constitutions "contained an explicit reference to God in their preambles." Calabresi & Agudo, Individual Rights Under State Constitutions When the Fourteenth Amendment Was Ratified in 1868: What Rights Are Deeply Rooted in American History and Tradition?, 87 Tex. L. Rev. 7, 12, 37 (2008). In addition to the preamble references, 30 State Constitutions contained other references to the divine, using such phrases as "Almighty God," "[O]ur Creator," and "Sovereign Ruler of the Universe." *Id.* Moreover, the state constitutional provisions that prohibited religious "comp[ulsion]" made clear that the relevant sort of compulsion was legal in nature, of the same type that had characterized founding-era establishments. These provisions strongly suggest that, whatever nonestablishment principles existed in 1868, they included no concern for the finer sensibilities of the "reasonable observer."

Thus, to the extent coercion is relevant to the Establishment Clause analysis, it is actual legal coercion that counts—not the "subtle coercive pressures" allegedly felt by respondents in this case, *ante*. The majority properly concludes that "[o]ffense . . . does not equate to coercion," since "[a]dults often encounter speech they find disagreeable[,] and an Establishment Clause violation is not made out any time a person experiences a sense of affront from the expression of contrary religious views in a legislative forum." *Ante*. I would simply add, in light of the foregoing history of the Establishment Clause, that "[p]eer pressure, unpleasant as it may be, is not coercion" either. *Newdow* (opinion of Thomas, J.).

JUSTICE BREYER, dissenting. . . .

As both the Court and Justice Kagan point out, we are a Nation of many religions. And the Constitution's Religion Clauses seek to "protec[t] the Nation's social fabric from religious conflict." *Zelman v. Simmons-Harris* (2002) (Breyer, J., dissenting). The question in this case is whether the prayer practice of the town of Greece, by doing too little to reflect the religious diversity of its citizens, did too much, even if unintentionally, to promote the "political division along religious lines" that "was one of the principal evils against which the First Amendment was intended to protect." *Lemon v. Kurtzman* (1971).

In seeking an answer to that fact-sensitive question, "I see no test-related substitute for the exercise of legal judgment." *Van Orden v. Perry* (2005) (Breyer, J., concurring in judgment). Having applied my legal judgment to the relevant facts, I conclude, like Justice Kagan, that the town of Greece failed to make reasonable efforts to include prayer givers of minority faiths, with the result that, although it is a community of several faiths, its prayer givers were almost exclusively persons of a single faith. Under these circumstances, I would affirm the judgment of the Court of Appeals that Greece's prayer practice violated the Establishment Clause.

I dissent from the Court's decision to the contrary.

JUSTICE KAGAN, with whom JUSTICE GINSBURG, JUSTICE BREYER, and JUSTICE SOTOMAYOR join, dissenting.

For centuries now, people have come to this country from every corner of the world to share in the blessing of religious freedom. Our Constitution promises that they may worship in their own way, without fear of penalty or danger, and that in itself is a momentous offering. Yet our Constitution makes a commitment still more remarkable—that however those individuals worship, they will count as full and equal American citizens. A Christian, a Jew, a Muslim (and so forth)—each stands in the same relationship with her country, with her state and local communities, and with every level and body of government. So that when each person performs the duties or seeks the benefits of citizenship, she does so not as an adherent to one or another religion, but simply as an American.

I respectfully dissent from the Court's opinion because I think the Town of Greece's prayer practices violate that norm of religious equality—the breathtakingly generous constitutional idea that our public institutions belong no less to the Buddhist or Hindu than to the Methodist or Episcopalian. I do not contend that principle translates here into a bright separationist line. To the contrary, I agree with the Court's decision in *Marsh*, upholding the Nebraska Legislature's tradition of beginning each session with a chaplain's prayer. And I believe that pluralism and inclusion in a town hall can satisfy the constitutional requirement of neutrality; such a forum need not become a religion-free zone. But still, the Town of Greece should lose this case. The practice at issue here differs from the one sustained in *Marsh* because Greece's town meetings involve participation by ordinary citizens, and the invocations given—directly to those citizens—were predominantly sectarian in content. Still more, Greece's Board did nothing to recognize religious diversity: In arranging for clergy members to open each meeting, the Town never sought (except briefly when this suit was filed) to involve, accommodate, or in any way reach out to adherents of non-Christian religions. So month in and month out for over a decade, prayers steeped in only one faith, addressed toward members of the public, commenced meetings to discuss local affairs and distribute government benefits. In my view, that practice does not square with the First Amendment's promise that every citizen, irrespective of her religion, owns an equal share in her government.

I

. . . "The clearest command of the Establishment Clause," this Court has held, "is that one religious denomination cannot be officially preferred over another." *Larson v. Valente*, 456 U.S. 228, 244 (1982). Justices have often differed about a further issue: whether and how the Clause applies to governmental policies favoring religion (of all kinds) over non-religion. . . .

II

[B]efore I dispute the Town and Court, I want to give them their due: They are right that, under *Marsh*, legislative prayer has a distinctive constitutional warrant by virtue of tradition. As the Court today describes, a long history, stretching back to the first session of Congress (when chaplains began to give prayers in both Chambers), "ha[s] shown that prayer in this limited context could 'coexis[t] with the principles of disestablishment and religious freedom.' " Relying on that "unbroken" national tradition, *Marsh* upheld (I think correctly) the Nebraska Legislature's practice of opening each day with a chaplain's prayer as "a tolerable acknowledgment of beliefs widely held among the people of this country." And so I agree with the majority that the issue here is "whether the prayer practice in the Town of Greece fits within the tradition long followed in Congress and the state legislatures."

Where I depart from the majority is in my reply to that question. The town hall here is a kind of hybrid. Greece's Board indeed has legislative functions, as Congress and state assemblies do—and that means some opening prayers are allowed there. But . . . the Board's meetings are also occasions for ordinary citizens to engage with and petition their government, often on highly individualized matters. That feature calls for Board members to exercise special care to ensure that the prayers offered are inclusive—that they respect each and every member of the community as an equal citizen.[4] But the Board, and the clergy members it selected, made no such effort. Instead, the prayers given in Greece, addressed directly to the Town's citizenry, were *more* sectarian, and *less* inclusive, than anything this Court sustained in *Marsh*. For those reasons, the prayer in Greece departs from the legislative tradition that the majority takes as its benchmark.

4. Because Justice Alito questions this point, it bears repeating. I do not remotely contend that "prayer is not allowed" at participatory meetings of "local government legislative bodies"; nor is that the "logical thrust" of any argument I make. *Ante*. Rather, what I say throughout this opinion is that in this citizen-centered venue, government officials must take steps to ensure—as none of Greece's Board members ever did—that opening prayers are inclusive of different faiths, rather than always identified with a single religion.

A

Start by comparing two pictures, drawn precisely from reality. The first is of Nebraska's (unicameral) Legislature, as this Court and the state senators themselves described it. The second is of town council meetings in Greece, as revealed in this case's record.

It is morning in Nebraska, and senators are beginning to gather in the State's legislative chamber: It is the beginning of the official workday, although senators may not yet need to be on the floor. The chaplain rises to give the daily invocation. That prayer, as the senators emphasized when their case came to this Court, is "directed only at the legislative membership, not at the public at large." Any members of the public who happen to be in attendance—not very many at this early hour—watch only from the upstairs visitors' gallery.

The longtime chaplain says something like the following (the excerpt is from his own *amicus* brief supporting Greece in this case): "*O God,* who has given all persons talents and varying capacities, Thou dost only require of us that we utilize Thy gifts to a maximum. In this Legislature to which Thou has entrusted special abilities and opportunities, may each recognize his stewardship for the people of the State." The chaplain is a Presbyterian minister, and "some of his earlier prayers" explicitly invoked Christian beliefs, but he "removed all references to Christ" after a single legislator complained. The chaplain also previously invited other clergy members to give the invocation, including local rabbis.

Now change the channel: It is evening in Greece, New York, and the Supervisor of the Town Board calls its monthly public meeting to order. Those meetings (so says the Board itself) are "the most important part of Town government." They serve assorted functions, almost all actively involving members of the public. The Board may swear in new Town employees and hand out awards for civic accomplishments; it always provides an opportunity (called a Public Forum) for citizens to address local issues and ask for improved services or new policies (for example, better accommodations for the disabled or actions to ameliorate traffic congestion); and it usually hears debate on individual applications from residents and local businesses to obtain special land-use permits, zoning variances, or other licenses.

The Town Supervisor, Town Clerk, Chief of Police, and four Board members sit at the front of the meeting room on a raised dais. But the setting is intimate: There are likely to be only 10 or so citizens in attendance. A few may be children or teenagers, present to receive an award or fulfill a high school civics requirement.

As the first order of business, the Town Supervisor introduces a local Christian clergy member—denominated the chaplain of the month—to lead the assembled persons in prayer. The pastor steps up to a lectern (emblazoned with the Town's seal) at the front of the dais, and with his back to the Town officials, he faces the citizens present. He asks them all to stand and to "pray as we begin this evening's town meeting." (He does not suggest that anyone should feel free not to participate.) And he says:

"The beauties of spring . . . are an expressive symbol of the new life of the risen Christ. The Holy Spirit was sent to the apostles at Pentecost so that they would be courageous witnesses of the Good News to different regions of the Mediterranean world and beyond. The Holy Spirit continues to be the inspiration and the source of strength and virtue, which we all need in the world of today. And so . . . [w]e pray this evening for the guidance of the Holy Spirit as the Greece Town Board meets."

After the pastor concludes, Town officials behind him make the sign of the cross, as do some members of the audience, and everyone says "Amen." The Supervisor then announces the start of the Public Forum, and a citizen stands up to complain about the Town's contract with a cable company.

B

Let's count the ways in which these pictures diverge. First, the governmental proceedings at which the prayers occur differ significantly in nature and purpose. The Nebraska Legislature's floor sessions—like those of the U.S. Congress and other state assemblies—are of, by, and for elected lawmakers. Members of the public take no part in those proceedings; any few who attend are spectators only, watching from a high-up visitors' gallery. (In that respect, note that neither the Nebraska Legislature nor the Congress calls for prayer when citizens themselves participate in a hearing—say, by giving testimony relevant to a bill or nomination.) Greece's town meetings, by contrast, revolve around ordinary members of the community. Each and every aspect of those sessions provides opportunities for Town residents to interact with public officials. And the most important parts enable those citizens to petition their government. In the Public Forum, they urge (or oppose) changes in the Board's policies and priorities; and then, in what are essentially adjudicatory hearings, they request the Board to grant (or deny) applications for various permits, licenses, and zoning variances. So the meetings, both by design and in operation, allow citizens to actively participate in the Town's governance—sharing concerns, airing grievances, and both shaping the community's policies and seeking their benefits.

Second (and following from what I just said), the prayers in these two settings have different audiences. In the Nebraska Legislature, the chaplain spoke to, and only to, the elected representatives. Nebraska's senators were adamant on that point in briefing *Marsh,* and the facts fully supported them: As the senators stated, "[t]he activity is a matter of internal daily procedure directed only at the legislative membership, not at [members of] the public." The same is true in the U.S. Congress and, I suspect, in every other state legislature. As several Justices later noted (and the majority today agrees),[5] *Marsh* involved "government officials

5. For ease of reference and to avoid confusion, I refer to Justice Kennedy's opinion as "the majority." But the language I cite that appears in Part II-B of that opinion is, in fact, only attributable to a plurality of the Court.

invok[ing] spiritual inspiration entirely for their own benefit without directing any religious message at the citizens they lead." *Lee* (Souter, J., concurring).

The very opposite is true in Greece: Contrary to the majority's characterization, the prayers there are directed squarely at the citizens. Remember that the chaplain of the month stands with his back to the Town Board; his real audience is the group he is facing—the 10 or so members of the public, perhaps including children. And he typically addresses those people, as even the majority observes, as though he is "directing [his] congregation." He almost always begins with some version of "Let us all pray together." Often, he calls on everyone to stand and bow their heads, and he may ask them to recite a common prayer with him. He refers, constantly, to a collective "we"—to "our" savior, for example, to the presence of the Holy Spirit in "our" lives, or to "our brother the Lord Jesus Christ." In essence, the chaplain leads, as the first part of a town meeting, a highly intimate (albeit relatively brief) prayer service, with the public serving as his congregation.

And third, the prayers themselves differ in their content and character. *Marsh* characterized the prayers in the Nebraska Legislature as "in the Judeo-Christian tradition," and stated, as a relevant (even if not dispositive) part of its analysis, that the chaplain had removed all explicitly Christian references at a senator's request. And as the majority acknowledges, *Marsh* hinged on the view that "that the prayer opportunity ha[d] [not] been exploited to proselytize or advance any one . . . faith or belief"; had it been otherwise, the Court would have reached a different decision.

But no one can fairly read the prayers from Greece's Town meetings as anything other than explicitly Christian—constantly and exclusively so. From the time Greece established its prayer practice in 1999 until litigation loomed nine years later, all of its monthly chaplains were Christian clergy. And after a brief spell surrounding the filing of this suit (when a Jewish layman, a Wiccan priestess, and a Baha'i minister appeared at meetings), the Town resumed its practice of inviting only clergy from neighboring Protestant and Catholic churches. About two-thirds of the prayers given over this decade or so invoked "Jesus," "Christ," "Your Son," or "the Holy Spirit"; in the 18 months before the record closed, 85% included those references. Many prayers contained elaborations of Christian doctrine or recitations of scripture. And the prayers usually close with phrases like "in the name of Jesus Christ" or "in the name of Your son."

Still more, the prayers betray no understanding that the American community is today, as it long has been, a rich mosaic of religious faiths. The monthly chaplains appear almost always to assume that everyone in the room is Christian (and of a kind who has no objection to government-sponsored worship). The Town itself has never urged its chaplains to reach out to members of other faiths, or even to recall that they might be present. And accordingly, few chaplains have made any effort to be inclusive; none has thought even to assure attending members of the public that they need not participate in the prayer session. Indeed, as the majority forthrightly recognizes, when the plaintiffs here began to voice concern over prayers that excluded some Town residents, one pastor pointedly thanked the Board "[o]n behalf of all God-fearing people" for holding fast, and another declared the objectors "in the minority and . . . ignorant of the history of our country."

C

Those three differences, taken together, remove this case from the protective ambit of *Marsh* and the history on which it relied. To recap: *Marsh* upheld prayer addressed to legislators alone, in a proceeding in which citizens had no role—and even then, only when it did not "proselytize or advance" any single religion. It was that legislative prayer practice (not every prayer in a body exercising any legislative function) that the Court found constitutional given its "unambiguous and unbroken history." But that approved practice, as I have shown, is not Greece's. None of the history *Marsh* cited—and none the majority details today—supports calling on citizens to pray, in a manner consonant with only a single religion's beliefs, at a participatory public proceeding, having both legislative and adjudicative components. Or to use the majority's phrase, no "history shows that th[is] specific practice is permitted." And so, contra the majority, Greece's prayers cannot simply ride on the constitutional coattails of the legislative tradition *Marsh* described. The Board's practice must, in its own particulars, meet constitutional requirements.

And the guideposts for addressing that inquiry include the principles of religious neutrality I discussed earlier. The government (whether federal, state, or local) may not favor, or align itself with, any particular creed. And that is nowhere more true than when officials and citizens come face to face in their shared institutions of governance. In performing civic functions and seeking civic benefits, each person of this nation must experience a government that belongs to one and all, irrespective of belief. And for its part, each government must ensure that its participatory processes will not classify those citizens by faith, or make relevant their religious differences.

To decide how Greece fares on that score, think again about how its prayer practice works, meeting after meeting. . . . Let's say that a Muslim citizen of Greece goes before the Board to share her views on policy or request some permit. Maybe she wants the Board to put up a traffic light at a dangerous intersection; or maybe she needs a zoning variance to build an addition on her home. But just before she gets to say her piece, a minister deputized by the Town asks her to pray "in the name of God's only son Jesus Christ." She must think—it is hardly paranoia, but only the truth—that Christian worship has become entwined with local governance. And now she faces a choice—to pray alongside the majority as one of that group or somehow to register her deeply felt difference. She is a strong person, but that is no easy call—especially given that the room is small and her every action (or inaction) will be noticed. She does not wish to be rude to her neighbors, nor does she wish to aggravate the Board members whom she will soon be trying to persuade. And yet she does not want to acknowledge Christ's divinity, any more than many of her neighbors would want to deny that tenet. So assume she declines to participate with the others in the first act of the meeting—or even, as the majority proposes, that she stands up and leaves the room altogether. At the least, she becomes a different kind of citizen, one who will not join in the religious practice that the Town Board has chosen as reflecting its own and the community's most cherished beliefs. And she thus stands at a remove, based solely on religion, from her fellow citizens and her elected representatives.

Everything about that situation, I think, infringes the First Amendment. (And of course, as I noted earlier, it would do so no less if the Town's clergy always used the liturgy of some other religion.) That the Town Board selects, month after month and year after year, prayergivers who will reliably speak in the voice of Christianity, and so places itself behind a single creed. That in offering those sectarian prayers, the Board's chosen clergy members repeatedly call on individuals, prior to participating in local governance, to join in a form of worship that may be at odds with their own beliefs. That the clergy thus put some residents to the unenviable choice of either pretending to pray like the majority or declining to join its communal activity, at the very moment of petitioning their elected leaders. That the practice thus divides the citizenry, creating one class that shares the Board's own evident religious beliefs and another (far smaller) class that does not. And that the practice also alters a dissenting citizen's relationship with her government, making her religious difference salient when she seeks only to engage her elected representatives as would any other citizen.

None of this means that Greece's town hall must be religion- or prayer-free. "[W]e are a religious people," *Marsh* observed, and prayer draws some warrant from tradition in a town hall, as well as in Congress or a state legislature. What the circumstances here demand is the recognition that we are a pluralistic people too. When citizens of all faiths come to speak to each other and their elected representatives in a legislative session, the government must take especial care to ensure that the prayers they hear will seek to include, rather than serve to divide. No more is required—but that much is crucial—to treat every citizen, of whatever religion, as an equal participant in her government.

And contrary to the majority's (and Justice Alito's) view, that is not difficult to do. If the Town Board had let its chaplains know that they should speak in nonsectarian terms, common to diverse religious groups, then no one would have valid grounds for complaint. Priests and ministers, rabbis and imams give such invocations all the time; there is no great mystery to the project. (And providing that guidance would hardly have caused the Board to run afoul of the idea that "[t]he First Amendment is not a majority rule," as the Court (headspinningly) suggests; what does that is the Board's *refusal* to reach out to members of minority religious groups.) Or if the Board preferred, it might have invited clergy of many faiths to serve as chaplains, as the majority notes that Congress does. When one month a clergy member refers to Jesus, and the next to Allah or Jehovah—as the majority hopefully though counterfactually suggests happened here, the government does not identify itself with one religion or align itself with that faith's citizens, and the effect of even sectarian prayer is transformed. So Greece had multiple ways of incorporating prayer into its town meetings—reflecting all the ways that prayer (as most of us know from daily life) can forge common bonds, rather than divide.

But Greece could not do what it did: infuse a participatory government body with one (and only one) faith, so that month in and month out, the citizens appearing before it become partly defined by their creed—as those who share, and those who do not, the community's majority religious belief. In this country, when citizens go before the government, they go not as Christians or Muslims or Jews (or what have you), but just as Americans (or here, as Grecians). That is what it means to be an equal citizen, irrespective of religion. And that is what the Town of Greece precluded by so identifying itself with a single faith.

III

How, then, does the majority go so far astray, allowing the Town of Greece to turn its assemblies for citizens into a forum for Christian prayer? The answer does not lie in first principles: I have no doubt that every member of this Court believes as firmly as I that our institutions of government belong equally to all, regardless of faith. Rather, the error reflects two kinds of blindness. First, the majority misapprehends the facts of this case, as distinct from those characterizing traditional legislative prayer. And second, the majority misjudges the essential meaning of the religious worship in Greece's town hall, along with its capacity to exclude and divide. . . .

When the majority analyzes the "setting" and "audience" for prayer, it focuses almost exclusively on Congress and the Nebraska Legislature; it does not stop to analyze how far those factors differ in Greece's meetings. The majority thus gives short shrift to the gap—more like, the chasm—between a legislative floor session involving only elected officials and a town hall revolving around ordinary citizens. And similarly the majority neglects to consider how the prayers in Greece are mostly addressed to members of the public, rather than (as in the forums it discusses) to the lawmakers. "The District Court in *Marsh,*" the majority expounds, "described the prayer exercise as 'an internal act' directed at the Nebraska Legislature's 'own members.'" Well, yes, so it is in Lincoln, and on Capitol Hill. But not in Greece, where as I have described, the chaplain faces the Town's residents—with the Board watching from on high—and calls on them to pray together.

And of course—as the majority sidesteps as well—to pray in the name of Jesus Christ. . . . In . . . Greece only Christian clergy members speak, and then mostly in the voice of their own religion; no Allah or Jehovah ever is mentioned. So all the majority can point to in the Town's practice is that the Board "maintains a policy of nondiscrimination," and "represent[s] that it would welcome a prayer by any minister or layman who wishe[s] to give one." But that representation has never been publicized; nor has the Board (except for a few months surrounding this suit's filing) offered the chaplain's role to any non-Christian clergy or layman, in either Greece or its environs; nor has the Board ever provided its chaplains with guidance about reaching out to members of other faiths, as most state legislatures and Congress do. The majority thus errs in assimilating the Board's prayer practice to that of Congress or the Nebraska Legislature. Unlike those models, the Board is determinedly—and relentlessly—noninclusive.[6]

. . . A person's response to the doctrine, language, and imagery contained in those invocations reveals a core aspect of identity—who that person is and how she faces the world. And the responses of different individuals, in Greece and across this country, of course vary. Contrary to the majority's apparent view, such sectarian prayers are not "part of our expressive idiom" or "part of our heritage and tradition," assuming the word "our" refers to all Americans. They express beliefs that are fundamental to some, foreign to others—and because that is so they carry the ever-present potential to both exclude and divide. The majority, I think, assesses too lightly the significance of these religious differences, and so fears too little the "religiously based divisiveness that the Establishment Clause seeks to avoid." *Van Orden v. Perry* (Breyer, J., concurring in judgment). I would treat more seriously the multiplicity of Americans' religious commitments, along with the challenge they can pose to the project—the distinctively American project—of creating one from the many, and governing all as united.

IV

In 1790, George Washington traveled to Newport, Rhode Island, a longtime bastion of religious liberty and the home of the first community of American Jews. Among the citizens he met there was Moses Seixas, one of that congregation's lay officials. The ensuing exchange between the two conveys, as well as anything I know, the promise this country makes to members of every religion.

Seixas wrote first, welcoming Washington to Newport. He spoke of "a deep sense of gratitude" for the new American Government—"a Government, which to bigotry gives no sanction, to persecution no assistance—but generously affording to All liberty of conscience, and immunities of Citizenship: deeming every one, of whatever Nation, tongue, or language, equal parts of the great governmental Machine." Address from Newport Hebrew Congregation (Aug. 17, 1790). The first phrase there is the more poetic: a government that to "bigotry gives no sanction, to persecution no assistance." But the second is actually the more startling and transformative: a government that, beyond not aiding persecution, grants "immunities of citizenship" to the Christian and the Jew alike, and makes them "equal parts" of the whole country.

Washington responded the very next day. Like any successful politician, he appreciated a great line when he saw one—and knew to borrow it too. And so

---

6. Justice Alito . . . takes great pains to show that the problem arose from a sort of bureaucratic glitch: The Town's clerks, he writes, merely "did a bad job in compiling the list" of chaplains. . . . Honest oversight or not, the problem remains: Every month for more than a decade, the Board aligned itself, through its prayer practices, with a single religion. That the concurring opinion thinks my objection to that is "really quite niggling," says all there is to say about the difference between our respective views.

he repeated, word for word, Seixas's phrase about neither sanctioning bigotry nor assisting persecution. But he no less embraced the point Seixas had made about equality of citizenship. "It is now no more," Washington said, "that toleration is spoken of, as if it was by the indulgence of one class of people" to another, lesser one. For "[a]ll possess alike . . . immunities of citizenship." Letter to Newport Hebrew Congregation (Aug. 18, 1790). That is America's promise in the First Amendment: full and equal membership in the polity for members of every religious group, assuming only that they, like anyone "who live[s] under [the Government's] protection[,] should demean themselves as good citizens."

For me, that remarkable guarantee means at least this much: When the citizens of this country approach their government, they do so only as Americans, not as members of one faith or another. And that means that even in a partly legislative body, they should not confront government-sponsored worship that divides them along religious lines. I believe, for all the reasons I have given, that the Town of Greece betrayed that promise. I therefore respectfully dissent from the Court's decision.

Chapter 10

Taking Private Property for Public Use

ASSIGNMENT S-13

What Is a "Taking"?

STUDY GUIDE:

- Do you agree with Justice Kagan that *Nollan* and *Dolan* do not apply here because no taking of private property has occurred? What is her theory of those two cases?
- Hasn't the government agency simply failed to allow a particular use of property rather than "taken" it?
- What work is the concept of "unconstitutional conditions" (and the First Amendment cases cited) doing in Justice Alito's analysis? What is the evil he seeks to prevent? Are you persuaded by Justice Kagan's reply to this?
- Why the discussion of taxes? (For that matter, why aren't taxes "takings"?)
- Put another way, could there be a difference between a "tax" and (in Justice Kagan's words) "requiring a person to pay money to the government, or spend money on its behalf"? Does her treatment of liens suggest a possible way to distinguish a "tax" from the monetary fee the government is charging here for the use of private property?
- Notice that the property owner requested permission to build in 1994, and this case is now being remanded for further consideration by the lower courts. How effective is this constitutional protection of private property?

KOONTZ v. ST. JOHNS RIVER WATER MANAGEMENT DISTRICT

No. 11-1447

Argued Jan. 15, 2013 | Decided June 25, 2013

ALITO, J., delivered the opinion of the Court, in which ROBERTS, C.J., and SCALIA, KENNEDY, and THOMAS, JJ., joined. KAGAN, J., filed a dissenting opinion, in which GINSBURG, BREYER, and SOTOMAYOR, JJ., joined.

JUSTICE ALITO delivered the opinion of the Court.

Our decisions in *Nollan v. California Coastal Comm'n* (1987), and *Dolan v. City of Tigard* (1994), provide important protection against the misuse of the power of land-use regulation. In those cases, we held that a unit of government may not condition the approval of a land-use permit on the owner's relinquishment of a portion of his property unless there is a "nexus" and "rough proportionality" between the government's demand and the effects of the proposed land use. In this case, the St. Johns River Water Management District (District) believes that it circumvented *Nollan* and *Dolan* because of the way in which it structured its handling of a permit application submitted by Coy Koontz, Sr., whose estate is represented in this Court by Coy Koontz, Jr. The District did not approve his application on the condition that he surrender an interest in his land. Instead, the District, after suggesting that he could obtain approval by signing over such an interest, denied his application because he refused to yield. The Florida Supreme Court blessed this maneuver and thus effectively interred those important decisions. Because we conclude that *Nollan* and *Dolan* cannot be evaded in this way, the Florida Supreme Court's decision must be reversed.

I

A

In 1972, petitioner purchased an undeveloped 14.9-acre tract of land on the south side of Florida State Road 50, a divided four-lane highway east of Orlando. The property is located less than 1,000 feet from that road's intersection with Florida State Road 408, a tolled expressway that is one of Orlando's major thoroughfares.

A drainage ditch runs along the property's western edge, and high-voltage power lines bisect it into northern and southern sections. The combined effect of the ditch, a 100-foot wide area kept clear for the power lines, the highways, and other construction on nearby parcels is to isolate the northern section of petitioner's property from any other undeveloped land. Although largely classified as wetlands by the State, the northern section drains well; the most significant standing water forms in ruts in an unpaved road used to access the power lines. The natural topography of the property's southern section is somewhat more diverse, with a small creek, forested uplands, and wetlands that sometimes have water as much as a foot deep. A wildlife survey found evidence of animals that often frequent developed areas: raccoons, rabbits, several species of bird, and a turtle. The record also indicates that the land may be a suitable habitat for opossums.

The same year that petitioner purchased his property, Florida enacted the Water Resources Act, which divided the State into five water management districts and authorized each district to regulate "construction that connects to, draws water from, drains water into, or is placed in or across the waters in the state." Under the Act, a landowner wishing to undertake such construction must obtain from the relevant district a Management and Storage of Surface Water

(MSSW) permit, which may impose "such reasonable conditions" on the permit as are "necessary to assure" that construction will "not be harmful to the water resources of the district."

In 1984, in an effort to protect the State's rapidly diminishing wetlands, the Florida Legislature passed the Warren S. Henderson Wetlands Protection Act, which made it illegal for anyone to "dredge or fill in, on, or over surface waters" without a Wetlands Resource Management (WRM) permit. Under the Henderson Act, permit applicants are required to provide "reasonable assurance" that proposed construction on wetlands is "not contrary to the public interest," as defined by an enumerated list of criteria. Consistent with the Henderson Act, the St. Johns River Water Management District, the district with jurisdiction over petitioner's land, requires that permit applicants wishing to build on wetlands offset the resulting environmental damage by creating, enhancing, or preserving wetlands elsewhere.

Petitioner decided to develop the 3.7-acre northern section of his property, and in 1994 he applied to the District for MSSW and WRM permits. Under his proposal, petitioner would have raised the elevation of the northernmost section of his land to make it suitable for a building, graded the land from the southern edge of the building site down to the elevation of the high-voltage electrical lines, and installed a dry-bed pond for retaining and gradually releasing stormwater runoff from the building and its parking lot. To mitigate the environmental effects of his proposal, petitioner offered to foreclose any possible future development of the approximately 11-acre southern section of his land by deeding to the District a conservation easement on that portion of his property.

The District considered the 11-acre conservation easement to be inadequate, and it informed petitioner that it would approve construction only if he agreed to one of two concessions. First, the District proposed that petitioner reduce the size of his development to 1 acre and deed to the District a conservation easement on the remaining 13.9 acres. To reduce the development area, the District suggested that petitioner could eliminate the dry-bed pond from his proposal and instead install a more costly subsurface stormwater management system beneath the building site. The District also suggested that petitioner install retaining walls rather than gradually sloping the land from the building site down to the elevation of the rest of his property to the south.

In the alternative, the District told petitioner that he could proceed with the development as proposed, building on 3.7 acres and deeding a conservation easement to the government on the remainder of the property, if he also agreed to hire contractors to make improvements to District-owned land several miles away. Specifically, petitioner could pay to replace culverts on one parcel or fill in ditches on another. Either of those projects would have enhanced approximately 50 acres of District-owned wetlands. When the District asks permit applicants to fund offsite mitigation work, its policy is never to require any particular offsite project, and it did not do so here. Instead, the District said that it "would also favorably consider" alternatives to its suggested offsite mitigation projects if petitioner proposed something "equivalent."

Believing the District's demands for mitigation to be excessive in light of the environmental effects that his building proposal would have caused, petitioner filed suit in state court. Among other claims, he argued that he was entitled to relief under Fla. Stat. §373.617(2), which allows owners to recover "monetary damages" if a state agency's action is "an unreasonable exercise of the state's police power constituting a taking without just compensation."

B

The Florida Circuit Court . . . held a 2-day bench trial. After considering testimony from several experts who examined petitioner's property, the trial court found that the property's northern section had already been "seriously degraded" by extensive construction on the surrounding parcels. In light of this finding and petitioner's offer to dedicate nearly three-quarters of his land to the District, the trial court concluded that any further mitigation in the form of payment for offsite improvements to District property lacked both a nexus and rough proportionality to the environmental impact of the proposed construction. It accordingly held the District's actions unlawful under our decisions in *Nollan* and *Dolan.*

The Florida District Court [of Appeals] affirmed, but the State Supreme Court reversed. A majority of that court distinguished *Nollan* and *Dolan* on two grounds. First, the majority thought it significant that in this case, unlike *Nollan* or *Dolan,* the District did not approve petitioner's application on the condition that he accede to the District's demands; instead, the District denied his application because he refused to make concessions. Second, the majority drew a distinction between a demand for an interest in real property (what happened in *Nollan* and *Dolan*) and a demand for money. . . .

Recognizing that the majority opinion rested on a question of federal constitutional law on which the lower courts are divided, we granted the petition for a writ of certiorari, and now reverse.

II

A

We have said in a variety of contexts that "the government may not deny a benefit to a person because he exercises a constitutional right." *Regan v. Taxation With Representation of Wash.* (1983). In *Perry v. Sindermann* (1972), for example, we held that a public college would violate a professor's freedom of speech if it declined to renew his contract because he was an outspoken critic of the college's administration. And in *Memorial Hospital v. Maricopa County* (1974), we concluded that a county impermissibly burdened the right to travel by extending healthcare benefits only to those indigent sick who had been residents of the county for at least one year. Those cases reflect an overarching principle, known as the unconstitutional conditions doctrine, that vindicates the Constitution's enumerated rights by preventing the government from coercing people into giving them up.

Nollan and *Dolan* "involve a special application" of this doctrine that protects the Fifth Amendment right to just compensation for property the government takes when owners apply for land-use permits. *Lingle v. Chevron U.S.A. Inc.* (2005). Our decisions in those cases reflect two realities of the permitting process. The first is that land-use permit applicants are especially vulnerable to the type of coercion that the unconstitutional conditions doctrine prohibits because the government often has broad discretion to deny a permit that is worth far more than property it would like to take. By conditioning a building permit on the owner's deeding over a public right-of-way, for example, the government can pressure an owner into voluntarily giving up property for which the Fifth Amendment would otherwise require just compensation. So long as the building permit is more valuable than any just compensation the owner could hope to receive for the right-of-way, the owner is likely to accede to the government's demand, no matter how unreasonable. Extortionate demands of this sort frustrate the Fifth Amendment right to just compensation, and the unconstitutional conditions doctrine prohibits them.

A second reality of the permitting process is that many proposed land uses threaten to impose costs on the public that dedications of property can offset. Where a building proposal would substantially increase traffic congestion, for example, officials might condition permit approval on the owner's agreement to deed over the land needed to widen a public road. Respondent argues that a similar rationale justifies the exaction at issue here: petitioner's proposed construction project, it submits, would destroy wetlands on his property, and in order to compensate for this loss, respondent demands that he enhance wetlands elsewhere. Insisting that landowners internalize the negative externalities of their conduct is a hallmark of responsible land-use policy, and we have long sustained such regulations against constitutional attack. See *Village of Euclid v. Ambler Realty Co.* (1926).

Nollan and *Dolan* accommodate both realities by allowing the government to condition approval of a permit on the dedication of property to the public so long as there is a "nexus" and "rough proportionality" between the property that the government demands and the social costs of the applicant's proposal. Our precedents thus enable permitting authorities to insist that applicants bear the full costs of their proposals while still forbidding the government from engaging in "out-and-out . . . extortion" that would thwart the Fifth Amendment right to just compensation. Under *Nollan* and *Dolan* the government may choose whether and how a permit applicant is required to mitigate the impacts of a proposed development, but it may not leverage its legitimate interest in mitigation to pursue governmental ends that lack an essential nexus and rough proportionality to those impacts.

B

The principles that undergird our decisions in *Nollan* and *Dolan* do not change depending on whether the government *approves* a permit on the condition that the applicant turn over property or *denies* a permit because the applicant refuses to do so. We have often concluded that denials of governmental benefits were impermissible under the unconstitutional conditions doctrine. See, *e.g., Perry* (explaining that the government "*may not deny* a benefit to a person on a basis that infringes his constitutionally protected interests" (emphasis added)). In so holding, we have recognized that regardless of whether the government ultimately succeeds in pressuring someone into forfeiting a constitutional right, the unconstitutional conditions doctrine forbids burdening the Constitution's enumerated rights by coercively withholding benefits from those who exercise them.

A contrary rule would be especially untenable in this case because it would enable the government to evade the limitations of *Nollan* and *Dolan* simply by phrasing its demands for property as conditions precedent to permit approval. Under the Florida Supreme Court's approach, a government order stating that a permit is "approved if" the owner turns over property would be subject to *Nollan* and *Dolan,* but an identical order that uses the words "denied until" would not. Our unconstitutional conditions cases have long refused to attach significance to the distinction between conditions precedent and conditions subsequent. To do so here would effectively render *Nollan* and *Dolan* a dead letter.

The Florida Supreme Court puzzled over how the government's demand for property can violate the Takings Clause even though "no property of any kind was ever taken," but the unconstitutional conditions doctrine provides a ready answer. Extortionate demands for property in the land-use permitting context run afoul of the Takings Clause not because they take property but because they impermissibly burden the right not to have property taken without just compensation. As in other unconstitutional conditions cases in which someone refuses to cede a constitutional right in the face of coercive pressure, the impermissible denial of a governmental benefit is a constitutionally cognizable injury.

Nor does it make a difference, as respondent suggests, that the government might have been able to deny petitioner's application outright without giving him the option of securing a permit by agreeing to spend money to improve public lands. Virtually all of our unconstitutional conditions cases involve a gratuitous governmental benefit of some kind. Yet we have repeatedly rejected the argument that if the government need not confer a benefit at all, it can withhold the benefit because someone refuses to give up constitutional rights. *E.g., United States v. American Library Assn., Inc.* (2003) ("[T]he government may not deny a benefit to a person on a basis that infringes his constitutionally protected . . . freedom of speech *even if he has no entitlement to that benefit*"); *Wieman v. Updegraff* (1952) (explaining in unconstitutional conditions case that to focus on "the facile generalization that there is no constitutionally protected right to public employment is to obscure the issue"). Even if respondent would have been entirely within its rights in denying the permit for some other reason, that greater authority does not imply a lesser power to condition permit approval on petitioner's forfeiture of his constitutional rights. See *Nollan* (explaining that "[t]he evident constitutional propriety" of prohibiting a land use "disappears . . . if the condition substituted for the prohibition utterly fails to further the end advanced as the justification for the prohibition"). . . .

C

. . . [R]espondent argues that we need not decide whether its demand for offsite improvements satisfied *Nollan* and *Dolan* because it gave petitioner another avenue for obtaining permit approval. Specifically, respondent said that it would have approved a revised permit application that reduced the footprint of petitioner's proposed construction site from 3.7 acres to 1 acre and placed a conservation easement on the remaining 13.9 acres of petitioner's land. Respondent argues that regardless of whether its demands for offsite mitigation satisfied *Nollan* and *Dolan,* we must separately consider each of petitioner's options, one of which did not require any of the offsite work the trial court found objectionable.

Respondent's argument is flawed because the option to which it points — developing only 1 acre of the site and granting a conservation easement on the rest — involves the same issue as the option to build on 3.7 acres and perform offsite mitigation. We agree with respondent that, so long as a permitting authority offers the landowner at least one alternative that would satisfy *Nollan* and *Dolan,* the landowner has not been subjected to an unconstitutional condition. But respondent's suggestion that we should treat its offer to let petitioner build on 1 acre as an alternative to offsite mitigation misapprehends the governmental benefit that petitioner was denied. Petitioner sought to develop 3.7 acres, but respondent in effect told petitioner that it would not allow him to build on 2.7 of those acres unless he agreed to spend money improving public lands. Petitioner claims that he was wrongfully denied a permit to build on those 2.7 acres. For that reason, respondent's offer to approve a less ambitious building project does not obviate the need to determine whether the demand for offsite mitigation satisfied *Nollan* and *Dolan*.

III

We turn to the Florida Supreme Court's alternative holding that petitioner's claim fails because respondent asked him to spend money rather than give up an easement on his land. A predicate for any unconstitutional conditions claim is that the government could not have constitutionally ordered the person asserting the claim to do what it attempted to pressure that person into doing. For that reason, we began our analysis in both *Nollan* and *Dolan* by observing that if the government had directly seized the easements it sought to obtain through the permitting process, it would have committed a *per se* taking. The Florida Supreme Court held that petitioner's claim fails at this first step because the subject of the exaction at issue here was money rather than a more tangible interest in real property. Respondent and the dissent take the same position, citing the concurring and dissenting opinions in *Eastern Enterprises v. Apfel* (1998) for the proposition that an obligation to spend money can never provide the basis for a takings claim.

We note as an initial matter that if we accepted this argument it would be very easy for land-use permitting officials to evade the limitations of *Nollan* and *Dolan*. Because the government need only provide a permit applicant with one alternative that satisfies the nexus and rough proportionality standards, a permitting authority wishing to exact an easement could simply give the owner a choice of either surrendering an easement or making a payment equal to the easement's value. Such so-called "in lieu of" fees are utterly commonplace, and they are functionally equivalent to other types of land use exactions. For that reason and those that follow, we reject respondent's argument and hold that so-called "monetary exactions" must satisfy the nexus and rough proportionality requirements of *Nollan* and *Dolan*.

A

In *Eastern Enterprises,* the United States retroactively imposed on a former mining company an obligation to pay for the medical benefits of retired miners and their families. A four-Justice plurality concluded that the statute's imposition of retroactive financial liability was so arbitrary that it violated the Takings Clause. Although Justice Kennedy concurred in the result on due process grounds, he joined four other Justices in dissent in arguing that the Takings Clause does not apply to government-imposed financial obligations that "d[o] not operate upon or alter an identified property interest." Relying on the concurrence and dissent in *Eastern Enterprises,* respondent argues that a requirement that petitioner spend money improving public lands could not give rise to a taking.

Respondent's argument rests on a mistaken premise. Unlike the financial obligation in *Eastern Enterprises,* the demand for money at issue here did "operate upon . . . an identified property interest" by directing the owner of a particular piece of property to make a monetary payment. In this case, unlike *Eastern Enterprises,* the monetary obligation burdened petitioner's ownership of a specific parcel of land. In that sense, this case bears resemblance to our cases holding that the government must pay just compensation when it takes a lien—a right to receive money that is secured by a particular piece of property. The fulcrum this case turns on is the direct link between the government's demand and a specific parcel of real property.[1] Because of that direct link, this case implicates the central concern of *Nollan* and *Dolan*: the risk that the government may use its substantial power and discretion in land-use permitting to pursue governmental ends that lack an essential nexus and rough proportionality to the effects of the proposed new use of the specific property at issue, thereby diminishing without justification the value of the property. . . .

1. Thus, because the proposed offsite mitigation obligation in this case was tied to a particular parcel of land, this case does not implicate the question whether monetary exactions must be tied to a particular parcel of land in order to constitute a taking. That is so even when the demand is considered "outside the permitting process." The unconstitutional conditions analysis requires us to set aside petitioner's permit application, not his ownership of a particular parcel of real property.

B

Respondent and the dissent argue that if monetary exactions are made subject to scrutiny under *Nollan* and *Dolan,* then there will be no principled way of distinguishing impermissible land-use exactions from property taxes. We think they exaggerate both the extent to which that problem is unique to the land-use permitting context and the practical difficulty of distinguishing between the power to tax and the power to take by eminent domain.

It is beyond dispute that "[t]axes and user fees . . . are not 'takings.'" [*Brown v. Legal Foundation of Wash.* (2003)] (Scalia, J., dissenting). . . . This case therefore does not affect the ability of governments to impose property taxes, user fees, and similar laws and regulations that may impose financial burdens on property owners.

At the same time, we have repeatedly found takings where the government, by confiscating financial obligations, achieved a result that could have been obtained by imposing a tax. Most recently, in *Brown,* we were unanimous in concluding that a State Supreme Court's seizure of the interest on client funds held in escrow was a taking despite the unquestionable constitutional propriety of a tax that would have raised exactly the same revenue. . . . Perhaps most closely analogous to the present case, we have repeatedly held that the government takes property when it seizes liens, and in so ruling we have never considered whether the government could have achieved an economically equivalent result through taxation.

Two facts emerge from those cases. The first is that the need to distinguish taxes from takings is not a creature of our holding today that monetary exactions are subject to scrutiny under *Nollan* and *Dolan*. Rather, the problem is inherent in this Court's long-settled view that property the government could constitutionally demand through its taxing power can also be taken by eminent domain.

Second, our cases show that teasing out the difference between taxes and takings is more difficult in theory than in practice. *Brown* is illustrative. Similar to respondent in this case, the respondents in *Brown* argued that extending the protections of the Takings Clause to a bank account would open a Pandora's Box of constitutional challenges to taxes. But also like respondent here, the *Brown* respondents never claimed that they were exercising their power to levy taxes when they took the petitioners' property. Any such argument would have been implausible under state law; in Washington, taxes are levied by the legislature, not the courts.

The same dynamic is at work in this case because Florida law greatly circumscribes respondent's power to tax. If respondent had argued that its demand for money was a tax, it would have effectively conceded that its denial of petitioner's permit was improper under Florida law. Far from making that concession, respondent has maintained throughout this litigation that it considered petitioner's money to be a substitute for his deeding to the public a conservation easement on a larger parcel of undeveloped land.

This case does not require us to say more. We need not decide at precisely what point a land-use permitting charge denominated by the government as a "tax" becomes "so arbitrary . . . that it was not the exertion of taxation but a confiscation of property." *Brushaber v. Union Pacific R. Co.* (1916). For present purposes, it suffices to say that despite having long recognized that "the power of taxation should not be confused with the power of eminent domain," *Houck v. Little River Drainage Dist.* (1915), we have had little trouble distinguishing between the two.

C

Finally, we disagree with the dissent's forecast that our decision will work a revolution in land use law by depriving local governments of the ability to charge reasonable permitting fees. Numerous courts—including courts in many of our Nation's most populous States—have confronted constitutional challenges to monetary exactions over the last two decades and applied the standard from *Nollan* and *Dolan* or something like it. Yet the "significant practical harm" the dissent predicts has not come to pass. That is hardly surprising, for the dissent is correct that state law normally provides an independent check on excessive land use permitting fees.

The dissent criticizes the notion that the Federal Constitution places any meaningful limits on "whether one town is overcharging for sewage, or another is setting the price to sell liquor too high." But only two pages later, it identifies three constraints on land use permitting fees that it says the Federal Constitution imposes and suggests that the additional protections of *Nollan* and *Dolan* are not needed. In any event, the dissent's argument that land use permit applicants need no further protection when the government demands money is really an argument for overruling *Nollan* and *Dolan*. After all, the Due Process Clause protected the Nollans from an unfair allocation of public burdens, and they too could have argued that the government's demand for property amounted to a taking under the *Penn Central* framework. We have repeatedly rejected the dissent's contention that other constitutional doctrines leave no room for the nexus and rough proportionality requirements of *Nollan* and *Dolan*. Mindful of the special vulnerability of land use permit applicants to extortionate demands for money, we do so again today.

* * *

We hold that the government's demand for property from a land-use permit applicant must satisfy the requirements of *Nollan* and *Dolan* even when the government denies the permit and even when its demand is for money. The Court expresses no view on the merits of petitioner's claim that respondent's actions here failed to comply with the principles set forth in this opinion and those two cases. The Florida Supreme Court's judgment is reversed, and this case is remanded for further proceedings not inconsistent with this opinion.

It is so ordered.

JUSTICE KAGAN, with whom JUSTICE GINSBURG, JUSTICE BREYER, and JUSTICE SOTOMAYOR join, dissenting.

In the paradigmatic case triggering review under *Nollan v. California Coastal Comm'n* (1987), and *Dolan v. City of Tigard* (1994), the government approves a building permit on the condition that the landowner relinquish an interest in real property, like an easement. . . . [T]he *Nollan–Dolan* test applies only when the property the government demands during the permitting process is the kind it otherwise would have to pay for—or, put differently, when the appropriation of that property, outside the permitting process, would constitute a taking. That is why *Nollan* began by stating that "[h]ad California simply required the Nollans to make an easement across their beachfront available to the public . . . , rather than conditioning their permit to rebuild their house on their agreeing to do so, we have no doubt there would have been a taking" requiring just compensation. And it is why *Dolan* started by maintaining that "had the city simply required petitioner to dedicate a strip of land . . . for public use, rather than conditioning the grant of her permit to [d]evelop her property on such a dedication, a taking would have occurred." Even the majority acknowledges this basic point about *Nollan* and *Dolan*: It too notes that those cases rest on the premise that "if the government had directly seized the easements it sought to obtain through the permitting process, it would have committed a *per se* taking." Only if that is true could the government's demand for the property force a landowner to relinquish his constitutional right to just compensation.

Here, Koontz claims that the District demanded that he spend money to improve public wetlands, not that he hand over a real property interest. . . . The key question then is: Independent of the permitting process, does requiring a person to pay money to the government, or spend money on its behalf, constitute a taking requiring just compensation? Only if the answer is yes does the *Nollan–Dolan* test apply.

But we have already answered that question no. *Eastern Enterprises v. Apfel*, as the Court describes, involved a federal statute requiring a former mining company to pay a large sum of money for the health benefits of retired employees. Five Members of the Court determined that the law did not effect a taking, distinguishing between the appropriation of a specific property interest and the imposition of an order to pay money. Justice Kennedy acknowledged in his controlling opinion that the statute "impose[d] a staggering financial burden" (which influenced his conclusion that it violated due process). Still, Justice Kennedy explained, the law did not effect a taking because it did not "operate upon or alter" a "specific and identified propert[y] or property right[ ]." Instead, "[t]he law simply imposes an obligation to perform an act, the payment of benefits. The statute is indifferent as to how the regulated entity elects to comply or the property it uses to do so." Justice Breyer, writing for four more Justices, agreed. He stated that the Takings Clause applies only when the government appropriates a "specific interest in physical or intellectual property" or "a specific, separately identifiable fund of money"; by contrast, the Clause has no bearing when the government imposes "an ordinary liability to pay money." (dissenting opinion).

Thus, a requirement that a person pay money to repair public wetlands is not a taking. Such an order does not affect a "specific and identified propert[y] or property right[ ]"; it simply "imposes an obligation to perform an act" (the improvement of wetlands) that costs money. (opinion of Kennedy, J.). To be sure, when a person spends money on the government's behalf, or pays money directly to the government, it "will reduce [his] net worth"—but that "can be said of any law which has an adverse economic effect" on someone. Because the government is merely imposing a "general liability" to pay money, (Breyer, J., dissenting)—and therefore is "indifferent as to how the regulated entity elects to comply or the property it uses to do so," (opinion of Kennedy, J.)—the order to repair wetlands, viewed independent of the permitting process, does not constitute a taking. And that means the order does not trigger the *Nollan–Dolan* test, because it does not force Koontz to relinquish a constitutional right.

The majority tries to distinguish *Apfel* by asserting that the District's demand here was "closely analogous" (and "bears resemblance") to the seizure of a lien on property or an income stream from a parcel of land. . . . But the majority's citations succeed only in showing what this case is *not*. When the government dissolves a lien, or appropriates a determinate income stream from a piece of property—or, for that matter, seizes a particular "bank account or [the] accrued interest" on it—the government indeed takes a "specific" and "identified property interest." *Apfel* (opinion of Kennedy, J.). But nothing like that occurred here. The District did not demand any particular lien, or bank account, or income stream from property. It just ordered Koontz to spend or pay money. . . . Koontz's liability would have been the same whether his property produced income or not—*e.g.*, even if all he wanted to build was a family home. And similarly, Koontz could meet that obligation from whatever source he chose—a checking account, shares of stock, a wealthy uncle; the District was "indifferent as to how [he] elect[ed] to [pay] or the property [he] use[d] to do so." *Id.* No more than in *Apfel,* then, was the (supposed) demand here for a "specific and identified" piece of property, which the government could not take without paying for it.

The majority thus falls back on the sole way the District's alleged demand related to a property interest: The demand arose out of the permitting process for Koontz's land. But under the analytic framework that *Nollan* and *Dolan* established, that connection alone is insufficient to trigger heightened scrutiny. As I have described, the heightened standard of *Nollan* and *Dolan* is not a freestanding protection for land-use permit applicants; rather, it is "a special application of the doctrine of unconstitutional conditions, which provides that the government may not require a person to give up a constitutional right—here the right to receive just compensation when property is taken"—in exchange for a land-use permit. [*Lingle v. Chevron U.S.A. Inc.* (2005).] As such, *Nollan* and *Dolan* apply only if the demand at issue would have violated the Constitution independent of that proposed exchange. Or put otherwise, those cases apply only if the demand would have constituted a taking when executed *outside* the permitting process. And here, under *Apfel,* it would not.[2]

The majority's approach, on top of its analytic flaws, threatens significant practical harm. By applying *Nollan* and *Dolan* to permit conditions requiring monetary payments — with no express limitation except as to taxes — the majority extends the Takings Clause, with its notoriously "difficult" and "perplexing" standards, into the very heart of local land-use regulation and service delivery. Cities and towns across the nation impose many kinds of permitting fees every day. Some enable a government to mitigate a new development's impact on the community, like increased traffic or pollution — or destruction of wetlands. Others cover the direct costs of providing services like sewage or water to the development. Still others are meant to limit the number of landowners who engage in a certain activity, as fees for liquor licenses do. All now must meet *Nollan* and *Dolan*'s nexus and proportionality tests. The Federal Constitution thus will decide whether one town is overcharging for sewage, or another is setting the price to sell liquor too high. And the flexibility of state and local governments to take the most routine actions to enhance their communities will diminish accordingly.

That problem becomes still worse because the majority's distinction between monetary "exactions" and taxes is so hard to apply. The majority acknowledges, as it must, that taxes are not takings. But once the majority decides that a simple demand to pay money — the sort of thing often viewed as a tax — can count as an impermissible "exaction," how is anyone to tell the two apart? The question, as Justice Breyer's opinion in *Apfel* noted, "bristles with conceptual difficulties." And practical ones, too: How to separate orders to pay money from . . . well, orders to pay money, so that a locality knows what it can (and cannot) do. State courts sometimes must confront the same question, as they enforce restrictions on localities' taxing power. And their decisions — contrary to the majority's blithe assertion, struggle to draw a coherent boundary. Because "[t]here is no set rule" by which to determine "in which category a particular" action belongs, *Eastern Diversified Properties, Inc. v. Montgomery Cty.* (Md. 1990), courts often reach opposite conclusions about classifying nearly identical fees. . . . Compare, *e.g., Coulter v. Rawlins* (Wyo. 1983) (holding that a fee to enhance parks, imposed as a permit condition, was a regulatory exaction), with *Home Builders Assn. v. West Des Moines* (Iowa 2002) (rejecting *Coulter* and holding that a nearly identical

2. The majority's sole response is that "the unconstitutional conditions analysis requires us to set aside petitioner's permit application, not his ownership of a particular parcel of real property." That mysterious sentence fails to make the majority's opinion cohere with the unconstitutional conditions doctrine, as anyone has ever known it. That doctrine applies only if imposing a condition directly — *i.e.*, independent of an exchange for a government benefit — would violate the Constitution. Here, *Apfel* makes clear that the District's condition would not do so: The government may (separate and apart from permitting) require a person — whether Koontz or anyone else — to pay or spend money without effecting a taking. The majority offers no theory to the contrary: It does not explain, as it must, why the District's condition was "unconstitutional."

fee was a tax). Nor does the majority's opinion provide any help with that issue: Perhaps its most striking feature is its refusal to say even a word about how to make the distinction that will now determine whether a given fee is subject to heightened scrutiny. . . .

At bottom, the majority's analysis seems to grow out of a yen for a prophylactic rule: Unless *Nollan* and *Dolan* apply to monetary demands, the majority worries, "land-use permitting officials" could easily "evade the limitations" on exaction of real property interests that those decisions impose. But that is a prophylaxis in search of a problem. No one has presented evidence that in the many States declining to apply heightened scrutiny to permitting fees, local officials routinely short-circuit *Nollan* and *Dolan* to extort the surrender of real property interests having no relation to a development's costs. And if officials were to impose a fee as a contrivance to take an easement (or other real property right), then a court could indeed apply *Nollan* and *Dolan*. That situation does not call for a rule extending, as the majority's does, to *all* monetary exactions. Finally, a court can use the *Penn Central* framework, the Due Process Clause, and (in many places) state law to protect against monetary demands, whether or not imposed to evade *Nollan* and *Dolan,* that simply "go[ ] too far." [*Pennsylvania Coal Co. v. Mahon* (1922).][3]

In sum, *Nollan* and *Dolan* restrain governments from using the permitting process to do what the Takings Clause would otherwise prevent—*i.e.,* take a specific property interest without just compensation. Those cases have no application when governments impose a general financial obligation as part of the permitting process, because under *Apfel* such an action does not otherwise trigger the Takings Clause's protections. By extending *Nollan* and *Dolan*'s heightened scrutiny to a simple payment demand, the majority threatens the heartland of local land-use regulation and service delivery, at a bare minimum depriving state and local governments of "necessary predictability." *Apfel* (opinion of Kennedy, J.). That decision is unwarranted—and deeply unwise. I would keep *Nollan* and *Dolan* in their intended sphere and affirm the Florida Supreme Court. . . .

---

3. Our *Penn Central* test protects against regulations that unduly burden an owner's use of his property: Unlike the *Nollan–Dolan* standard, that framework fits to a T a complaint (like Koontz's) that a permitting condition makes it inordinately expensive to develop land. And the Due Process Clause provides an additional backstop against excessive permitting fees by preventing a government from conditioning a land-use permit on a monetary requirement that is "basically arbitrary." *Eastern Enterprises v. Apfel* (1998) (Breyer, J., dissenting). My point is not, as the majority suggests, that these constraints do the same thing as *Nollan* and *Dolan*, and so make those decisions unnecessary. To the contrary, *Nollan* and *Dolan* provide developers with enhanced protection (and localities with correspondingly reduced flexibility). The question here has to do not with "overruling" those cases, but with extending them. My argument is that our prior caselaw struck the right balance: heightened scrutiny when the government uses the permitting process to demand property that the Takings Clause protects, and lesser scrutiny, but a continuing safeguard against abuse, when the government's demand is for something falling outside that Clause's scope.

III

Nollan and *Dolan* are important decisions, designed to curb governments from using their power over land-use permitting to extract for free what the Takings Clause would otherwise require them to pay for. But . . . the government commits a taking only when it appropriates a specific property interest, not when it requires a person to pay or spend money. Here, the District never took or threatened such an interest; it tried to extract from Koontz solely a commitment to spend money to repair public wetlands. . . . The majority's errors here are consequential. The majority turns a broad array of local land-use regulations into federal constitutional questions. It deprives state and local governments of the flexibility they need to enhance their communities—to ensure environmentally sound and economically productive development. It places courts smack in the middle of the most everyday local government activity. As those consequences play out across the country, I believe the Court will rue today's decision. I respectfully dissent.

Study Guide:

- The next case treats the issue of whether a taking of private property must be permanent to constitute a "taking" for purposes of the Fifth Amendment.
- Just as the previous case discussed the difference between a "taking" and a "tax," how does the Court distinguish between a "taking" and a "government interference with property"?

ASSIGNMENT S-14

ARKANSAS GAME AND FISH COMMISSION v. UNITED STATES

No. 11-597

Argued Oct. 3, 2012 | Decided Dec. 4, 2012

Ginsburg, J., delivered the opinion of the Court, in which all other Members joined, except Kagan, J., who took no part in the consideration or decision of the case.

Justice Ginsburg delivered the opinion of the Court.

Periodically from 1993 until 2000, the U.S. Army Corps of Engineers (Corps) authorized flooding that extended into the peak growing season for timber on forest land owned and managed by petitioner, Arkansas Game and Fish Commission (Commission). Cumulative in effect, the repeated flooding damaged or destroyed more than 18 million board feet of timber and disrupted the ordinary use and enjoyment of the Commission's property. The Commission sought compensation from the United States pursuant to the Fifth Amendment's instruction: "[N]or shall private property be taken for public use, without just compensation." The question presented is whether a taking may occur, within the meaning of the Takings Clause, when government-induced flood invasions, although repetitive, are temporary.

Ordinarily, this Court's decisions confirm, if government action would qualify as a taking when permanently continued, temporary actions of the same character may also qualify as a taking. In the instant case, the parties and the courts below divided on the appropriate classification of temporary flooding. Reversing the judgment of the Court of Federal Claims, which awarded compensation to the Commission, the Federal Circuit held, 2 to 1, that compensation may be sought only when flooding is "a permanent or inevitably recurring condition, rather than an inherently temporary situation." 637 F.3d 1366, 1378 (2011). We disagree and conclude that recurrent floodings, even if of finite duration, are not categorically exempt from Takings Clause liability.

I

A

The Commission owns the Dave Donaldson Black River Wildlife Management Area (Management Area or Area), which comprises 23,000 acres along both banks of the Black River in northeast Arkansas. The Management Area is forested with multiple hardwood timber species that support a variety of wildlife habitats. The Commission operates the Management Area as a wildlife and hunting preserve, and also uses it as a timber resource, conducting regular harvests of timber as part of its forest-management efforts. Three types of hardwood oak species — nuttall, overcup, and willow — account for 80 percent of the trees in the Management Area. The presence of these hardwood oaks is essential to the Area's character as a habitat for migratory birds and as a venue for recreation and hunting.

The Clearwater Dam (Dam) is located 115 miles upstream from the Management Area. The Corps constructed the Dam in 1948, and shortly thereafter adopted a plan known as the Water Control Manual (Manual) to determine the rates at which water would be released from the Dam. The Manual sets seasonally varying release rates, but permits planned deviations from the prescribed rates for agricultural, recreational, and other purposes.

In 1993, the Corps approved a planned deviation in response to requests from farmers. From September to December 1993, the Corps released water from the Dam at a slower rate than usual, providing downstream farmers with a longer harvest time. As a result, more water than usual accumulated in Clearwater Lake behind the Dam. To reduce the accumulation, the Corps extended the period in which a high amount of water would be released. The Commission maintained this extension yielded downstream flooding in the Management Area, above historical norms, during the tree-growing season, which runs from April to October. If the Corps had released the water more rapidly in the fall of 1993, in accordance with the Manual and with past practice, there would have been short-term waves of flooding which would have receded quickly. The lower rate of release in the fall, however, extended the period of flooding well into the following spring and summer. While the deviation benefited farmers, it interfered with the Management Area's tree-growing season.

The Corps adopted similar deviations each year from 1994 through 2000. The record indicates that the decision to deviate from the Manual was made independently in each year and that the amount of deviation varied over the span of years. Nevertheless, the result was an unbroken string of annual deviations from the Manual. Each deviation lowered the rate at which water was released during the fall, which necessitated extension of the release period into the following spring and summer. During this span of years the Corps proposed Manual revisions that would have made its temporary deviations part of the permanent water-release plan. On multiple occasions between 1993 and 2000, the Commission objected to the temporary deviations and opposed any permanent revision to the Manual, on the ground that the departures from the traditional water-release plan adversely impacted the Management Area. Ultimately, the Corps tested the effect of the deviations on the Management Area. It thereupon abandoned the proposal to permanently revise the Manual and, in 2001, ceased its temporary deviations.

B

In 2005, the Commission filed the instant lawsuit against the United States, claiming that the temporary deviations from the Manual constituted a taking of property that entitled the Commission to compensation. The Commission maintained that the deviations caused sustained flooding of its land during the tree-growing season. The cumulative impact of this flooding over a six-year period between 1993 and 1999, the Commission alleged, resulted in the destruction of timber in the Management Area and a substantial change in the character of the terrain, which necessitated costly reclamation measures. Following a trial, the Court of Federal Claims ruled in favor of the Commission and issued an opinion and order containing detailed findings of fact.

The Court of Federal Claims found that the forests in the Management Area were healthy and flourishing before the flooding that occurred in the 1990's, and that the forests had been sustainably managed for decades under the water-release plan contained in the Manual. It further found that the Commission repeatedly objected to the deviations from the Manual and alerted the Corps to the detrimental effect the longer period of flooding would have on the hardwood timber in the Management Area.

As found by the Court of Federal Claims, the flooding caused by the deviations contrasted markedly with historical flooding patterns. Between 1949 and 1992, the river level near the Management Area reached six feet an average of 64.7 days per year during the growing season; the number of such days had been even lower on average before the Clearwater Dam was built. Between 1993 and 1999, however, the river reached the same level an average of 91.14 days per year, an increase of more than 40 percent over the historic average. Although the Management Area lies in a floodplain, in no previously recorded time span did comparable flooding patterns occur. Evidence at trial indicated that half of the nuttall oaks in the Management Area were saturated with water when the river level was at six feet; the evidence further indicated that the saturation of the soil around the trees' root systems could persist for weeks even after the flooding had receded.

The court concluded that the Corps' deviations caused six consecutive years of substantially increased flooding, which constituted an appropriation of the Commission's property, albeit a temporary rather than a permanent one. Important to this conclusion, the court emphasized the deviations' cumulative effect. The trees were subject to prolonged periods of flooding year after year, which reduced the oxygen level in the soil and considerably weakened the trees' root systems. The repeated annual flooding for six years altered the character of the property to a much greater extent than would have been shown if the harm caused by one year of flooding were simply multiplied by six. When a moderate drought occurred in 1999 and 2000, the trees did not have the root systems necessary to sustain themselves; the result, in the court's words, was "catastrophic mortality." More than 18 million board feet of timber were destroyed or degraded.

This damage altered the character of the Management Area. The destruction of the trees led to the invasion of undesirable plant species, making natural regeneration of the forests improbable in the absence of reclamation efforts. To determine the measure of just compensation, the Court of Federal Claims calculated the value of the lost timber and the projected cost of the reclamation and awarded the Commission $5.7 million.

The Federal Circuit reversed. It acknowledged that in general, temporary government action may give rise to a takings claim if permanent action of the same character would constitute a taking. But it held that "cases involving flooding and [flowage] easements are different." Government-induced flooding can give rise to a taking claim, the Federal Circuit concluded, only if the flooding is "permanent or inevitably recurring." . . . We granted certiorari to resolve the question whether government actions that cause repeated floodings must be permanent or inevitably recurring to constitute a taking of property.

II

The Takings Clause is "designed to bar Government from forcing some people alone to bear public burdens which, in all fairness and justice, should be borne by the public as a whole." *Armstrong v. United States* (1960). And "[w]hen the government physically takes possession of an interest in property for some public purpose, it has a categorical duty to compensate the former owner." *Tahoe-Sierra Preservation Council, Inc. v. Tahoe Regional Planning Agency* (1951)). These guides are fundamental in our Takings Clause jurisprudence. We have recognized, however, that no magic formula enables a court to judge, in every case, whether a given government interference with property is a taking. In view of the nearly infinite variety of ways in which government actions or regulations can affect property interests, the Court has recognized few invariable rules in this area.

True, we have drawn some bright lines, notably, the rule that a permanent physical occupation of property authorized by government is a taking. *Loretto v. Teleprompter Manhattan CATV Corp.* (1982). So, too, is a regulation that permanently requires a property owner to sacrifice all economically beneficial uses of his or her land. *Lucas v. South Carolina Coastal Council* (1992). But aside from the cases attended by rules of this order, most takings claims turn on situation-specific factual inquiries. With this in mind, we turn to the question presented here — whether temporary flooding can ever give rise to a takings claim.

The Court first ruled that government-induced flooding can constitute a taking in *Pumpelly v. Green Bay Co.* (1872). . . . [T]he Court held that "where real estate is actually invaded by superinduced additions of water, earth, sand, or other material . . . so as to effectually destroy or impair its usefulness, it is a taking, within the meaning of the Constitution." Following *Pumpelly,* the Court recognized that seasonally recurring flooding could constitute a taking. . . .

Furthermore, our decisions confirm that takings temporary in duration can be compensable. This principle was solidly established in the World War II era, when "[c]ondemnation for indefinite periods of occupancy [took hold as] a practical response to the uncertainties of the Government's needs in wartime." *United States v. Westinghouse Elec. & Mfg. Co.* (1950). In support of the war effort, the Government took temporary possession of many properties. These exercises of government authority, the Court recognized, qualified as compensable temporary takings. Notably in relation to the question before us, the takings claims approved in these cases were not confined to instances in which the Government took outright physical possession of the property involved. A temporary takings claim could be maintained as well when government action occurring outside the property gave rise to "a direct and immediate interference with the enjoyment and use of the land." *United States v. Causby* (1946) (frequent overflights from a nearby airport resulted in a taking, for the flights deprived the property owner of the customary use of his property as a chicken farm).

Ever since, we have rejected the argument that government action must be permanent to qualify as a taking. Once the government's actions have worked a taking of property, "no subsequent action by the government can relieve it of the duty to provide compensation for the period during which the taking was effective." [*First English Evangelical Lutheran Church of Glendale v. County of Los Angeles* (1987).]

Because government-induced flooding can constitute a taking of property, and because a taking need not be permanent to be compensable, our precedent indicates that government-induced flooding of limited duration may be compensable. No decision of this Court authorizes a blanket temporary-flooding exception to our Takings Clause jurisprudence, and we decline to create such an exception in this case.

III

. . . There is . . . no solid grounding in precedent for setting flooding apart from all other government intrusions on property. And the Government has presented no other persuasive reason to do so. Its primary argument is of the in for a penny, in for a pound genre: reversing the decision below, the Government worries, risks disruption of public works dedicated to flood control. "[E]very passing flood attributable to the government's operation of a flood-control project, no matter how brief," the Government hypothesizes, might qualify as a compensable taking. To reject a categorical bar to temporary-flooding takings claims, however, is scarcely to credit all, or even many, such claims. It is of course incumbent on courts to weigh carefully the relevant factors and circumstances in each case, as instructed by our decisions.

The slippery slope argument, we note, is hardly novel or unique to flooding cases. Time and again in Takings Clause cases, the Court has heard the prophecy that recognizing a just compensation claim would unduly impede the government's ability to act in the public interest. We have rejected this argument when deployed to urge blanket exemptions from the Fifth Amendment's instruction. While we recognize the importance of the public interests the Government advances in this case, we do not see them as categorically different from the interests at stake in myriad other Takings Clause cases. . . .

IV

We rule today, simply and only, that government-induced flooding temporary in duration gains no automatic exemption from Takings Clause inspection. When regulation or temporary physical invasion by government interferes with private property, our decisions recognize, time is indeed a factor in determining the existence *vel non* of a compensable taking. Also relevant to the takings inquiry is the degree to which the invasion is intended or is the foreseeable result of authorized government action. For example, the Management Area lies in a floodplain below a dam, and had experienced flooding in the past. But the trial court found the Area had not been exposed to flooding comparable to the 1990's accumulations in any other time span either prior to or after the construction of the Dam.

The Court of Federal Claims found that the flooding the Commission assails was foreseeable. In this regard, the court noted the Commission's repeated complaints to the Corps about the destructive impact of the successive planned deviations from the Water Control Manual. Further, the court determined that the interference with the Commission's property was severe: The Commission had been deprived of the customary use of the Management Area as a forest and wildlife preserve, as the bottomland hardwood forest turned, over time, into a "headwater swamp."

The Government, however, challenged several of the trial court's factfindings, including those relating to causation, foreseeability, substantiality, and the amount of damages. Because the Federal Circuit rested its decision entirely on the temporary duration of the flooding, it did not address those challenges. As earlier noted, preserved issues remain open for consideration on remand.

* * *

For the reasons stated, the judgment of the Court of Appeals for the Federal Circuit is reversed, and the case is remanded for further proceedings consistent with this opinion.

It is so ordered.

JUSTICE KAGAN took no part in the consideration or decision of this case.

35047758R00136

Made in the USA
Lexington, KY
28 August 2014